WALKS & HIKES ON THE

BEACHES

AROUND PUGET SOUND

Harvey Manning

&

Penny Manning

THE
MOUNTAINEERS

*For our leader, Benella Caminiti,
and our legal counsel, Henry David Thoreau*

Published by
The Mountaineers
1011 SW Klickitat Way,
Seattle, Washington 98134

9 8 7 6 5
5 4 3 2 1

Published simultaneously in Canada by Douglas & McIntyre, Ltd.,
1615 Venables Street, Vancouver, B.C. V5L 2H1

Published simultaneously in Great Britain by Cordee, 3a DeMontfort Street,
Leicester, England, LE1 7HD

Manufactured in the United States of America

Edited by Dana Lee Fos
Maps by Gary Rands and Gray Mouse Graphics
Photos by Bob and Ira Spring
Cover design by Watson Graphics
Book design and layout by Gray Mouse Graphics
Typesetting by The Mountaineers Books

Cover photographs: *background image* deserted section of coastline, by
Kirkendall/Spring; *insets:* Edmonds ferry dock; tidal pools on Puget Sound
beach, by Bob & Ira Spring

Library of Congress Cataloging in Publication Data
Manning, Harvey
    Walks and hikes on the beaches around Puget Sound / Harvey Manning &
Penny Manning.
            p.   cm.
        Includes bibliographical references and index.
        ISBN 0-89886-411-9
        1. Walking--Washington (State)--Puget Sound--Guidebooks. 2.
Beaches--Washington (State)--Puget Sound--Guidebooks. 3. Puget Sound
(Wash.)--Guidebooks. I. Manning, Penny. II. Title.
GV199.42.W22P834   1995
796.5'3'097977--dc20   94-41025
                                        CIP

CONTENTS

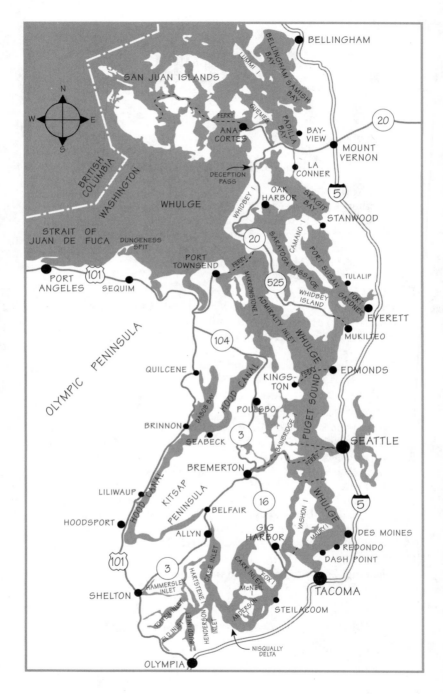

ISLANDS IN THE SOUTH SOUND: FOX, MCNEIL, ANDERSON, HARTSTENE   142

THE WESTERN ISLES: BAINBRIDGE, VASHON, MAURY, BLAKE   152

THE NORTHERN ISLES: INDIAN–MARROWSTONE, CAMANO, WHIDBEY, FIDALGO, GUEMES, SAMISH, LUMMI   173

PUBLISHER'S NOTE ON "PUBLIC" AND "PRIVATE" PROPERTY

In this book the author, Harvey Manning, advocates an interpretation of the law under what has been called the Public Trust Doctrine. He argues that private property owners hold shorelands in trust for the public and should not be allowed to prevent members of the public from walking the beaches. This argument has some support from recent court cases and legal commentaries, but the doctrine has not yet been applied in a direct confrontation between a property owner and an alleged trespasser. As of this writing, the only safe approach for the hiker is to secure permission before crossing any land posted as private property.

Even if one agrees with the author's position on this issue, the risks involved in ignoring private property notices should not be underestimated. A property owner who misreads a situation, a walker who strays too near to a house, or a confrontation that gets out of hand—all may lead to arrest or worse consequences. The hiker who chooses to cross property marked "Private" does so at his or her own risk.

Similar cautions should be taken with passages describing travel along the railroad tracks of the "Jim Hill Trail." The author argues that the rails traditionally have been used for foot traffic, but he also notes, correctly, that the railroads consider this to be private property, and those who do walk the tracks will be treated as trespassers. Again, even if one agrees with the author, the hiker who chooses to follow railroad tracks assumes the risks of both legal consequences and injury. The decision to follow this course should not be taken lightly.

The Mountaineers encourage and support authors in speaking their minds and advocating constructive changes in the law. It is in this spirit that we have decided to publish Harvey Manning's *Walks and Hikes on the Beaches Around Puget Sound* in its present form. However, Mr. Manning's advocacy of civil disobedience as a means to force such changes represents his own personal views and not the views of The Mountaineers.

PHOTOGRAPHERS' NOTE ON "PUBLIC" AND "PRIVATE" PROPERTY

Public Trust Doctrine or Private Property Rights?

For fifty years our parents lived near the saltwater. They always assumed people's right to walk their beach was the law of the land. It wasn't until involvement in these books that we became aware of a conflict between the two given rights, Public Trust Doctrine and private property. Until the issue is resolved in the courts, we cannot condone ignoring "no trespassing" edicts.

Aerial view of the Longbranch Peninsula and Carr Inlet (page 222). From bottom to top: Von Geldern Cove, Mayo Cove (on the far shore is Penrose Point State Park, page 226), Delano Beach, Pitt Passage, and McNeil Island. Fox Island is at upper left.

INTRODUCTION

"The Saltwater We Know"

Captain George Vancouver, in 1792, placed "Puget's Sound" south of "The Narrows," and there it remained while the Hudson's Bay Company established a post on the Nisqually and pioneers snuffled around for riches. The fur market had gone bad when silk replaced beaver in the Boston toffs' toppers. Gold was hard to find and hard work to dig. Farming was slow. Real estate speculation, *that* was the mother lode. The royal road to fortune and a page in the history books was "townbooming." But late-arriving boomers found the choice sites on Vancouver's Puget Sound already taken. They were forced north, beyond Puget Sound, to Admiralty Inlet and other waters of the inland sea. However, the bonanza of their fevered dreams lay in obtaining the western terminus of the projected Northern Pacific Railroad, and Congress had stipulated this was to be on Puget Sound, the only waterway north of the Columbia River Congress ever had heard about. The boomers nagged Congress into agreeing that *strictly for purposes of the railroad* "Puget Sound" could drift as far north as it might be blown by the hot boomer air.

Railroad terminus or not, boomers couldn't have a town without townfolks. Easterners who itched to move West were as ignorant as Congress. Boomers therefore advertised their plats as being on Puget Sound; the press, as ignorant as everybody else, expanded Puget Sound north to Whidbey Island.

That has been a done deed for better than a century, and it would be futile to try to convince Seattle it actually is on Admiralty Inlet. Villagers of the infant hamlet just in from the East, unable to see farther than the nearest clam, and transients of today's adolescent megalopolis, with no notion of where they are and one foot always at Sea-Tac International Airport for a quick getaway, have pushed Puget Sound steadily toward Canada and the ocean.

Those who stick around long enough to gain rudimentary orientation (California is that way, New York that way, Canada and Oregon are— well, who cares?) may grow aware that though the inland sea is a unity of a myriad named parts, as a whole it has no name. Geographers long have discussed, debated, wrangled, and never agreed on an umbrella name. Laymen newly in from the subways and the tall corn could not be expected to do better. Yet for a great many purposes a comprehensive name is essential to communication. In the lack, Puget Sound has been pressed into service, has moved inexorably toward embracing everything wet except rain and root beer.

The good, gray *Seattle Times* blushed to its toes in the mid-1980s when an editor from Alabama headlined an article on the San Juans, "Islands in the Sound." When the press whooped it up for the admirable intentions of the Puget Sound Alliance and People for Puget Sound, old settlers asked who was looking after Possession Sound, Port Susan, Saratoga Passage, Skagit Bay, Padilla Bay, Samish Bay, and Bellingham Bay, to name a few. The terms "Greater Puget Sound" and "North Puget Sound" have been heard. The one falls as sweetly on the ear as "Greater Seattle." The other is what old settlers call the waters off Edmonds. Television weathermen, not as pretty as the "weather girls" of old or as entertaining as the outmoded weather-cartooners, and aspiring to be considered scientists, have begun referring to "Puget Sound and northern waters."

Better. But not good enough. In walking beaches from Allyn to Fairhaven, the surveyors of this volume became consumed by the need for a Big Umbrella. They wondered, Do the people whose ancestors have lived beside and on these waters for thousands of years have a name for the waters?

Yes. Several, in fact. In Lushootseed, the language spoken from the Skagit River to the south end of the inland sea (by some three-quarters of its aboriginal population), the word for "sea, ocean, sound, saltwater, the saltwater we know," has been variously Englished as *whulj, whulch, whole-itch, khwulch,* and *whulge.* If the population majority is permitted to rule, Lushootseed has the best claim to the Umbrellaship. The spelling least troublesome to our foreign tongues is *Whulge.*

The Wildness Within

The Wilderness Act of 1964 defines "national wilderness" as a place where "the earth and its community of life are untrammeled by man, where man himself is a visitor who does not remain." Far from the madding crowd, this is "the wildness without." The closer and more madding the crowd, the more intense the need for another sort of wilderness, near urban homes, "the wildness within." Largest and grandest in Washington, in the Pacific Northwest, in the nation, is the Whulge.

The wildness of the Whulge itself is in the long, wide waters where man is never more than a lonely anomaly. The wildness of the Whulge edge, the beach, is the legacy of the Canadian glacier. The northern ice, in retreating, left dumps of debris that buried the pre-glacial lowlands. This debris, weakly consolidated, is easy cheese for storms. The wind-pushed waves batter down debris which then is relocated by wind-driven currents; most of the Whulge is thereby shored by sand-shingle strands, continuous walkways. The battering provides the beaches; it also, in those lengthy stretches where the bluffs are so unstable they force houses to stay prudently back from the ever-retreating brink, preserves beach wildness beside the water wildness.

Except in the spots (fortunately, few) where the bluffs are relatively stable, permitting ragtag, importunate accretions on the brink or even between brink and beach, bluffs of 200 feet or more generally are perfect keepers of the waterside peace; houses cannot be seen and residents descend to the beach infrequently. Houses atop lower bluffs, still usually out of sight, connect to the water (mainly on blue-sky summer Sundays) via tramway-elevators (which sometimes lose their brakes, causing serious injuries and lawsuits); timber stairways (which always ultimately lose their bottoms and deadend in air); well-graded, railing-guarded trails (most winters overwhelmed by bluff-slumps); toboggan-slide mudchutes (children squeal, adults quail); rotten ladders missing every other rung (each vacancy remembering contusions and fractures); and—heaven help us!—rope ladders dangling from overhangs.

As the bluff lowers more, houses approach the water, but even a few feet of bank can blind Private picture-window eyes to passage of a quiet Public stranger. It's when the bank dwindles to naught that trammelers run amok. Few spits and bars in and near Puget Sound City (our term for the urban area from Olympia through Tacoma–Seattle to Everett) lack cheek-by-jowl rows of houses. The mortal enemy of the beachwalker (and, more important, of the natural shore) is the bulkheading which invades and obliterates beaches. This "armoring" is a spectacularly stupid attack on the very values the Privatizers presumably seek by "owning" a beach. Interfering with the physical processes of the water–land interface by constructing homes, planting lawns, and building badminton courts, they violate the laws of the Nature they presumably love—else why are they on the Whulge at all? Armoring obliterates habitats of fish, shellfish, and shorebirds, narrows the beach, lowers the beach profile, and by denying bluff-derived sediments to longshore currents impacts the beaches downcurrent. The government process for regulating armoring is such a farce it is nothing more than Private theft of Public values abetted by official neglect. In Thurston County, where a third of the shores are armored, the amount of shoreline thus denaturalized doubled between 1977 and 1993; each year sees an additional 2600 feet vandalized.

As with kayaking, the crux of beachwalking is the "put-in." The first essential is a spot to park the car. (Where possible, take the bus; in these pages the transit line, where one exists, is noted along with driving instructions.) The parking place or bus stop needn't be at the beach. If a walk of several miles is intended, an extra half-mile is no sweat. (The clogging of residential streets and blocking of driveways is thoughtless, selfish, illegal, and rude.)

Second, there must be access from road to beach that does not entail climbing a fence or darting through a garden party. The *horizontal access* to Whulge beaches ordinarily is easy—one beach connects to another, only here and there obstructed by bulkheads, marinas, and the Ports of Seattle, Tacoma, Des Moines, et cetera. Housefolks effectively Privatize the beach by cutting off the *vertical access* from the upland. A common community strategy is the Great Wall, the gaps between houses closed by thorny hedges, chain-link fence, timber palisades, or stone walls with broken bottles concreted atop.

The most ubiquitous strategy of the Privatizer, employed both horizontally and vertically, is signing, which may be as mild as "Private Beach. Passage Subject to Permission. Please Be Nice," or stern, "No Trespassing. RCW 666-00-666. Fines and Imprisonment," or terrifying, "Savage Dogs in Ambush. Police on the Way. They Will Cut off Your Right Hand and Deport You to a Penal Colony." Beachdwellers native to the Whulge don't truly believe, deep inside, that a beach *can* be Private; in friendly conversation with walkers, they will half-apologize for what their lawyers tell them are their property rights.

Inlanders just arrived on the beach from Illinois know only what they've been told by their real estate agent and the local branch of the Private Property Rights League. Let it be recognized that beach residents are much put upon by walkers who are not saintly worshippers of Nature but blithering louts or arrogant slobs. Residents often feel they have no recourse except vigilante action, first cousin to civil disobedience. In addition to erecting "bluff" signs, they conspire to conceal the incontestable Public accesses to the beach: utility corridors, as for underwater cables; road rights-of-way, as in street-ends and roads that once led to ferry slips; port districts organized to build docks for the mosquito fleet and that endure as Public ownerships though docks and mosquitoes are gone; the Public boat-launches provided by the State Wildlife Department and parks departments; and undeveloped state, county, and city parks. Park signs are ripped out. Generations-old Public trails are heaped over with brush so their starts cannot be seen from the road. Fences are built. Public roads are signed "Private"—illegal signs, bluff signs. Especially in the 17 years since the beginning of our systematic survey of Whulge beaches, Big Lie signing has increased manifold. Added to the blockages by bulkheads and docks predating passage of the Shorelines Management Act of 1971, it adds insult to injury.

The Tide Waits Not

The beachwalker with a poor head for mathematics and a profound disinterest in the golf course on the moon should skip this section for now and return to it only when freshly escaped from being pinned by a spring tide against a vertical clay bluff.

Understanding the mechanism of tides rarely is essential to safe beachwalking. Caused by the moon (most important) and sun (very helpful), they are shaped by some 250 factors only digestible by a computer. But the habits of tides are easily observed—and surely will be by a walker who has become an involuntary surfer or cliff-clamberer.

Of the several types that occur around the world, our Whulge has a *mixed tide,* two high–low cycles in a period of approximately 24 hours 50 minutes (so, each day the tides are about 50 minutes later than the day before); alternate highs are nearly equal in feet and lows very unequal, or vice versa.

A tide is not, as commonly imagined, a ridge of water dogging the moon around the globe, but an up-and-down, thus in-and-out, motion in a tide basin—in our case, the Pacific Ocean. The tide enters and leaves the Whulge mainly through the Strait of Juan de Fuca, to a minor extent through the Strait of Georgia. The tides thus are earlier near the ocean. The tide table for Seattle, published in the daily newspapers along with moon phases, is the reference used here. To correct for other areas, subtract 30 minutes for Dungeness Spit, 20 minutes for Quimper Peninsula and Whidbey Island's west coast, and 10 minutes for Everett; add 6 minutes for Tacoma and 35 minutes for Steilacoom.

The difference on the open ocean between *high water,* the highest level of a tide cycle, and *low water,* the lowest, is much less than on the Whulge, where narrowing shores constrict the tidal current and "pile up" the water. At the mouth of Admiralty Inlet, the *mean tide range* (the year's mean of the vertical differences between daily high and low waters) is a meager 4 feet; at Olympia it's a whopping 10.5 feet. At Seattle the *daily tide range* builds to around 16 feet in June and January and dwindles to as little as 1.7 feet in May and October–November.

Highs and lows vary a lot, depending on the mix of those 250 factors. In a recent year, Seattle's highest forecast highs (14 feet) came in December–January (and slightly less in June–July), and the lowest high (7.4 feet) in May (nearly matched in fall). The lowest lows (–3.3 feet) were in June and January, and the highest lows (7.2 feet) in December–February. As can be seen, some highs are virtually the same as some lows. At Seattle, during a month the highs may vary up or down 4 feet or more, the lows 8 feet or more.

The greatest difference between high and low comes on a *spring tide,* which has nothing to do with the season but occurs twice every month, near new moon and full moon, when sun, moon, and earth are in line. The tide range at Seattle is then as much as 16 feet (a whole lot). The least difference is in a *neap tide,* near the first and last quarters of the moon, when the heavenly bodies are farthest out of line. The tide range at Seattle is then less than 2 feet (hardly anything).

Those are the numbers. Which affect a beach walk?

First is the *height of the high water.* Since that's how beaches are made, at the highest highs the waves are pummeling the cliff and anybody who gets in the way. Generally, then, when the high forecast for Seattle is 12 or 14 feet, there is going to be dang little beach anywhere on the Whulge. (Note: The forecast tides published in tide tables are the *astronomical tides* determined by moon, sun, et cetera. The actual tides usually are to some extent *meteorological tides,* responding to differences in atmospheric pressure and force of winds and perhaps to a glut of water from flooding rivers; in the high atmospheric pressure of "sunshine tides," levels are

South Whidbey Island (page 194)

under the forecast, whereas in storm tides the levels may be several feet over the forecast, surprising the heck out of beachdwellers and delta farmers and marina operators and ferryboat captains.) With a forecast of 10 or 11 feet, and good weather, considerable stretches of beach will be easy-open at the high—but will be skinny and have many obstacles, such as bulkheads and fallen trees and pieces of slid-down bluff. With a forecast of 9 feet or less, most beaches will be mostly negotiable, though some obstacles may remain until the tide ebbs to 7 or 6 feet or less. Except on feeble-wave beaches, at that level the main obstacle may be human constructions.

Second is the *height of the low water*. Feeble-wave beaches are best walked at quite a low level to avoid a brushfight; however, an adjoining exposed mudflat can be a boot-sucking snare and delusion. (Note: The mudflat immediately adjoining the beach commonly is a soupy quickmud, due to the underground drainage of freshwater from the upland, while outside this narrow belt the mud/sand is wet and sticky but solid and easy-walking.) Strong-wave beaches may be most effortlessly walked on the wide, firm sands of a wave-built terrace exposed at low tide, much easier going than a sloping shingle beach.

Third is the *time of the high water.* In a neap tide, the high may be so low there's nothing to worry about. In a spring tide, look out—some of those so-and-so's flood scarily fast and practically climb the cliffs. When it is suspected the beach may be wiped out by the day's high, the better part of valor is to schedule the trip for an outgoing tide. If the high is around 8:00 to 10:00 in the morning, a person can set out then or soon after and, though perhaps forced to clamber the bank a little or crawl over logs or wait for a while at obstacles, can journey relaxed and comfortable in the knowledge the beach will grow steadily; the return will be a cinch. Walking on an incoming tide can be nervous business but is not irrational if the high is low, if the beach will be left well before the high, or if an escape is available leading to a decent overland return.

What do you do if there's no daytime neap or afternoon low? Head for the all-tides-walkable "complete beaches" of benches-terraces, baymouth bars, and spits. Or hie thee to a delta dike or a handy shoreside railroad trail.*

The Once and Future Glacier

Four *glaciations* by the Juan de Fuca and Puget Lobes of the Cordilleran Ice Sheet, which in the Pleistocene epoch invaded from Canada, have been identified in Western Washington lowlands. First were the Orting and Stuck Glaciations, of unknown dates (but less than 2–3 million years ago); their handiwork has been obscured by successors. The Salmon Springs Glaciation culminated prior to 38,000 years ago with a maximum reach of 15–20 miles south of Olympia. After the Olympia Interglaciation came the Fraser Glaciation, with three *stades* (intervals of advance). Between 15,000 and 13,500 years ago, during the second, the Vashon Stade, Seattle was under 3300–4000 feet of ice. (Maximum ice depth in the Bellingham area was about 5250–7000 feet; Olympia, about 1200–1400 feet; the terminus, 100 feet.) The glacier pushed beyond the Nisqually River but stayed only briefly in its southernmost extension, and Vashon drifts thus are scanty there. The Everson Interstade was succeeded by the Sumas Stade of 11,000 years ago; this time the Canadian ice barely got over the border.

Only in several areas does hard rock outcrop on this book's described shores, which mainly are of *glacial drift,* a term inclusive of all materials transported by the ice and its meltwater. An *erratic* is a boulder that rode the glacier until ultimately dumped. *Till* is an unsorted mixture of particles of every size from clay to boulders; the concretelike "hardpan" characteristically erodes into vertical walls. *Stratified drift* has been sorted

---

*See the publisher's note on private property on page 11.

by meltwater; the *sand* and *gravel* in the mix is deposited by water of lesser or greater velocity in riverbeds or deltas; the *clay* from ice-milled rock milk settles out in lakes. Drift overridden by the glacier during its advance was compressed and hardened. Organic materials from trees and plants that grew during the glacial lulls were sealed up by clay, preserved from total oxidation and rot, and became blackish layers of *peat*. The walker sees peat beds containing branches and logs, cedar bark and fir cones, that appear to have come from the woods mere months ago.

Fraser-Vashon drift, the most abundant, is relatively unconsolidated and new-looking when it dates from the retreat, quite compact if from the advance. Whether a lay walker can readily distinguish the older of the Vashon drifts from the Salmon Springs is debatable. However, he/she will frequently observe old-looking drift, more compacted (by weight of later ice) or even folded or faulted, often somewhat cemented by yellow-orange iron oxides, getting along toward becoming mudstones, shales, sandstones, and conglomerates; cliffs of this "nearly rock" may be quite tall and vertical.

Whulge beaches weren't always where they are now. The glacier from the north formed an ice dam stretching from the Olympics to the Cascades, impounding Lake Russell. This lake, fed by mountain streams and meltwater from the glacier front, had to rise hundreds of feet to overflow south to the Chehalis River, its outlet to the ocean. At various levels above the modern Whulge, the scientific eye identifies bluffs cut by waves of the old lake.

When the ice retreated and let the salt flow in, there wasn't as much ocean water as now; much of the world's supply was still locked up in glaciers. Arriving from Asia a dozen millennia ago, the Original Settlers found no Whulge; they hunted mastodons and woolly mammoths in the broad valley savannah of the Puget Trough, which resembled today's mid-northern Alaska. Forests advanced from the south. The sea flowed in from the north, its level rising some 300 feet from the Pleistocene low of 15,000 years ago, reaching today's approximate level perhaps 4000–5000 years ago. That's how long people have been walking the beaches we now walk.

Of the Building of Beaches There Is No End

The *coast* is an indefinite strip landward from the shore. The *shore* is the narrow zone between low-tide shoreline and high-tide shoreline. The *shoreline* is the intersection of water and land at any given moment.

The chief agents in eroding the shore are *wind-generated waves* that carve *wave-cut cliffs* whose debris forms *beaches* of gravel, also called shingle (cobbles, pebbles, and granules), sand (coarse to fine), and mud (silt and clay). Waves that strike the shore obliquely have a component of motion along the shore; the resulting *longshore currents* transport materials, depositing some on beaches and using some to build *spits and bars*.

In any locality the orientation of spits and bars is determined by the direction of the dominant longshore current, a result of the dominant winds and the orientation of the shore. *Tidal currents* go back and forth and accomplish relatively little; similarly, the *swash and backwash,* in and out, of surf.

As waves erode inland the beach widens. The retreating cliff leaves behind a *wave-cut bench,* a platform of rock (or, in most of our area, drift) usually covered with sand and gravel that gradually are moved seaward by the undertow and dumped in deep water, forming a *wave-built terrace,* at whose outer edge is the drop-off that wading children are warned against.

Width of the bench and terrace and thus the beach they constitute depends partly on how long the waves have been at it; the Whulge isn't old enough for much erosion of the hard-rock shores and that's why there's so little beachwalking in such places as the San Juan Islands and the west side of Hood Canal.

Beach width depends on vigor of the waves, which depends on strength of the wind. Weather shores (in our area, mainly south and west) tend to have the wider beaches, lee shores (north and east) the narrower; in fiordlike estuaries the wave action on all shores may be so feeble the beach is mere inches wide. Beaches of protected shores with meek waves are uncleanly green: trees typically lean horizontally far over and close to the beach; fallen logs, instead of being churned around and abraded to splinters or floated away, just lie placidly where they fall, growing seaweed and barnacles. Walking such beaches, narrow and perhaps steep, cobbles weed-slimy, can be a misery of slithering and brushfighting and log-crawling and pulling seaweed out of your hair.

Beach width also depends on the vigor of longshore currents. Where these are very strong they sweep away the materials from the bluff, drastically slimming the beach.

Not all shores have beaches. Rock cliffs may plunge directly to deep water. Delta and estuary *saltmarshes* may merge with bay-bottom *tideflats;* some of these vast low-tide expanses of sand or mud, also found in shallow bays perhaps rimmed by skinny beaches, can be walked a long way from shore, far out in birdland.

As wave-cut bench plus wave-built terrace grow, the widening beach may become "complete." Above regularly washed sands and gravels, a *driftwood line* of logs is thrown up by big storms and remains untouched by ordinary high tides, perhaps jostled once or twice a decade. Behind the driftwood is a sand ridge rising above the high-tide shoreline, a *dune line* of particles blown from sun-dried beach. Though usually not resembling the classic marching dunes of deserts, being mostly vegetation-anchored, the sand ridge often impounds a lagoon. The lagoon may be freshwater, fed by a creek or seepage, and may be dry in summer. It may be partly freshwater marsh or it may be tidal, connected to the sea by a channel. It may be sometimes tideflat or may be partly saltmarsh. Normally a lagoon harbors a raft of old, bleached driftwood cast up by big storms.

A longshore current picks up material when it hits the shore and drops material when it runs out in the deep water of a *sink* and loses momentum. When a current manages to fill an offshore area, creating a shallows, breaking waves then build an *offshore bar* that may be raised above the normal high-tide line by storm tides and ultimately shaped by waves and connected to the shore, enclosing a lagoon—such a *looped bar* is another route to a complete beach.

Longshore currents work to straighten out shores, by this process: When the shore bulges abruptly out or curves abruptly in, the currents tend to keep going straight, soon losing momentum in a sink and dropping loads. Thus, *spits* are built. When one terminates in open water, it forms a *point*. When it connects mainland to an island, the latter becomes a *tombolo*. When a spit reaches across the mouth of a bay and nearly or completely closes it off, it's called a *baymouth bar*—here are the great big lagoons, marshes, dredged boat basins, fancy yacht-and-mansion subdivisions, and ecological disasters. A delta pushed out in open water and subjected to the spit-building process typically becomes a *cuspate hybrid*.

Tolmie State Park (page 63)

In a narrow band of several hundred feet from low tide to upland, a complete beach may compress eight distinct ecosystems, eight different communities of plants and animals—"infinite riches in little room." A row of mansions and stinkpots is a single ecosystem, wealth reduced to stark poverty.

Ups and Downs

Venice did not always have canals, nor Holland dikes.

When lands of Western Washington were released from the burden of ice, they rebounded; this is *isostasy*. Thus, while the sea was rising, so was the land. Often one was rising faster than the other, and sometimes the pace of the rises varied from one spot to another nearby. Bewildering. Above today's beach there are *fossil shores,* usually obscured by bluff-slumps and vegetation but in some cases plainly identifiable as wave-cut benches. Below today's beach, unseen, lie *drowned shores.* For the past 4000–5000 years, the flooding and rebounding have pretty much evened out and the beach has been about where it is now.

Over and above such local factors, worldwide the sea level has been rising for 17,000 years, the result of a global warming that has accelerated in the past half-century. The greenhouse effect? Politicians and scientists may debate the cause; the fact is beyond dispute. The ice sheets of Greenland and Antarctica are shrinking. The federal Environmental Protection Agency estimates that by the year 2100 the sea, worldwide, will be 4–7 feet, possibly as many as 10 feet, higher than today. That would be plenty to do in Venice, Holland, and the subways of New York and Boston. In 1989 the Washington Department of Ecology sponsored a Northwest Sea Level Rise Conference, at which it was predicted that by 2100 the Whulge will be at least 5 feet higher.

One speaker at the conference cried out, "GET THOSE HOUSES OFF THE BEACH!"

A cynic responded, "Government can prohibit development. That causes a political uproar. It can buy all the private shores. This is enormously costly. It can do nothing—the popular solution."

Shake, Rattle, and Roll

Plate theory instructs us that our local Juan de Fuca Plate has the potential to generate an earthquake of magnitude 6 or 7, and the collision zone of that plate and the North American Plate, an 8 or 9. In 1949 the Whulge experienced a 7.1, the epicenter 33 miles beneath the surface, just east of McNeil Island. The 6.5 of 1965 was centered just east of Maury Island, 38 miles down.

Since 1980 a new field of study, *paleoseismology,* has probed the past. In 1992 a feature that long had stirred curiosity was found to have generated a major quake 1100 years ago from an epicenter just west of Seattle and fewer than 5 miles underground. The mind reels! Shocking! The probable maximum quake from this newly named Seattle Fault is calculated at 7.5; a 7.5 so near the surface and so close to a major population center would be magnitudes more destructive than a 7.5 at depth or at a distance. Catastrophic!

Restoration Point, on Bainbridge Island, caught Vancouver's eye in 1792. The wave-cut bench is so large, and perched so far above high tide, that it served as the site of an Original Settlers' village and, later, as a golf course for the nabobs who built mansions on the hill (formerly a tombolo) it ringed. The older surveyor of this book used to get dizzy hypothesizing a belated frenzy of isostasy. Wrong. On that fine day or dark night of A.D. 900 when forests slid into Lake Washington, where the trees were so pickled in cold water they recently have been scuba-logged for prime lumber, the Restoration Point bench lurched up 20 feet; the corresponding bench across the Whulge at Alki Point, 13 feet.

North of this east–west fault (an anomaly, other faults of the area run north–south), which has been traced to Issaquah and Fall City, the land fell—at West Point, 3 feet. The resulting saltmarsh has been filled for the heinous Metro sewage plant. The quake stirred up a *tsunami* (tidal wave) that swept over West Point; a repeat next Sunday would do it for Metro's atrocity as well as for the Navy's "Home Port" in Everett. As far north as Whidbey, the tsunami deposited a sheet of sand 5–15 centimeters thick over Cultus Bay; a repeat would do wholesale wholesome cleansing of spits and bars.

The Conjunction of Four

The morning of December 16, 1977, the older surveyor's father looked out the window of his home on Hood Canal and was confounded to see that his large, sturdy dock had disappeared. There had been no storm, no night of howling winds. The water, in fact, was glassy calm. As he watched, his dock reappeared in the ebbing of a 14.63-foot (Seattle) tide, the highest on record (equaled on January 27, 1983). He was witnessing a Conjunction of Three (C/3): (1) a spring tide (a twice-monthly event); (2) heavy, warm, snow-melting rains in the mountains that caused rivers to dump more water in the Whulge than it could quickly flush to the ocean (which happens two or three times in a normal winter); and (3) a deep storm centered offshore in the Pacific, its extremely low pressure extending inland over the Whulge (an event of every other winter or so).

This C/3 carried driftwood onto the porches of spit houses and into the privies of public parks, flowed over the tops of Skagit delta dikes, and set the more thoughtful beach residents to brooding over what would have happened had that deep storm not held steady in the Pacific but (4) moved in on the Whulge. They knew the glassy water would have been stirred to furious waves pounding the spits and dikes.

This surveyor's hunch is that when paleometeorologists get to it they will find firm evidence for perhaps two C/4s in the past century. In olden times when the small amount of building done on spits was of summer cabins, disposable and cheaply replaced, a spit-cleansing storm elicited a local shrug of the shoulders, no headlines in city newspapers, no record by historians. After World War II, the developers thoroughly ticky-tacked the spits, never a murmur of objection from government. As a result, the C/2s which are routine in winter soak a lot of living room rugs. The National Weather Service has begun issuing "high-tide warnings." Cousins of the ignorants who build on banks of the Mississippi whine for the TV. Boy Scouts and the Kiwanis fill sandbags. The Red Cross serves coffee and doughnuts.

Thanks to warnings by the National Weather Service, few lives will be lost in the next C/4, the first since the empty-beach, pre-historical era before World War II; but more than rugs will get wet, and insurance companies will take a whipping. The probability verges on certainty that the catastrophe will come within the lifetimes of folks now living on the spits. There, winter is not the season to be jolly.

People laughed when an earlier version of this book described the Hood Canal Floating Bridge as temporary. The book scarcely had reached bookstore shelves when, on February 13, 1979, Bridge No. 1 went to the bottom.

Sayeth this surveyor, "High water is the Lord's way of saying, 'If you can't stand My waves, get off My beach.' "

The Common Law and the Public Trust Doctrine*

In A.D. 533 the Institutes of Justinian, codification of Roman law dating to Romulus and Remus, declared that "by the law of nature" the air, the running water, the sea, and the seashore are "common to all mankind." In 1215, at Runnymede, the Magna Carta reaffirmed the Public right dating from before the coming of the Normans, and of the Danes, and of the Anglo-Saxons, and doubtless of the Kelts to beds and water of navigable streams, tidelands, and sea. It was a right that not even the Crown could abrogate. The Public Trust Doctrine (PTD) was a central tenet of the English common law which was taken over as a whole by the Founders of the United States to provide the unwritten foundation of the Constitution. The people of the new nation, as its sovereign, inherited the rights and duties of the Crown.

With the PTD embodied in the common law came the "Private Greed Doctrine" (PGD) embodied in human nature. Not being written down, the common law is subject to misinterpretation to serve Privatizer ends and, frequently, is unknown to or ignored by the legislative and executive branches of government. Citizens seeking their rights under the common law often must have recourse to the courts.

In 1821 the New Jersey courts defined the basic feature of the PTD as

---

*See the publisher's note on private property on page 11.

we know it today, ruling that the state "cannot ... make a direct and absolute grant of the waters of the state, divesting all the citizens of their common right." In 1892 the U.S. Supreme Court, in the landmark Illinois Central case, affirmed that "the state cannot abdicate its trust over property in which the whole people are interested ... [any more than it can] abdicate its police powers." In 1988 the U.S. Supreme Court confirmed state ownership of the tidelands of Mississippi. In its 1992 Lucas decision, the court ruled that the state of South Carolina's common law doctrines so limit a landowner's property rights as to insulate regulatory bodies from claims for "taking" what never had been owned by the "owner" in the first place.

In 1969 the Gallaghers, residents of the Lake Chelan shore, prepared for a major commercial construction by filling a portion of the lake bottom. Their neighbors, the Wilbours, brought suit and won from the Washington State Supreme Court a decision citing the Public right to navigation, a common law right. In a footnote, the court expressed wonderment "at the absence of any representation in this action by the Town or County of Chelan, or the State of Washington." By silence, every level of government had condoned this attempted Privatization, this "taking" of Public rights for Private profit. The footnote stimulated the Washington Environmental Council to an initiative campaign that resulted in the Shoreline Management Act (SMA) of 1971. Limitations are placed on Private intrusions, and Public policy defined, for lands from extreme low tide to 200 feet inland from extreme high tide.

The SMA of 1971 was not the measure drafted by the citizens. As rewritten by the legislature, it recognized values enshrined in the PTD—but imperfectly. Nevertheless, it was a step. If it did not resolve competing demands on shorelines but simply set out the competing interests and left them to fight it out, primarily in local governments usually dominated by Privatizer lobbyists, it ended the uncontestable divestiture and abdication of powers of the state. Further, in 1971 the legislature put a stop to the selling of tidelands and shorelands granted to the new state by Congress in 1889.

In 1987 the Washington Supreme Court affirmed the PTD as the law of the state. The legislature had passed a measure that amounted to an egregious gift to shoreline residential property owners. Benella Caminiti, co-founder of the Seattle Shorelines Coalition and first Chairperson of the Coast and Shoreline Committee of the Washington Environmental Council, filed suit. Peter Jenkins, veteran of legal combat to preserve the Nisqually delta from industrialization, took the case pro bono. The victory for the Public in *Caminiti* v. *Boyle* placed 1987 in shoreline history together with 1971. But the year was not finished. The Orion Corporation sought to convert Padilla Bay into a Venetian-style community of lagoons, fancy houses, and fancy stinkpots. In *Orion Corporation* v. *State,* the Supreme Court prevented residential development of the tideflats and declared that Private property owners cannot claim compensation for the "taking" of property where their proposed action violates the Public Trust. When the first Privatizers obtained these lands from the state, their land rights did not include a right to extinguish Public rights. The state had no power to transfer or alienate such Public rights.

The 1987 rulings by the state Supreme Court may be summarized as saying that any property rights people may think they have in tidelands are limited. In effect, the Public has an easement over the property to do certain things with which the Private owner cannot interfere. Public and Private rights coexist. Unfortunately, in 1987 the court did not address the right of the Public to set foot on property the court clearly defined as, in all essentials, Public. More courts lie ahead. The Public must hope for more Caminitis, more Jenkinses.

The Public to benefit from reclamation of ignored and derogated rights is much larger than beachwalkers pure and simple: recreational fishermen, kayakers and canoeists, birdwatchers, water-watchers, sunsets-over-the-Olympics-watchers. In addition to actions in the courts, there must be actions by the legislative and executive branches. How many legislators, mayors, governors, Congressmen, and leaders of environmental organizations know the meaning of PTD?

A scholar has written, "… the Public Trust interest in these lands and waters is so strong that government can defeat the Public right only by express legislation, and then only to promote other Public, rather than private, values" (Johnson, *Washington Law Review,* Vol. 67, No. 3 [July 1992]: 524). Legal scholars put it succinctly, "There's a lot more law in the PTD than has been squeezed out so far."

That the squeezing must and will continue is certain. The 1984 report of the Governor's Recreation Resource Advisory Committee gives results of an October 1983 survey of 600 randomly selected Washington voters. When asked what they thought would be the "most important areas or facilities to you during the next 5 years," 50 percent said public beaches and waterfronts. Playgrounds, for comparison, were named by 13 percent, athletic facilities by 10 percent.

The Golden Rule

The movement to compel government at every level to recognize and enforce the PTD might be viewed as a crusade. If so, it is not a crusade for a "taking" of private property rights. Rather, it seeks to undo a taking of Public rights, to restore the balance of Private and Public property rights under the rule of law.

Crusaders, being True Believers, have a tendency to be rude, as do infidels under attack. We do not, here, take a position on the comparative virtues of the medieval Christians and Muslims who did battle in the Holy Land. (We agree that Saladin was a much nicer fellow than Richard the Lion-Hearted, who was, after all, a Norman.) At places in these pages, we surveyors may sound angry, as perhaps is excusable when we kindly and peaceful folks have been harried from beaches by howling women brandishing garden tools and men bellowing threats of cruel and unusual punishment. Yet in walking thousands of miles of "Private" beaches, these surveyors have encountered more friendlies than hostiles. In our experience and judgment, beach people (ourselves included, of course) have more soul than inlanders who never have awakened in morning with the aroma of salt and seaweed in their noses, the lapping of waves in their ears. For every expression of suspicion, distrust, and hatred, we have a hundred times met tolerance, welcome, and camaraderie.

Our counsel to beachwalkers is to be of good cheer, have no fear. Do unto beach residents as you would wish done to you if you were one. Misled though they may be by lawyers who know only half (the profitable half) of the law, they nearly always will answer a smile with a smile. They understand your love of the beach—after all, that's where they *live*.

Whatever limits there may be on property rights of beach residents, they have human rights—to live in peace, to sleep at night undisturbed by bachanals, to sunbathe free from alien ogling, to not be forced by sad experience to suspect passing eyes as those of burglars casing the house, to walk the beach in front of their house without stepping in human or canine body wastes.

The Golden Rule and common courtesy embrace a host of virtues. *Be quiet.* No shouting when passing houses. Stifle the little children. *Be clean.* Carry and use a litterbag. Keep Rover leashed, if not in the doghouse at home. *Keep your eyes to yourself.* In short, *be nice.*

It is better, of course, to walk where houses are not. Seek out a goodly bluff. Avoid dense habitation. If you cannot, go at low tide, when you can walk the outer beach distant from picture windows. Choose the off-seasons and off-days and off-weather. On a drizzly Wednesday morning in February, a person can walk even city beaches invisibly.

Should a resident burst from a house breathing fire, screaming "Git off my beach!" remember that a soft answer turneth away wrath. No smart talk. You might politely ask which way he/she wishes you to git.

Maps and Books

Our guidebooks aim to teach a citizen how to tie the lands and waters together by use of his/her feet in order that he/she may have the knowledge to do something useful about it.

U.S. Geological Survey maps are listed for each section of this book. The inland hiker much prefers the Green Trails maps, USGS sheets overprinted to show current roads and trails and updated by the publisher every other year. Beaches don't change that much.

Pictorial landform maps are superb for regional orientation. *Puget Sound Region, Washington,* by Dee Molenaar, was produced specifically at the nagging of this surveyor to cover the area from the Olympics to the Cascades, Canada to Tenino. No harassment was needed to get Richard

Pargeter to publish his *The Puget Sound Country: A View from the North-west* and *Washington's Northwest Passage: A View from the Southwest.* These are both published by their respective authors and are periodically revised.

Public Trust Doctrine/Common Law Reading List

In 1983 came *Evaluation of Public Access to Washington's Shorelines Since Passage of the Shoreline Management Act of 1971,* by James W. Scott (Olympia: Washington Department of Ecology). Scott found that of the state's 2421 miles of marine shorelines, only 17 percent were accessible to the Public; excluding ocean beaches, only 10 percent. (Note: In Scott's study, "accessible" is used in a very narrow sense compared to the far broader definition in the present volume.)

Published by the Northwestern School of Law of Lewis and Clark College, *Environmental Law* carried an article by prominent authorities, "Symposium on the Public Trust and the Waters of the American West: Yesterday, Today, and Tomorrow" (19 [Spring 1989]: 425–735).

The Department of Ecology participated in a national study that in November 1990 culminated in the book *Putting the Public Trust Doctrine to Work: Applications to the Management of Lands, Waters, and Living Resources of the Coastal States.* Washington cases figure prominently.

As part of its aggressive consideration of the Public Trust Doctrine, the department's Shorelands Program supported Professor Ralph W. Johnson of the University of Washington School of Law, who had been researching the subject for 30-odd years. In July 1992, a seminal article was published in *Washington Law Review,* "The Public Trust Doctrine and Coastal Zone Management in Washington State" (pp. 521–97), by Ralph W. Johnson, Craighton E. Goeppele, David Jansen, and Rachel Paschael.

Not letting any seaweed grow under its feet, on November 18, 1992, the Shorelands Program sponsored a day-long symposium by Professor Johnson and four other legal scholars, introduced by State Land Commissioner Brian Boyle and managed by James Scott and Douglas Canning. The overflow attendance of 250 included officials (great, good, and bad), what appeared to be just about every Privatizer-employed attorney in the West, and a representation of citizen environmentalists. The proceedings of the symposium, a 120-page volume that belongs in every beach-walker's library, may be obtained free of charge by writing to Douglas Canning, Department of Ecology, Shorelands Program, P.O. Box 47690, Olympia, WA 98504-7690.

The Department of Natural Resources has published the four-volume *Your Public Beaches,* describing, mapping, and photographing those beaches that were not sold off by the DNR prior to the 1971 legislative ban on sales.

Living with the Shore of Puget Sound and the Georgia Strait (Durham, N.C.: Duke University Press, 1987), by Thomas A. Terich, is a review of the dangers of building on the beach and has a short (and curiously incomplete) bibliography useful to walkers.

The beachwalker *must* own *Washington Public Shore Guide: Marine Waters* (Seattle: University of Washington Press, 1986), by James W. Scott, M. A. Reuling, and Don Bates. This county-by-county guide revealed to this book's surveyors how many "Private Property" signs are bare-faced lies and gave them directions to Public accesses that (thanks to the neighbors' habit of tearing down signs) had evaded their surveys.

Modesty ought to (but won't) prevent us from mentioning *Walking the Beach to Bellingham*—not a guidebook, but a memoir of half a century of trudging beside the waters, now out of print. The original publisher fell on hard times. Others who might have picked up the rights have wimpishly failed to do so, frightened off by Privatizer attorneys. Try the library.

About This Book

The order of presentation of trips in this book is based on Seattle as ground (or beach) zero. First, the mainland beaches, Seattle to Tacoma and onward to the end of Puget Sound, then Seattle to Everett and onward to Bellingham. Next, the islands, in three groups, southern, western, and northern. Then the Kitsap Peninsula, the eastern shore from south to north, and the Hood Canal shore. Finally the Olympic Peninsula, the northeast of it only, and only a sampling.

Elliott Bay from Myrtle Edwards Park (page 79)

Certain facts and figures help a reader choose the hike suiting his/her needs and desires of the moment. In this book we do not separate them out from the text in information blocks: the "high point" of a beach walk never is a great deal more than sea level, and the "elevation gain" only occasionally has significance, and where such information matters it is easy to find in the text. "Hikable" is not determined on beaches by time of year so much as by stage of tide; all beaches are essentially open to feet the entire year. So few of these beaches offer the option of "backpack," the "one day" pretty much goes without saying. What about "roundtrip" and "hiking time"? Well, a beach is not a trail. On a trail a person covers a certain number of miles to and from a destination, in a certain number of hours/days. On a beach a person may set out in high gear and go all the way around Maury Island in a day, as did the older surveyor, or he/she may walk to the edge of the waves and sit there counting them all day, as did the younger surveyor when accompanied by her very young (crawling and toddling) assistant surveyor. In the text we note some mileages from access points to appealing destinations, but beach trips are not, as are trail trips, cookbook recipes so much as lists of ingredients available to the ingenious chef.

The trip descriptions vary in the amount of detail. The general rule is the closer to the population center (Seattle) and the more distinctive the features of the beach, the more is said about it ("Take the whites of two eggs, sprinkle in a teaspoon of garlic, put in a 300-degree oven ..."). At the other end of explicitness, little more may be given than the access ("Take one buffalo, preferably dead ..."). Discovery Park, Point Defiance Park, Blake Island, Ebey's Landing—these are examples of classics where we're so afraid you'll miss something great we take you by the hand and lead you from treasure to treasure. The South Sound, the east shore of Whidbey Island—these are examples of fine beaches (all beaches are fine) where we say, "There's the water. Make your own day."

The driving directions to beach accesses have been carefully thought out by the surveyors based on their own experiences in driving to those accesses. Generally, we expect the reader to depend heavily on maps, both those in this book and the highway and city-street maps sold wherever you buy gas or books. An inordinate amount of our precious space in these pages would be required were we to guide you from I-5 to Alki Avenue, and nobody competent to hold a steering wheel should have any trouble getting there on his/her own. On the other hand, the driving to Discovery Park has a few tricky turns and we've been kind enough to save you wrong turns. In a few cases the routes are so intricate we've lit a torch and led you step by step through the darkness—which at certain points in our area is deepened by conspiracy of parties Public and Private who do not wish the Public to get to "Private" water: official signs installed by parks departments are torn down; official-looking signs are installed declaring Public streets to be "Private Road—No Trespassing." In some cases the routes are too intricate to describe; the surveyors can walk to Steilacoom (you just follow the edge of the water) but can't drive there; trust the highway map, watch for signs, and tear your hair out.

Buses. Public transit. There is—there *must be*—the future of pedestrian re-creation, or much of it, in urban-suburban areas. But the future is not yet. To be sure, Metro buses lead to Discovery Park. And a fleet of Tacoma buses to Point Defiance Park. The bus enables splendid walks on Vashon and Maury Islands, the private car never ferried from the mainland. People who on principle do not own cars have walked from Everett to Discovery Park in several stages, dropped off and picked up by bus. The elder surveyor adventured by foot and bus from Cougar Mountain to Tacoma to Seattle and back to Cougar Mountain (backpacking, yet, sleeping 3 nights in three illegal and potentially dangerous places which will not be here divulged).

However, the traveler who trusts this guidebook for precise bus information is going to be sorry. Where service presently exists, the option is promoted by citing a route number. But do not rely for such information on a book that is revised only every several years. The bus situation is too fluid. Routes are added and deleted annually. To catch a bus, call the local bus company for up-to-date routes and times of service. Which company do you call? Well, if in King County, Metro. And so on.

By all means, check out the buses. Here we can do little more than point you in that direction.

Harvey   Manning

November 1993 and May 1994

A Note About Safety

Safety is an important concern in all outdoor activities. No guidebook can alert you to every hazard or anticipate the limitations of every reader. Therefore, the descriptions of roads, trails, routes, and natural features in this book are not representations that a particular place or excursion will be safe for your party. When you follow any of the routes described in this book, you assume responsibility for your own safety. Under normal conditions, such excursions require the usual attention to traffic, road and trail conditions, weather, terrain, the capabilities of your party, and other factors. Because many of the lands in this book are subject to development and/or change of ownership, conditions may have changed since this book was written that make your use of some of these routes unwise. Always check for current conditions, obey posted private property signs, and avoid confrontations with property owners or managers. Keeping informed on current conditions and exercising common sense are the keys to a safe, enjoyable outing.

The Mountaineers

MAINLAND: SEATTLE TO TACOMA

The Whulge Trail, close to the homes of just about everybody, is an all-year route, never blocked by snow except during the infrequent Ice Ages. Due to a partial rainshadow of the Olympics, the weather is better than farther east in—say—the Issaquah Alps. When storms are chasing each other's tails over the Northwest, mountains and foothills never freeing themselves of one storm's murk before the next obscures, blue holes open above the beach. These interludes are the most exciting times to go walking—clouds boiling around the Olympics, whitecaps flashing in the sun, surf rattling the gravel, wind nipping the nose. Of course, when the inland weather is sunny-blue, fogs may linger long on the water. That's not bad walking either, foghorns mourning, ghost ships sliding through mists, gulls wailing at the mystery of it all.

In the 20 crow-flying miles from Duwamish Head to Browns Point, the shore curves in and swings out for some 35 foot miles. Much beach is open at medium-high tide and just about all at low, save lighthouses,

West Point Lighthouse

bulkheads grandfathered in from the freely Privatizing era before 1971, and the Godzilla of dockage at Des Moines. However, in that thank-God-gone time when any owner of abutting uplands could build structures out over tidelands as he/she pleased, some 40,000 docks were built, and golly knows how many miles of "armoring" bulkheads. These latter so invade the gray trail that a walker striding along a beach 50 feet wide may suddenly find himself forced out, and out, until he is up to his knees in the salt. The bulkheads also, in guarding houses from waves, prevent those waves from attacking the bluff and bringing down to the beach the nutriments of gravel and sand which feed the longshore currents. A starved beach results, the surface 2 feet or more lower than before the armoring and studded with materials the longshore currents have difficulty carrying away—cobbles, big and round and slippery. A pace of a mile an hour may be too fast on a cobble beach. Lacking good boots, a person may develop miseries in the Achilles tendons.

There are all too many bulkheads and cobbles between Seattle and Tacoma. But as a result of what brought them, there also is more recent human history here than on any other stretch of the Whulge. Many a house has been built here over the years, only to slide down to the beach on a clump of bluff, or be slid down upon. Many a house has survived and grown into the landscape. The era of the mosquito fleet, of middy blouses and straw boaters and mandolins, is recalled by boxy clapboard houses with sleeping porches and verandas, by cabins that might have been chopped up for kindling a half-century ago but instead were lovingly preserved for the family memories. Sadly, a new generation has moved in from Kansas, come to Oz to see the Emerald City, and each family has more money than a Third World nation, enough to enrich a new generation of architects and engineers. The old homes with the salt blown deep in their woodwork by the winds of a half-century, wallpaper that smells of kelp and clams, are being demolished to make room for space-age technology—technology that also atttacks those wild-jungled bluffs we used to think of as the greenbelts of God.

Of the 35 beach miles from Seattle to Tacoma, better than 7 are in city, county, and state parks. Seven of these are major beach accesses, not bothered by Privates who truly believe they own the beach as fully as they do their bathtubs and by the police who leave to the judges enforcement (or not) of the common law. Those 7 park miles are mob scenes except on rainy Tuesday mornings in February. However, people mainly like to play in sand and waves close to the parking lot; even on bright summer Sundays, a few steps suffice to find a spot to pick your nose undisturbed.

Some twenty lesser accesses (small parks, street-ends) usually are better starts for crowd-free walks, largely because few have enough parking to accommodate many vehicles. Keep the bus alternatives in mind.

USGS maps: Duwamish Head, Vashon, Des Moines, Poverty Bay, Tacoma North

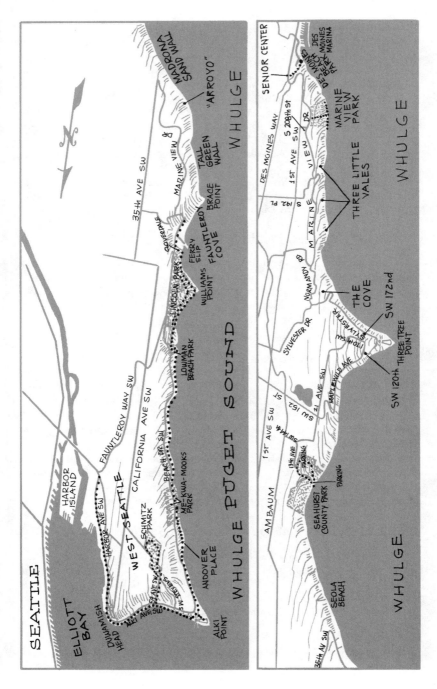

ALKI BEACH PARK

Bus: 37

Drive Alki Avenue SW.

The 154-acre park, 13,000 feet of shoreline, is Seattle's most famous beach. Winter storms draw TV cameras to gasp at ocean-size breakers smashing over the seawall. Spring sunshine ushers in the mating season, gals promenading the sidewalk in scanties, guys parading the avenue in pickups and muscle vans, tongues hanging out. In summer the sands are brightened by rows of sunburnt-red bikini bottoms. At low tide the beach is the water-lover's choice, the seawall berming out sidewalk and avenue. Give the avenue this—it keeps the beach housefree most of the way to the Alki Point Lighthouse (visiting hours, 1:00–4:00 P.M.).

Northeast from Alki Point to Duwamish Head, 2½ miles

The headland is the premier spot for watching ferries to Bainbridge Island and Bremerton, ships and barges and tugs to and from Duwamish Waterways, and playboats to and from marinas. Vistas of downtown Seattle, Queen Anne Hill, Magnolia Bluff, West Point, and the Olympics.

Inland from Alki Point to Schmitz Park

A few steps on SW Stevens Street or 59 Avenue SW lead to the lower end of Schmitz Park, one of only two ancient forests in Seattle (the other is Seward Park on Lake Washington). Nearly 2 miles of paths intertwine the 50-acre park. Big trees. A creek that is not in a pipe.

The Birthplace of Seattle Monument on Alki Point at 63 Avenue SW brings to mind that when the schooner *Exact* debarked the first band of roving townboomers in 1851 (the men began to plat, the women to weep, the Original Residents to shake their heads) the forested ravine of Schmitz Park was just about exactly as it is now. And this was what Puget Sound country looked like all the way to the mountains. Bless Ferdinand and Emma Schmitz for preserving this remembrance of things past.

South from Alki Point to Lincoln Park, 3 miles

At Alki Point, Alki Avenue SW changes name to Beach Drive SW and lets Privates cross the street to squat by the water. At a very low tide the whole beach can be walked. Why bother? The Great Wall of Alki, houses shoulder-to-shoulder, keeps the Public at bay. However, several gaps provide ways through from Public street to Public water.

Andover Place

Street right-of-way path to beach.

Me-Kwa-Mooks Park

At Oregon Street, another Schmitz gift. Half the 34 acres is wooded bluff, half is 2000 feet of beach. Glacier droppings top sandstone, one of the few outcrops of non-glacial rock in the area. The earthquake from the Seattle Fault, 1100 years ago, jolted this formation 13 feet up.

Lowman Beach Park

A short strip of sand and shingle where Public lips can wrap around a sandwich without being shouted at. An alley-street allows the Public to sneak between beach houses and bluff to Lincoln Park.

LINCOLN PARK

Bus: 54

Drive Fauntleroy Avenue SW to Cloverdale.

The 5350 feet of beach, views from the 130 acres of forest atop the 175-foot bluff, and good bus service place this on everybody's list of Seattle favorites.

Steps and ramp descend from Fauntleroy parking to a bulkhead walkway which violates the beach but does permit high-tide walking. On Williams Point the primeval spit has been civilized by Colman Pool, a concrete tub of warm, chlorinated water for swimmers afraid of cold saltwater and jellyfish. Walk the 1 mile of beach/bulkhead north to houses, return to one of three safe paths up the bluff, and climb to views across broad waters to the Vashon ferry, Bainbridge ferry, and Olympics.

South from Lincoln Park to Seahurst (Ed Munro) Park, 4 miles

The Privates at Fauntleroy Cove guard their Great Wall, ever vigilant. The only practical way for Publics to set foot on the beach is from Lincoln Park at low tide, walking under the ferry dock.

Until recently the shore walk was a visit to times gone by. Summer cabins from the 1920s. Two-storey-plus-garret clapboard-and-shingle boxes from early in the century. Front porches for pre-TV evening entertainment. Second-floor sleeping porches whose windows wide open to the winds kept lungs safe at night from germs of the White Plague. Steamer races between Seattle and Tacoma. Mandolins and ukuleles around the beachfire. Going, going, gone.... The land is too valuable to be wasted on cheap old houses. Glass-and-cedar monuments to ego are more valued by the gypsy wealthy than history, which isn't *theirs* anyway.

Generations of Seattleites rejoiced in their heritage of "unbuildable" bluffs. But when views were transmuted by overpopulation to pure gold, with which the overpopulators were richly supplied, no terrain could frustrate the costly ingenuity of engineers and the cupidity of developers for whom the land is only real estate. Some bluffs can be somewhat stabilized by underground drainage pipes and pumps. Steel pilings driven deep in the beach can support a platform connected to the bluff by breakaway timbers which, on a rainy winter night, slide with the bluff to the beach, passing harmlessly beneath the picture windows on stilts. The other environmental cost is more fundamental. Bulkheads and seawalls. Armoring. The starved beach. Masses of cobbles. Crippled walkers.

Brace Point, third in the southward succession of vandalized spits, is a crowd of houses. The next ¼ mile, however, has been kept wild by a bluff rising 300 steep and unstable feet. This Tall Green Wall catches the eye from far away. But the engineers cometh.

On the next spit are piling stubs, relict of a dock. At the base of the bluff, deeply scooped by an ancient gravel mine (thus the dock), are houses of Arroyo Beach, connected by a switchback road to Arroyo Heights; the developer was advised by his sales manager that "arroyo" was classier than "Gravel Pit Estates."

In the 1 mile beyond the "arroyo" are houses of Seola Beach, then one of the most magnificent madrona forests of the Whulge on one of its finest walls of sand (but there do cometh the engineers, yes), then a pretty little valley breaching the bluff. The final ¼ mile to Inglesea, at the boundary of Seahurst Park, is a row of beach houses.

The distance north from Seahurst Park to Lincoln Park is also 4 miles, of course. But the first 2½ miles, to the Tall Green Wall, are the most scenic, least housed, and easiest on the ankles. Put it on the short list of great little urban-area beach walks.

Driftwood at Seahurst (Ed Munro) Park

SEAHURST (ED MUNRO) PARK

Bus: 136 to SW 144 Street, then walk a few blocks

Drive Ambaum Boulevard in Burien via SW 144 Street.

When King County voters of the 1960s approved the Forward Thrust bond issue, several bits of beach had not yet been profiteered. Creeks in deep tanglewood gulches. Bluffs appallingly tall or unstable. Among these were the 185 acres of forest and 5000 feet of beach acquired for Seahurst (Ed Munro) Park.

Trails tour some 3 miles of big forests and babbling creek. The creek-mouth parking gives access to an upper concrete seawall protecting a picnic area–pathway open at the highest tides, a lower gabion wall topped by a perched beach walkable at middle tides, and natural beach open at low tides. A noble bluff enwildens the beach scene ½ mile north to park's end and houses' start.

South from Seahurst (Ed Munro) Park to Des Moines Beach Park, 7 miles

Park beach continues ¼ mile from the creek. In the next ¼ mile houses are hidden by a tall bluff, route of slumping clumps of trees, boughs forming a canopy over the sands. Houses crowd the water the following 2 miles to Three Tree Point.

Three Tree Point (Point Pully)

On the north side of the point is the street-end of SW 120. On the south side SW 172 edges the driftwood. Both are approached via Maplewild Avenue SW. But no parking at either. A Public would have to park at a considerable distance or—better—take bus 136 to Marine View Drive and walk from SW 170. The navigation light is on private property and cannot be visited.

Onward South. The jut of Three Tree Point (another heavenly spit converted to earthly real estate) is a landmark for miles. Rounding the tip, Alki Point is lost from sight and Rainier is revealed. The first 1 mile of beach is closely paralleled by road and mostly lined by houses. Then a ¼-mile-wide valley breaches the bluff and houses briefly are few. A delightful little park by the creek mouth belongs to Normandy Park Community Club.

For ½ mile houses are solid-packed. Then, gloryosky, the longest stretch of lonesome shore between Seattle and Tacoma, 2½ miles of as grand a "wildness within" as the civilized Whulge has to offer. Not as wild as it was recently. Forward Thrust didn't win 'em all. Three little vales break through from upland to beach. In 1977 they had a total of half a dozen modest homes. The northernmost now is a baronial estate and the southernmost is chock-a-block with millions of dollars' worth of trophy mansions. A baymouth bar across the middle of the three has newly blossomed out in spiffiness, but pristinity of the marsh enclosed by the bar is protected (we trust) by wetlands law; this and Dumas Bay are the only preserved examples of this type of ecosystem between Seattle and Tacoma. The best of this best stretch of shore ensues south of the valley trio.

Marine View Park

Acquired by King County's Forward Thrust, this ½ mile of beach defended by a formidable 200-foot bluff is now administered by the City of Normandy Park. Bluff north and south brings the total wildness to nearly

1 mile. Drive 1 Avenue S, then S 208 Street, then turn south a few feet on Marine View Drive. Or take bus 130 or 132 and walk ¼ mile. The parking area is so tiny that visitors must always be few. The trail (signed "steep and 1200 feet long") plummets to the brink of a beachside precipice which was very perilous until construction of the tower staircase.

Onward South. Just south of Marine View Park, a private road snakes down to a rumple in the bluff which temporarily accommodates "Fancy Houses Estates." The next neighborhood south is less fancy, a half-dozen houses tucked atop bulkheads at bluff base, low-tide-only vehicle access by driving the beach. On the first survey, in 1977, the older surveyor was joined on his journey north by the whole neighborhood of dogs from dozens of ramshackles on pilings. But the Health Department cometh. The ramshackles that couldn't hook to sewer are gone.

Starting from the south, at Des Moines Beach Park, the first 1¼ miles to Marine View Park and the first of the Three Little Vales are as fine a lonesome beach as one can find in Puget Sound City. The succeeding 1¼ miles also make the Excellent List.

DES MOINES BEACH PARK

Bus: 130 and 132

Drive to the north end of Des Moines Marina.

Des Moines Creek exits from a green gorge at the north edge of Des Moines Marina. Here was the Covenant Beach Bible Camp, bought by King County in 1987. The quaint old buildings were converted to a senior center and picnic shelter, old roads closed to give some 2 miles of greenwood strolling up the creek. A Public pier at the north edge of the marina gives vistas north and south and west.

SALTWATER STATE PARK

Bus: 130 to South 28, then walk ¼ mile

Drive Marine View Drive SW (Highway 509).

This 88-acre park, with 1445 feet of beach, bears the weight of 1 million visitors a year. Trails wind through forest in the valley of Smith Creek, culminating in a superb blufftop view.

North from Saltwater State Park to Des Moines Marina, 1½ miles

The bluff leaps up 150 feet, exceptionally vertical, hard sandstones-shales and, atop an unconformity, gravels. Layers of peat—a black, partly carbonized wood—are an early step toward coal. Large granite erratics dropped from icebergs are imbedded in the gravels. Clumps of trees from

Des Moines Beach Park

the blufftop continue to grow on the beach until winter storms batter them to driftwood.

For 1 mile the beach is free from the sight of houses, and pretty much the bodies, of Privates, few of whom have chiseled paths in the bluff. At Des Moines valley, turn back. Not without trauma and peril can a walker get by the Des Moines Marina, the one great huge beach obliterator between Duwamish Head and Browns Point. For ½ mile it protrudes beyond not only the high-tide line but also the low-tide line, out into deep water. Privates on its south boundary are so uptight that Publics trying to sneak through their yards trigger silent alarms and the police cars come a-screaming.

South from Saltwater State Park to Redondo Waterfront Park, 1¾ miles

Beyond a handful of houses begins a lovely long stretch of mostly empty beach. For ½ mile a 125-foot cliff keeps Privates safely distant. A short strip of houses has access via a narrow, piling-protected road from Woodmont Beach on the south. The bluff dwindles to a bank, with solid houses the final scant 1 mile.

REDONDO WATERFRONT PARK

Drive from Highway 509 down Redondo Way.

In the 1920s Redondo Beach was a summer-long carnival: two dance halls, a bowling alley, a merry-go-round and ferris wheel, games of skill

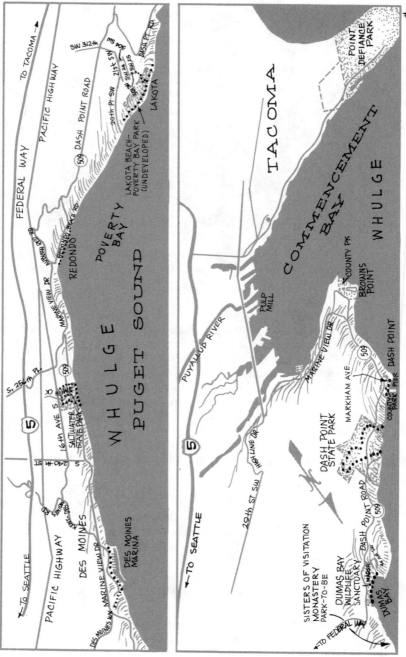

and chance, cotton candy and hot dogs and ice cream sodas. The mosquito fleet steamed south from Seattle, north from Tacoma, to a convergence of 5000 merrymakers at a time. The action never gets that frantic nowadays, but 1060 feet of King County Parks beach (2.3 acres of upland!) get a good stomping. You can still buy fish and chips or, at the grocery store, an ice cream bar and a six-pack of cold root beer.

Puget Sound is narrow here in its East Passage, the island bluffs close across the water. To the southwest appears Point Defiance. The stack of the ASARCO smelter is gone and so the south winds no longer bring to the nose the sharp bite of sulfur dioxide, but still wafting is the privy stench of pulpmill hydrogen sulfide.

The beach route is open north to Saltwater State Park, 1¾ miles, but is best walked from the north.

South from Redondo Waterfront Park to Dash Point State Park, 4 miles

Though not the lonesomest, this surely has the most variety of any beach between Seattle and Tacoma. Major parks at each end and four intervening accesses to the beach accommodate jaunts of any length, from an hour to all day.

In December 1990 a storm demolished the timber seawall of a long ½ mile of Redondo Beach Road South. Commuters accustomed to saving several minutes by doubling the speed limit demanded reconstruction. Residents newly accustomed to the sound of waves wished not to revive the twice-daily Grand Prix. In the spring of 1993 the racers lost. King County accepted easements from homeowners for a machine-free beach park. In 1994 the racers won, got their road replaced.

Where the commuters' course turns uphill and inland, waterfront houses continue another ½ mile, succeeded by ½ mile of high bluff and wild beach, ending in Adelaide valley.

20 Place Street-End

At 1½ miles from Redondo, a street-end touches the beach. The display of signs is hostile to the max ("Beware of Killer Dogs"). From 21 Avenue SW (see Lakota Beach–Poverty Bay Park), turn right on narrow, twisty 20 Place SW (signed "Beach"), down a cute little ravine. Parking at the driftwood for two cars. Carry a cudgel for self-defense in case the dogs are loose.

Lakota Beach–Poverty Bay Park*

South from the street-end park is ½ mile of 300-foot bluff. The south half is county park. Undeveloped. Naught to offer funseekers but a maze of trails in wildland forest, a cathedral choir of birds, and a lonesome

*See the publisher's note on private property on page 11.

beach in broad view of the Gravel Coast of Maury Island.

Finding the park is a challenge. Where SW 312 intersects Dash Point Road (Highway 509) at a stoplight just south of a small shopping center, turn west on 21 Place SW, which bends north as 21 Avenue SW. Turn left on 304 Street SW, which bends right as 24 Avenue. Turn left on 301 Place, which at a jog becomes 25 Avenue. At the jog is space to park a car or two. The Privates have heaped up lawn-clippings and hedge-trimmings and logs to artfully conceal from Publics the start of a very decent, unsigned trail a scant ½ mile down to the beach.

Onward South. The wild bluff of Lakota Beach Park yields at the boundary to the low bank and densely inhabited valley of Lakota Beach. Picture windows and plastic seagulls and stinkpots terminate at a point embellished by granite boulders, gift of the Canadian glacier. This is the east end of Dumas Bay. From here to "Biltgood Point" the shoreline is about 1 mile; at low tide the bay empties and the flats permit a shortcut across the bay mouth. Three creeks enter the bay. The southernmost is in Dumas Bay Wildlife Sanctuary.

Sisters of Visitation Monastery

But first, just south of the northernmost creek, is the site of an abandoned monastery, a dozen blufftop acres bought by the City of Federal Way. Development for public access is expected by 1995.

Dumas Bay Wildlife Sanctuary

Though the City of Federal Way, in accepting the Forward Thrust property from King County, has renamed it "park," it is *not* a playground. The 23 acres, 450 feet of shore, mostly a baymouth bar enclosing a marvelous lagoon marsh, are not for kinetic recreation but respectful birding.

Cattails and reeds extend inland from the driftwood ¼ mile; in season there's such a racket of redwing blackbirds and frogs that the crows and gulls hardly can be heard. As for the shallow little bay, its seaweeds and creek-deposited mucks nourish such tasty bites that at times one hardly can see the water. One fine April afternoon the surveyor found fleets of black brants, terns, mallards, and goldeneyes, the motley mob dominated by a solitary white-fronted goose. Mergansers and surf scoters patrolled offshore, cormorants posed on rocks, the sands were alive with killdeer and peep, and kingfishers scolded, not to mention the great blue herons standing in the water pretending to be driftwood. The sanctuary has a fifty-nest heronry (nesting area) whose existence in an urban area testifies to the natural defenses of the wetland.

From Dash Point Road turn onto 44 Avenue SW 0.25 mile. At the only gap in houses, at 310 Street SW, is the parking lot. Walk the trail ¼ mile down through alder forest, beside the creek that feeds the marsh, to a little meadow by the driftwood.

Onward South. From the baymouth bar the shore curves north, then west, a scant ½ mile, houses atop the slope at first, then not, to the hulk of a beached barge, the *Biltgood,* whose hull declares its home port to have been Tacoma. A 150-foot bluff rises to Camp Kilworth of the Boy Scouts of America (off Highway 509 on 48th) and Palisades Retreat. The final ¾ mile to Dash Point State Park has houses atop the precipitous bluff and, somehow, a dozen at the base accessible solely by trails hacked in the 150-foot cliff. Fascinating. Do they flush their toilets? Where?

Backward North. This Redondo–Dash Point shore is some of the best urban beachwalking. Dash Point is the sweetest start because the best of the best is to the *Biltgood,* Dumas Bay, and Lakota Beach Park. Take a whole day for the birds and omit the final mile to Redondo.

DASH POINT STATE PARK

Bus: Tacoma 61A

Drive Highway 509, turn right on 47th, and finally left on Dash Point Road.

The 297 acres, 3500 feet of sandy beach beneath a 225-foot bluff of vertical clay and sand topped by forest, have 3 miles or more of trails looping up and down and around the park's central ravine.

The shore, having trended southerly from Alki to Redondo, then bending southwesterly to Dash Point, sharply swings more southerly, opening new views past the tip of Vashon Island to Point Defiance and Gig Harbor. Maury Island blocks out the North Sound.

West and South to Beach-End in Commencement Bay, 4 miles

A traveler from afar north finds the scenery stranger and stranger, just as it becomes homelier to folks of the south who do most of the walking here, exploiting the quick access from Tacoma domiciles.

Some ¾ mile from the state park is Dash Point. To walk there at any but the lowest tides requires wading past a bulkhead. The tip of the point is a home, closely jostled by a park.

Dash Point State Park

Bus: 61A, then walk

From Highway 509 turn off on Markham Avenue, guided by no visible sign announcing the park but a prominent sign soliciting patronage of Dash Point Lobster Shop.

The pride of this Pierce County parklet is a fishing pier giving views northward nearly to Three Tree Point (Point Robinson on Maury Island blocks it out), across the mouth of Commencement Bay (not yet quite seen) to Point Defiance, and across East Passage to Vashon and Maury Islands and Dalco Passage.

Onward South. Beach houses continue past Dash Point ¼ mile. A

Browns Point Lighthouse

175-foot cliff then leaps up, secluding the waterside for ½ mile, to the resumption of houses on the out-bulging flat of Browns Point, last in the Seattle-to-Tacoma sorry succession of ravaged spits.

Browns Point Park

The lighthouse is photogenic, the lawns manicured, the views superb. Popular for outdoor weddings. Getting there is half the fun. The best bet is Tacoma bus 61A. Alternately, drive Highway 509 to a big sign, "Welcome to Browns Point Shopping Center," and a tiny shrubbery-obscured sign pointing parkward on ¼ mile of cute-named lanes.

Onward South. From the lighthouse the shore rounds easterly to the first views directly into Commencement Bay and across to downtown Tacoma. For ¼ mile picture windows wall the beach. Then the bluff returns, 165 feet and stunningly vertical and absolutely pathless.

In this final scant 1 mile to a marina and the beginning of industrial trash is a major surprise—a "complete" beach—driftwood, dunes, and even a tiny lagoon marsh. Lonesome beachwalking and panoramas of a city, an unusual (unique?) combination. History, too—ancient barges rotting on the beach, others sinking into the bay, ships moving to and from the Port of Tacoma, and (in memory's eye) the tallest masonry construction in the world, grim reaper of nobody knows how many smelter employees and neighbors.

46

MAINLAND: TACOMA TO OLYMPIA TO ALLYN

The "South Sound": Peter Puget's Sound. North is Main Street, carrying traffic of the world. South is lonesomer, a few ships, some tugs–barges, mainly playboats. North is where the glaciers came from and stayed the longest. In the South the Vashon Stade of the Fraser Glaciation was relatively brief and its drift is more mixed with the older Salmon Springs deposits, the gravels partly iron-cemented to conglomerate, the sands nearly sandstone, the blue clays often iron-stained and compacted to rubbly shale, forming quite vertical walls—but not so tall as North, often mere banks that let houses crowd the water.

South is the hotbed of history: the State Historical Museum in Tacoma; the reconstruction of Fort Nisqually at Point Defiance; old homes of Steilacoom; the site of Fort Nisqually, first European settlement on Puget Sound; Treaty Tree, where were signed the Medicine Creek Treaties that started the "Indian" (White) Wars; and Tumwater, first American settlement on the Sound.

North is characterized by broad sweeps of water and wind, long views and violent storm surfs, high bluffs, often of naked drift, and wide beaches beaten from the cliffs—drama.

South is what Vancouver called "the sea in the forest." A complexity of bays and spits, a maze of passages and inlets and reaches and islands. Estuaries lovely to look at, delightful to boat, appalling to boot, the intermingling of muck and brush and water forming absolute route-stoppers. Birds enjoy the protected waters—everywhere in winter are small flocks, vast fleets—and the population of great blue herons and kingfishers may be the largest in the world. Seals, too, are happy here. So are people who appreciate the intimacy, the coziness, of narrow waterways where waves are feebler and thus beaches narrower. When trees slide down the bluff and topple to the sands they are not, North-like, battered to driftwood in a winter and carried away by longshore currents; they just lie there growing seaweed and barnacles, awful to crawl through. Vegetation grows to the edge of the beach, swordferns root in the sands, and maples and alders lean far over the shingle, enclosing green-lit alcoves of waterfalls and maidenhair fern; if they lean too low they halt any critter taller than a weasel. The shallow bays drain at low tide to become enormities of mudflats, sometimes providing detours around upland brush but often sucking in boots, and knees, if never entire hikers.

A Ruston marina and Mount Rainier from the Vashon ferry

As the crow flies, the distance from Tacoma to Olympia is about 30 miles; from Olympia to the geographically momentous if otherwise obscure Allyn, about the same. As the foot goes, who knows? The foot doesn't fly. South from Tacoma, whether on beach at low-medium tides or on the all-tides railway, the Whulge Trail is straightforward. Save for the occasional iron horse, whatever racket is made by humans is lost in the cries of gulls. Ships dwindle to naught. The incubus of commercial jets, so heavily burdening the North, lightens.

The Nisqually River ends the Whulge Trail. Beyond, the foot finds intermittent opportunities but no longer a continuous route. Yet there are wonders in the Deep South. As Vikings gawked through the streets of Constantinople gnawing dried herrings while envying alien sweetmeats, the North Sounder sees that man cannot live by boots alone. He must have boats, too. (Please—oars, paddles, sails. Stifle the stinkpots.)

Beyond the Nisqually these pages describe the beach selectively rather than comprehensively. Sampling. Folks from faraway are willing to spend the required torture time on highways only for choice bits. Folks who live nearby know these intimately and know, too, how to evade the Privatizers and their killer dogs and attorneys.

USGS maps: Tacoma South, Gig Harbor, Steilacoom, McNeil Island, Longbranch, Squaxin Island, Shelton, Mason Lake, Vaughn, Nisqually, Lacey, Tumwater

COMMENCEMENT BAY

Bus: 13

Drive Schuster Parkway to Ruston Way.

Tacoma grew up on dredged-filled tidal marshes of the Puyallup River and on glacier drift atop the adjoining bluffs. The city's birthplace in Old Town, on the shore of the open bay, was industrially begrimed and forgotten. Then rediscovered and prized. The busy shore was cleaned up, prettied up, and parked up for 2 full miles, from where Schuster Parkway descends the bluff at McCarver Street, to North 49 Street and the smelter ruins. When Tacoma eradicates the last poisonous residues of dead Ruston, it could hitch the 2 miles of bay parks to Point Defiance and become the envy of the Western world.

The bay shore already is well-hitched in the other direction. The Bayside Trail leads 2½ miles, more or less in this variant and that, to Stadium High School, a former railway hotel in French Provincial style, spires and turrets and garrets and Quasimodo; the stadium (a natural scoop in the bluff) itself, where the oratory of olden-day Fourth-of-July patriots still reverberates; the Washington State Historical Museum and Old City Hall. The forest path passes five rainy-day picnic shelters, views to the pulpmill steam plume and other industries of the Puyallup flats,

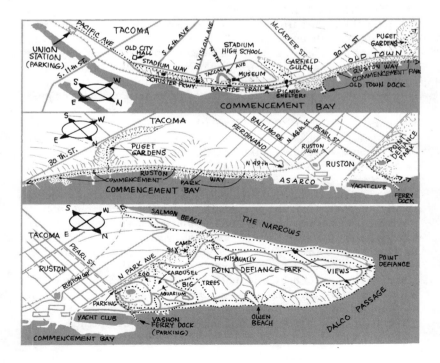

Commencement Park

ships in the bay, and skylines of the Cascades and Olympics. From McCarver a Schuster sidewalk goes 0.4 mile to Garfield Gulch Park, start of the greenwood climb up the bluff.

At McCarver is Commencement Park, the start of 2 continuous miles of shore parks and interspersed eateries. The pedestrian should fill a rucksack at Ocean Fish Company, walk out to the end of Old Town Dock, and peel shrimp while soaking up scenery and history. First seen by Europeans (Vancouver) in 1792 and named in 1841 by the Wilkes Exploring Expedition, which here commenced its work, Commencement Bay was settled in 1852. In the 1860s Job Carr homesteaded at Chebaulip (Old Town). As agent of the Northern Pacific Railroad, McCarver renamed the projected metropolis for The Mountain (Tahoma) and relocated the center to the blufftop.

Up the hill a block from the dock are the recently brick-paved streets and bright little shoppes of (new) Old Town. Next to the dock is rotting-away piling and planking, surely to be soon replaced by something very costly. The wide walkway, with viewpoints and benches, proceeds by Hamilton Park and a derelict building on piles awaiting rebirth, and three fancy restaurants in a row. From Puget Park a trail ascends the green gulch of Puget Creek. Two more restaurants; Fire Station No. 5 (a retired fireboat rests on dry land); Marine Park, the Lee Davis Pier, a vantage for views across the bay to Browns Point and out to Maury Island. Another expense-account restaurant. At 49th the City of Tacoma ends.

A huge sign, "ASARCO TACOMA," used to announce entry into the City of Ruston, the Butte of the Whulge. Built in 1887, closed in 1985, the smelter is alleged to have smitten golly knows how many employees who loyally accepted the highly questionable air (sniffable on a south wind as far as Seattle) for the sake of a steady job and how many neighbors whose kitchen gardens were anti-nutritious, receiving the fallout of 310 tons of airborne arsenic a year. The matter will be in the courts probably until everybody involved is long gone. Completed in 1917, the 571-foot smelter stack, 12,700 tons of brick and mortar, was the tallest in the world. On January 17, 1993, the 562-foot stack (9 feet had been sliced off after an earthquake), having been observed to be listing, the sides bulging and bricks falling, was dynamited. An audience of 100,000 watched 2.5 million bricks tumble into the 360-foot ditch dug to receive them. As of 1993 the entire 87-acre ASARCO property was being cleared of buildings, junk, and topsoil. Though the lawyers insist the arsenic-lead contamination is no danger, ASARCO has agreed to spend $80 million over 7 years digging up and replacing soil on more than 500 properties.

POINT DEFIANCE PARK

Bus: 10 or 11

Drive Highway 16 toward Narrows Bridge and turn right on Pearl Street.

The greatest city park in the nation? On the nomination list, anyhow. Acquired from the U.S. Army in 1888 (formal title transferred in 1906), this peninsula ¾ mile wide and nearly 2 miles long juts out between The Narrows and Dalco Passage. From 3 miles of mostly wild beach, the drift cliffs leap to an upland of ancient forest interweaving 50 miles of trails. There are gardens, a zoo, and an aquarium—and Camp Six and Fort Nisqually, by golly. As the second-largest municipal park in America, 698 acres, exceeded only by New York's Central Park, this is not merely a city asset but a regional treasure.

Five Mile Drive, looping the perimeter, has numerous parking areas for short walks on blufftop or in forest. For the beach, up to 6 miles round trip on a low-medium tide, drive to parking at the Vashon ferry dock or Owen Beach.

Upland Perimeter Loop, 7 miles

The recommended plan is to park (or get off the bus) at the Pearl Street entrance, head for the water but stop while still atop the bluff, and mainly stay there all around the peninsula. The trail system is not signed and there are a dozen times more paths than shown on maps—just take the outermost (nearest the bluff) and, that failing, walk the road or cross into forest. Following are the sights along the way.

Overlook of Vashon Island ferry dock, and the black-slag (from the smelter) peninsula of the Tacoma Yacht Club, and Commencement Bay, and the Cascades. Japanese Gardens. Job Carr Home, moved here from Old Tacoma, built in 1864, the settlement's first post office. A sign on Five Mile Drive, "Big Tree Trail—This Is the Forest Primeval," a ¾-mile loop up one side of a ravine, down the other, sampling old Douglas firs and other splendid wildland vegetables. Rhododendron Gardens. A major ravine, slicing the bluff, letting the road descend to Owen Beach. For perimeter purposes it is best to follow this road down to the beach and on the far side of the ravine find meager paths up the bluff. Vashon Island Viewpoint. Another superb green-riot ravine and the last decent trail to the beach. The Mountaineer Tree, a fir 220 feet tall, a circumference of 24 feet, about 400 years old. Another great vista, up Colvos Passage. Point Defiance Viewpoint, atop a sand-gravel cliff above the navigation light, views across to Gig Harbor. Here, in 1841, Lieutenant Wilkes declared that with a few cannon he could defy the fleets of the world; in 1868 President Johnson signed the order reserving the site for coast artillery, but guns never were emplaced. Walking distance to here, about 4 miles. Onward to ...

Madronas leaning over the bluff brink. Eagle-perch fir snags. Narrows Bridge Viewpoint. Never Never Land, a Mother Goose World. A viewpoint noting the camp made May 20, 1792, by Peter Puget, when detailed by Captain Vancouver to explore southward into the "sea in the forest."

Fort Nisqually—allow at least an hour here. The first fort, built in 1833 by Hudson's Bay Company, was destroyed by Indians and little about it is known except the location near the beach just north of the Nisqually River. The second fort was built in 1843 at a more inland site (now Dupont), 17 miles south of here. Remnants were moved here in 1933, and the entire fort was faithfully reconstructed. Among the fort's firsts: first European settlement on the Sound, first cattle, sheep, and chickens, first European marriage, first European child, first religious instruction, first murder. The only original buildings are the granary, the oldest surviving building (1843) in Washington, and the factor's house, now a museum, open afternoons, featuring pioneer furnishings and a souvenir shop. Replica structures exhibiting pioneer artifacts: blacksmith shop, two lookout towers, kitchen, washroom, Nisqually House (the warehouse that was located on the beach below the fort). Also original is the boiler of the wood-burning

Olden-time "lokie" (a sidewinder) at Point Defiance Park

Beaver, launched in England in 1835, arrived at Nisqually in 1837, the first steamship on the Northwest coast, wrecked off Vancouver, British Columbia, in 1888. Onward....

From a group camp just below the fort, bluff-near paths to the Salmon Beach community and Narrows Bridge.

Camp Six—allow another hour, especially if you've spent a lot of time in second-growth forests among evidences of railroad logging, for here are a logging railroad complete with locomotive, a Shay No. 7, invented in 1880, a huge Lidgerwood Skidder, a Dolbeer Donkey, a loaded log car, other donkeys, yarders, and loaders, a 110-foot fully rigged spar tree, and two complete logging camps, one (formerly Camp 7 on the slopes of Mount Rainier) resting on the ground, the other (Quinault Car Camp) on flat-cars. Onward, now inland, the bluff having been left at the fort....

Northwest Native Gardens. Via a detour left, the zoo (the owls are outstanding); the aquarium, best on a rainy winter day when the seals and walrus and otter are lonesome and will stage a swimming show for your solitary benefit; and the 1906 carousel. Rose gardens. A pond full of islands, bridges, and ducks. Waterfalls. And so back to the Pearl Street entrance, some 3 walking miles from Point Defiance.

Vashon Ferry Dock to Point Defiance, 2½ miles

From the park entrance descend road or path ¼ mile to the ferry dock and follow the shore on a closed-off road a scant 1 mile to Owen Bathing Beach. From here the beach is wild, and wilder, beneath the 200-foot jungled bluff of sand and blue clay, with views over Dalco Passage, north to the Issaquah Alps. In 1 mile is the last path up the bluff—the last easy beach escape in the park. In a long ½ mile more the shore curves around to Point Defiance and the light, at the base of a great sand precipice, 2½ miles from the Vashon ferry dock. An exciting place—Dalco currents colliding with Narrows currents, fishermen boated and winged clustered at the rip, views over the water to Gig Harbor and up and down the Sound.

South from Point Defiance to Titlow Beach Park, 4¾ miles*

The 1½ miles of beach south from the point, fairly safe and partly easy, are the wildest in the park, kept so by the lack of easy and safe ways down (or up) the bluff. A rude route blunders through chunks of alder forest slumped to the beach, awaiting winter storms to smash them to driftwood. On his first sortie in 1977, the oldest surveyor said the heck with *that* and waded past in The Narrows, the tidal race buffeting his belly.

At park's end, finding a way back up the bluff, the surveyor was startled to look down to half-a-hundred (eighty-one, the newspapers say) driftwood-looking dwellings on pilings at the base of the 120-foot precipice. The

---

*See the publisher's note on private property on page 11.

lifestyle of Salmon Beach is authentically Alternative. Since settlement at the turn of the century the residents flushed toilets into the Whulge. In 1993 sewers arrived.

A maze of paths weaves through the largest madrona forest on the Whulge. At 1 mile from the park the railroad emerges from Bennett Tunnel, where it has been since the ruins of Ruston. A safe path drops to the tunnel mouth. The route south is then unmistakably marked by two parallel strips of steel. On the left, the wildwood bluff. On the right, the tides of The Narrows rushing this way, then that way, to no useful purpose except the entertainment of grebes and gulls hitching rides on speeding driftwood.

At 2 miles from the tunnel the tracks cross under Narrows Bridge and in ¾ mile more reach the edge of Titlow Beach Park.

Narrows Bridge

Bus: 20

A valley forest shelters not a wildwood park but (what else?) a sewage plant. A gated road switchbacks up to War Memorial Park. Drive here on Highway 16.

Walk out on the bridge for views up and down The Narrows (skinniest segment of the main channel of Puget Sound) from Point Defiance to Steilacoom. Trucks set the entire structure to dancing. Exciting. The Pictorial Center in the toll plaza tells that The Narrows are 4600 feet wide, 120 feet deep, with 12-foot tides running as fast as 8 knots. A campaign begun in 1923 culminated in the 1940 completion of the first bridge. Called "Galloping Gertie," it walked and trotted in breezes, at winds of 35 mph galloped, and on November 7, 1940, at 42 mph, snapped. *Very* exciting. Too much so for a hysterical dog, which died in the fall. On October 14, 1950, was opened the present bridge, "Sturdy Gertie."

TITLOW BEACH PARK*

Bus: 20

Drive Highway 16, keep left on 6 Avenue.

For ¾ mile the park is on both sides of the tracks, the beach screened by a skinny forest, the wildwood bluff threaded by paths. Leave the rails to walk ⅓ mile on the beach. From the picnic tables follow the seawall and closed road ½ mile to park's end at 6 Avenue, at pilings of the pre-bridge ferry dock.

Inland are playfields, duck ponds, and the 1½-mile Fit Trail looping around Titlow Lagoon, up the hill into the woods, with signs at each of 20 "stations" commanding fanatics to perform specified gymnastic feats.

---

*See the publisher's note on private property on page 11.

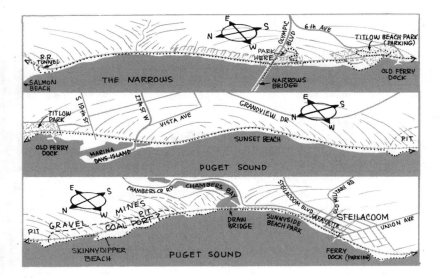

South from Titlow Beach Park to Steilacoom Ferry Dock, 6 miles

The rails pass 1 mile of boatworks and marinas in the baylet sheltered by house-covered Day's Island. The bluff then rears up for 1¼ miles of delightful wildland. Sunset Beach interrupts, a row of outside-the-tracks cottages on a bulkhead fill. Wild shore resumes for a long ½ mile.

Now for something completely different. The next 1½ miles used to be a bluff, but a century of digging the largest gravel mine on the Whulge and one of the five largest in the nation has remodeled the landscape to a pair of gigantic "cirques" reaching as far as a mile inland. Where are we? Not on the Whulge. Watch for the Foreign Legion marching at quickstep, pursued by snarling camels. The lode is about worked out; the clanking rumbling conveyor belts, the washers and sorters, the hoppers for loading rail cars, the docks for loading barges—all this is fated to be the past. As for the present, the good news is that the uproar is mainly confined to two spots; most of the 1½ miles are sandy beach, no houses, no people except giggling groups come for mixed skinnydipping. The future? A Japanese firm proposed to build a terminal for shipping 50 million tons of coal a year from Montana–Wyoming to the Greater East Asia Co-Prosperity Sphere. The schemers heard discouraging words and appear to be looking to the south, where Weyerhaeuser stockholders are hospitable, as are the 601 residents of the "City" of Dupont, enraptured by the prospective tax base.

The Fox Island views have yielded to those of McNeil Island and its penitentiary buildings. The gravel mines end at Chambers Bay, which the railroad crosses on a drawbridge.

Chambers Bay

Hard to believe, while in the tanglewood depths of Chambers Creek canyon, that metropolis surrounds. "Creek" is too small a word; the older name was "Steilacoom River." Four salmon runs (king, coho, chum, and pink) survive, as well as trout and steelhead. Otter, muskrat, mink, raccoon, coyote, deer, bobcat, porcupine, aplodontia. Birds, 136 species. Salamander, rubber boa, western fence lizard. Dragonflies and water beetles.

Primevally the river-creek emptied into the estuary of saltwater Chambers Bay; a lumber mill and other industry impact this lower portion of the canyon. A dam and tidegate have converted the upper bay to freshwater Chambers Lake. The south side of this canyon lake is Tacoma's grandest "wildness within." Pierce County Parks and Planning and the state Departments of Fisheries and Wildlife have a look-in. Since 1981 the Friends of Chambers Creek have been doing their best to drown out the sound of the cash register.

The canyon upstream from Chambers Lake is sampled by trails. For beach access, drive the Steilacoom–Chambers Creek Road to a parking shoulder south of the bay. Or take bus 21.

Onward South. Just south of the bay on an outside-the-tracks bulge of land is Steilacoom's Sunnyside Beach Park, featuring (where else would you put it?) a sewage plant. In the May/June 1993 issue of *Coastal Currents,* the state Department of Ecology declared, "Sunnyside Beach Park is virtually the only public access to Puget Sound in the vicinity." Wrong, DOE—read my lips.

The better with the bitter: winter storms of 1990 and 1991 washed away the timber bulkhead installed in the mid-1960s to "protect" the beach. DOE goes on, "The town was forced to fence off much of the park's shoreline for safety reasons." (Beware, beware the hungry waves, the vicious jellyfish, and shun the frumious Bandersnatch!) The city now "will remove the bulkhead and use environmentally sound techniques to protect the shore." From sewage plants?

Backward North. Skip the first ¾ mile by parking at Sunnyside Beach Park. The choice walk is the 1 mile to Chambers Bay (take a 3-mile

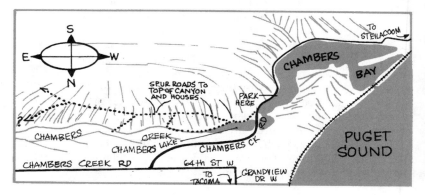

roundtrip sidetrip up the canyon to trail's end) and Skinnydipper Beach, where seals slap flippers, applauding the show.

STEILACOOM FERRY DOCK

Bus: 212

Go off I-5 on Exit 129 and follow signs (lots of luck).

Devote an hour or more to touring the town, one of the earliest European settlements on Puget Sound, incorporated 1854, and never growing to such size as to obliterate its past. From here to Bellingham ran the Military Road built in the Indian Wars (or, as Native American historians call them, the White Wars). Numerous houses have plaques identifying them as built in the 1850s. Pioneer Orchard Park is the site of a log cabin used as a school and an Indian Wars refuge. Visit the museum in the Town Hall on Lafayette and Main (1:00–4:00 P.M. Tuesday–Thursday, 1:00–5:00 P.M. Sunday).

Another thing to do at Steilacoom is ride the ferry to Anderson Island.

South from Steilacoom Ferry Dock to Solo Point, 3 miles

A bit south of the dock is Saltars Point Beach Park and in a long ⅓ mile, on Gordon Point, Steilacoom Bathing Beach Park. The dock of Steilacoom Marina reaches out to views north to Narrows Bridge, Fox Island, and Carr Inlet, westerly over McNeil Island to the Olympics.

To the right, narrow Cormorant Passage separates mainland from petite Ketron Island. To the left, bluff rears up to fend off picture windows. Soon there are no windows to be fended, no houses, because ¾ mile south of Gordon Point begins the Whulge's largest (future) park, presently on loan to the U.S. Army. From the rails rises 4th Infantry Bluff; inland is 30th Infantry Bluff. Will the buffalo ever roam here? Not likely. But pedestrians will ramble the prairies and forests once unexploded shells have been picked up. The army is quite environmentally sensitive (foreign battlegrounds aside) and here is taking reasonably good care of our heritage. Meanwhile, along the beach, the walker savors the bliss enjoyed by Lew Ayres in *All Quiet on the Western Front* just before a French sniper shot him in the head.

SOLO POINT

Go off I-5 on Exit 119. Turn right at the interchange stoplight to a second stoplight and turn right again, signed "Steilacoom." At 2 miles

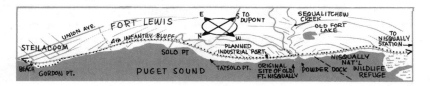

Anderson Island ferry arriving at the Steilacoom Ferry Dock

from the exit stoplight, turn left at a large State Wildlife sign, "Solo Point." In 1 more mile pass the Fort Lewis sewage plant and wind down a ravine and 4th Infantry Bluff to a large parking lot for fishermen's boat-trailers.

While driving here, note the crossing of Sequalitchew Creek, the "city" limits of Dupont, and the enormous sign announcing "Northwest Landing." If you want a house or an industrial site, call Weyerhaeuser. Operators standing by. Thanks to Fort Lewis, the entire way from I-5 to the beach is in forest—young forest invading former prairies. But beside the approach road is that "Landing." At present, Solo Point is as remote-feeling as any shore of the Whulge. Ketron Island, close enough to almost hit with a rock, has residents, but not visibly from here. None are on the steep forest wall and certainly not on the south tip, where winter storms batter the naked bluff and keep it from turning green. Anderson Island sprawls beyond, the very slow ferry creeping through the good-weather haze to and from Steilacoom. Gulls wade the little creek.

North from Solo Point to Steilacoom Ferry Dock, 3 miles*

The first 2 miles are so wild that a person standing on the railroad tracks (and forgetting they are there) can imagine himself in 1850, or 850, or B.C. No houses. No highway roar. The occasional train for nostalgia. Choice!

South from Solo Point to Nisqually Station, 6 miles

Also choice. Few ships proceed on Main Street south from Tacoma. Ketron and Anderson are not loud islands and in a good-weather saltwater haze appear uninhabited. The trains rarely molest the tracks. The U.S. Army keeps the peace inland. It's about as quiet as the Whulge ever gets. The unique treat is the change in upland vegetation. The standard-issue steep Whulge bluff of alder-maple growing on clay-sand-gravel-till is replaced by shrubby Douglas fir on a moderate slope of loose gravels, outwash from the final push of the Canadian glacier. The east-of-Cascades-like prairies of the South Puget Plain flower in spring to the very shore.

---

*See the publisher's note on private property on page 11.

Tatsolo Point is rounded and views open south past the tip of Anderson Island to the Black Hills. The Nisqually delta comes in sight. Ancient pilings are passed and an old wagonlike road—relic of a settlers' landing predating the fort?

When Fort Lewis falls to the rear the war zone begins. At 2 miles from Solo Point, the old Dupont powder dock speaks volumes. Here is the wilderness of the 3200 acres where explosives formerly were manufactured, beginning in 1909, an activity that required much empty land around, just in case. In 1949 the Port of Olympia planned a superport on the Nisqually delta. In 1964 the City of Seattle investigated using it as a garbage dump. In 1965 the Port of Tacoma proposed a deep-water port for huge bulk carriers and tankers. Weyerhaeuser Company acquired the property in 1976 and planned to build an enormous log-and-lumber-products warehousing and shipping port, and perhaps mills as well, and perhaps an "industrial park" with other companies as tenants. Environmentalists opposed the project for several reasons: immediately south is the Nisqually National Wildlife Refuge, crucial to the survival of wildfowl migrating on the Pacific Flyway, as well as resident wildlife; plentiful shipping facilities are available at Tacoma and north and elsewhere in the state, rendering unnecessary a major port on the South Sound, which ought to be left free of the risk of pollution catastrophes; this is the wildest, most peaceful portion of the Whulge; Sequalitchew Creek's canyon, down which the truck highway would come to the docks, is the largest and most magnificent wildland gulch on the Whulge; the site is among the most historic in the Northwest, with a major village of the Nisquallies, Nisqually House built in 1832 and the first Fort Nisqually in 1833, both at the canyon mouth, an American church mission in 1840, the second Fort Nisqually (see Point Defiance Park) in 1843, up on the bluff. Weyerhaeuser ignored all this but shelved the plans when the export market weakened. Temporarily. But in 1988 it announced plans to build a new town of 14,000 people, "Northwest Landing," on the property. See the start of subdivisions while driving to Solo Point.

In 1993 Weyerhaeuser staged a public relations stunt, donating 8 acres at the site of Fort Nisqually to the Archaeological Conservancy. That's right: *8 acres!*

Vultures of a feather flock together. In 1990 Lone Star Northwest announced plans to lease 400 acres from Weyerhaeuser, next to Sequalitchew Creek, under the banner of "Pioneer Aggregates," and spend 20–25 years (beginning possibly in 1994) mining some 90 million tons from a 300-foot-deep pit on 350 acres. The company identifies itself as "local," and, to be sure, a company of that name mined out the bluffs north of Chambers Bay; now, however, it is 97 percent owned by Onada Cement of Tokyo. The coal port formerly proposed at the gravel mine to the north likely will follow the crowd. Weyerhaeuser's older scheme has not died. In the cheering section is the "City" of Dupont, created by the 601 residents (at Weyerhaeusers's urging), and welcoming the prospective 14,000 new taxpayers, the jobs for 17,000 commuters, and golly knows how many bureaucrats.

The "City" of Dupont complacently issued a permit, naturally, but in late 1993 the state Department of Ecology denied a permit, judging the project to be inconsistent with the state Shoreline Management Act. The proposed use of barges would "result in unavoidable adverse imports."

The people of Dupont (Weyerhaeuser) and Tokyo surely won't take this lying down.

The Nisqually Delta Association, formed in 1970 as successor to the Washington Citizens Committee for Outdoor Resources, which was organized in 1965 by the late Margaret McKenny, went to court against Weyerhaeuser in 1976 and in 1994 is challenging Lone Star in a case pending before the state's Shoreline Hearing Board. (In August 1994, Weyerhaeuser–Lone Star and the environmentalists *tentatively* made a settlement, whereby the gravel port would be sited to the north, at Tatsolo Point.)

A few steps along the tracks past the Dupont dock a jetty marks the edge of the Nisqually Flats. The shore bluff reverts to Whulge "normal." Tracks swing inland from Nisqually Reach to the Nisqually valley. Wildwood bluff rises to the left. Below to the right are delta sloughs and marshes and pastures. Mount Road is crossed on a rail bridge, then the twin roars of I-5; at 3¼ miles from the powder dock is the site of the vanished Nisqually Station.

Though Solo Point is much more attractive, walks can start here. Go off I-5 on Exit 116, drive a scant 2 miles toward Old Nisqually, and soon after crossing the railroad spot the vacancy where was the station.

NISQUALLY NATIONAL WILDLIFE REFUGE

Go off I-5 on Exit 114, signed "Nisqually." Cross under I-5 and turn right 0.2 miles to the refuge entry.

The last major unspoiled estuary of its kind on the Pacific Coast of the United States, and an important stopover on the Pacific Flyway for migratory waterfowl, the Nisqually delta has recorded some 50 species of mammals, 200 of birds, 125 of fish, and 300 plants in its ecosystems of open freshwater and saltwater, mudflats, freshwater marshes, saltmarshes, mixed coniferous forests, deciduous woodlands, shrubs, grasslands, croplands, and the tidally influenced freshwaters of Nisqually River and McAllister Creek. On one winter trip the older surveyor saw a coyote dive from a dike into a slough, swim across, and run a mile over fields; he also saw (and was closely inspected by) a group of three otters; deer were numerous, and more birds than he knows. Led by Margaret McKenny and the Nisqually Delta Association, in 1974 a movement culminated in the establishment of a Nisqually National Wildlife Refuge, managed by the U.S. Fish and Wildlife Service, authorized for an ultimate 3780 acres.

It's not there yet. As of 1994 the acreage is 2800-odd. Of two crucial properties, at this writing the Nisqually Tribe is negotiating for the 400-acre Braget Farm on the east side of the refuge between the railroad and the river; if Congressional funding can be obtained, the tribe indicates the 315-acre lowland portion along Red Salmon Creek will become part of the refuge, and any uses of the upland area would be compatible with its proximity to the refuge. Another crucial property is the 150 or so acres of the Meek Logging parcel above McAllister Creek on the bluff to the west. The owner (since 1987 only, not what you'd call a pioneer) had expressed his intention to log the forest and subdivide the stumps as Meridian Heights, which would be neighbor to the Weyerhaeuser-intended "Meridian Campus," which would house 7000 residents and create 11,000 jobs, and be adjoined by a Glacier development of 1200 acres. In July 1994, the U.S. Fish and Wildlife Service reached an agreement to buy 112.5 acres of the holding for addition to the refuge. Meek would keep about 37 acres for a "cluster development."

The summer of 1993 brought issuance by concerned citizens of *The Delta Plan, a Citizen's Plan for Protecting the Greater Nisqually Delta*. The refuge would be completed by acquiring 930 acres of delta farms and bluff forest. (As of 1994, about half that goal seems to be near attainment.) Land-use regulations would be revised to extend the Stewardship Management Zone out from the refuge into the schemery range of Weyerhaeuser and confederates.

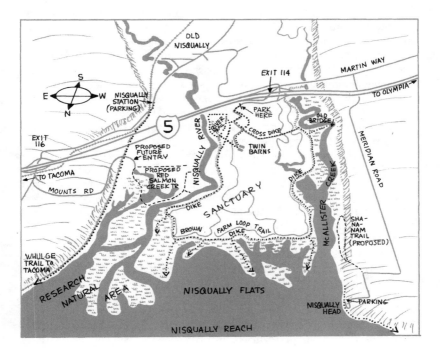

Small creek beside the Nisqually River trail

The visitor must keep in mind that the Nisqually Refuge is not a park. Acceptable human pleasures (only during daylight, to let the critters enjoy nocturnal pursuits): wildlife observation, nature study, photography, fishing, walking, lunching. Unacceptable: hunting, bicycling, jogging, "power walking," off-trail exploration, dog-exercising, kite-flying, Frisbee-throwing, boomboxes, blowing bugles, screaming and hollering.

For a very great short trip, walk past the open-air interpretive center ¼ mile to the Twin Barns Education Center and the start of the Nisqually River Trail, a ½-mile, self-guided, nature-trail loop over a slough, through cottonwoods to the river, and back.

The classic long walk is the 5-mile perimeter loop around the Outer Dike. Now named the Brown Farm Trail (the farming started by Alson L. Brown in 1904 continued to the mid-1960s), it remains the big show. But please keep in mind: until a controlled hunting program can be instituted, the dike will be closed, for the safety of walkers, during the waterfowl hunting season. To avoid disappointments call in advance: (206) 753-9467.

From Twin Barns walk to the dike, which follows the Nisqually, gray-green with rock milk from Rainier's glaciers, 1½ miles to the vicinity of the mouth, where diked freshwater marshes yield to saltmarshes open to the tides. Look north to Ketron Island, Steilacoom, and Narrows Bridge. Over Nisqually. Reach to the Olympics. Turn around and—holy cow!—that's Rainier!

The dike turns left (west). Saltmarsh reaches out in long, inviting fingers. The wildfowl display varies with the seasons. Nearly always there are clouds of peep. In a long 1 mile, at McAllister (Medicine) Creek, the dike turns left (south), following the slough back into the delta, the sluggish water meandering through tidal marshes. In 1½ miles the trail leaves the Outer Dike and turns east on the Cross Dike, which leads 1¼ miles back to the refuge entrance.

And what besides walking are you doing all that way? Watching herons blundering out of bulrushes into the air, hawks circling above, waterfowl feeding and flying, little birds flittering. And maybe coyotes running, otters swimming.

TOLMIE STATE PARK

Go off I-5 on Exit 111 and drive west 5 miles on Marvin Road.

In a stretch of shore so densely Privatized that the Public hardly can glimpse the water, this park is a gem beyond price. A delightful stroll of 1 mile can be assembled from these parts: the ¼ mile of beach to Sandy Point; the forest trail to Sandy Point (which nearly has been eroded away by longshore currents since Privatizer bulkheads were installed a half-mile distant); the grassy baymouth bar which nearly closes off charming (little) Big Slough; the path down a ravine from the bluff to the beach; a path up the lush-green, wild-tangled valley of Big Slough Creek.

A historical display tells how Dr. William Frazer Tolmie (1812–1866) served Hudson's Bay Company 16 years at Nisqually House and Fort Nisqually as physician, surgeon, botanist, and fur trader and, on a botanizing tour of 1833, was the first European to set foot on Rainier.

East from Tolmie State Park to Nisqually Head, 3 miles

The bank (no bluff) is a ½-mile crowd of houses, some slopping over onto beach-invading bulkheads. Butterball Cove is worth it, though, the baymouth bar (only two little houses, and cute) enclosing a ducky lagoon,

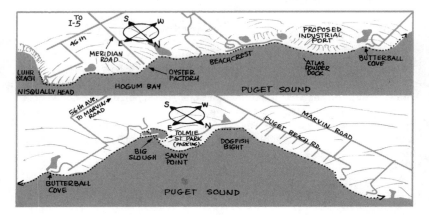

the charming vale bounded on each side by little cliffs of tawny, wavy-banded riverbar sands.

Then a long ½ mile of "wildness within." How can this be? From remnants of a derelict dock, an old road climbs through trees to the blufftop. Up there, amid the vast emptiness usual for such business, Atlas Powder competed with Dupont. The property was acquired by Burlington-Northern (née Northern Pacific, etc.) and spun off into the Glacier Park Company (so named in an attempt to spin off a dozen decades of evil reputation), which plans a 1200-acre development adjoining Weyerhaeuser's intended 1500-acre Meridian Campus adjoining the Nisqually National Wildlife Refuge. Refuge! Less for birds than for anachronistic nineteenth-century scoundrelism. The Nisqually Delta Association stands watch.

Beachcrest Beach puts houses on the shore. In a scant ½ mile there are a valley–estuary–lagoon–boat harbor (at low tide, walkers can leap the creek upstream and battle brush back to the beach); another dandy lagoon; and a dainty little vale. The next ½ mile of beach, wild for no visible reason, passes an estuary lagoon in a cove closed off by a grassy baymouth bar. A "point" of shells, midden of the Hogum Bay Oyster Mine, juts into Hogum Bay. In a final ½ mile houses descend to the beach; an enchanting tidal lagoon in an enchanting creek estuary is ideal for ambushing waterfowl with binoculars.

The bluff resumes, rising to Nisqually Head at the mouth of McAllister Creek, flowing at the edge of the Nisqually delta. The Audubon Nature Center is open from noon to 4:00 P.M., Wednesday, Saturday, and Sunday. Luhr Beach is a boat-launch entry to Nisqually National Wildlife Refuge as well as to the contiguous State Wildlife Department's Nisqually Habitat Management Area, where wildfowl that stray from their Refuge are liable to get shot and et.

To do this route in the reverse direction, go off I-5 on Exit 114 and drive Martin Way west 1 long mile from Nisqually Plaza. Turn right (north) on Meridian Way 2.5 miles. Turn right on 46th and in 0.2 mile left on D'Milluhr Drive to Luhr Beach.

West–North from Tolmie State Park to Mill Bight, 2 miles

From Commencement Bay to the Nisqually, the Whulge Trail is partly beach, partly railroad,* always a continuous footway. This briefly resumes at Nisqually Head. Then the hiker's pal, the beach-guarding bluff so nearly omnipresent on the Whulge to the north, shrinks, permitting houses next to or even on the beach. Further, the sheltered, feeble-wave beaches are narrow, not brushed out by the surfs of winter southerlies, and the way repeatedly is blocked by foot-stopping estuaries. Lastly, the Privates tend to take all this to signify that God is on their side and Devil take the Publics.

---

*See the publisher's note on private property on page 11.

A scant ¼ mile from the Tolmie parking lot is Sandy Point, the start of houses houses houses. In ½ mile more is the slough of Dogfish Bight, worth a look, though the enclosing bar is solid houses, as is the shore to Mill Bight, an estuary that means business.

A Public can touch the water at several marinas along the shore to Johnson Point at the mouth of Henderson Inlet. Why bother? The Whulge Trail has ended. But not the Whulge!

WOODARD BAY NATURAL RESOURCES CONSERVATION AREA

Bus: 20 to Woodard Bay Road NE, then walk 1.3 miles

Go off I-5 on Exit 105-B, drive Plum, which becomes East Bay Drive, which becomes Boston Harbor Road. At 3.4 miles from the end of Priest Point Park, turn right on Woodard Bay Road. In 1.1 miles turn left on Woodard Bay Road NE. In 0.5 mile, where the road crosses Woodard Bay, turn left to an unsigned road parking area.

Having walked the Whulge Trail south from Bellingham, the older surveyor was disgruntled by the frittering-away fingers of the South Sound where Nature and Man conspired to frustrate his feet. Then, in 1987, the benefactor wizards of the state Department of Natural Resources got the legislature to pass an act authorizing certain DNR lands to be converted to Natural Resources Conservation Areas. The NRCA concept is tantamount to a state version of the National Wilderness Act of 1964. Extractive uses are essentially excluded, ecosystem preservation and enhancement elevated to primacy, and recreation limited to "low impact."

Four areas were designated by the 1987 act, among them Woodard Bay, where Weyerhaeuser's railroad used to dump logs for floating to Everett. Additions through 1994 have brought the total to twenty-one NRCAs, 41,000 acres; an even more protective classification, the Natural Area Preserves, which in 1980 numbered three, have grown to thirty-seven,

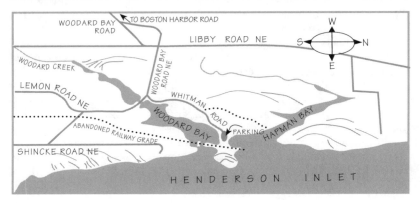

Woodard Bay trail

of 15,000 acres. To quote the valedictory of State Land Commissioner Brian Boyle, whose 16-year tenure oversaw all this, "We are building a legacy that will dominate the state's physical landscape for centuries to come."

As of 1993 the ecosystems of the 627-acre Woodard Bay NRCA are being inventoried. (On the day of the surveyor's visit, a team was counting seals, then in midst of pupping: total, 217. The management plan will see to it that the number is not diminished by bullying stinkpots—nor by friendly canoes and curious cameras.) The plan probably will be completed in 1994–95. For now we do no more than note the creation of this preserve and warn visitors not to get too familiar too soon.

The Woodard Bay "Trail" (*sic*) is being developed on the abandoned Weyerhaeuser railway grade. It will make a nice bikeway for local wheels. The last ½ mile from the parking area will be an easy and great walk on rainy Tuesday mornings in February.

The roadside views of Woodard Bay and Chapman Bay are intriguing. Two trails (foot only) lead to Chapman Bay. Don't expect beach. At high tide the Whulge climbs into the trees. At low tide the quickmud lusts after your boots, your ankles, your knees.

They nonetheless are superb (*no wheels*) trails. Machine-free quiet of the "sea in the forest": huge cedars—marvel at their size after little more than a century of growth! Gape at the stumps, *that's* how big a cedar gets in a number (how many?) of centuries; this forest is not ancient but *second-growth!* The tidewater logging was done by bullteams on puncheon skid roads. Booming grounds formed up rafts. Floated to mills. To docks for loading on windjammers bound for Australia, South Africa, Europe. Then came mountain-scalping, still continuing, but the logs now are trucked to the docks for shipment overseas. Space was insufficient here for the fleets of foreign log ships.

BURFOOT PARK

Bus: 20

Drive Boston Harbor Road from Olympia.

An interpretive trail twists and turns through lovely woods of a Thurston County park and descends a cool green ravine to a tiny cove nearly closed off by a miniature baymouth bar. How sweet it is.

North from Burfoot Park to Zangle Cove, 1¾ miles

The ¾ mile of beach to Dofflemyer Point at the mouth of Budd Inlet is a nice picnic walk, the bank-top houses not too intrusive. Beyond the quaint little old lighthouse the cozy old New England–like village of Boston Harbor snuggles up to the protected waters. A boat-launch (unsigned) is fenced on either side, signs crying "KEEP OUT. Private Tidelands." To get by the fence a walker would need a minus tide to keep knees dry. The thoroughly peopled shore might be strolled 1 mile to Dover Point at the mouth of Zangle Cove and perhaps beyond.

South from Burfoot Park to Percival Landing Park, 7 miles

Unlike the other finger inlets, Budd Inlet is walkable the full length, the east shore at least. For 1½ miles a bluff 60–100 feet tall (reminiscent of the North Sound!) keeps all but a few houses at a quiet distance. The

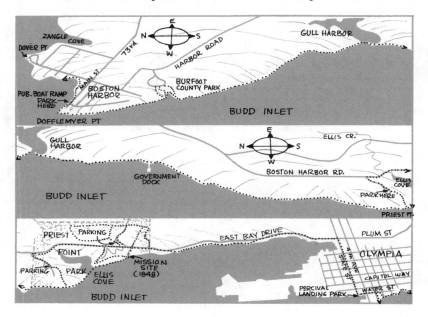

dome of the state Capitol is glimpsable. Once in a great while a ship passes, to or from the Port of Olympia. Beyond the waters rise the Black Hills. A naked till bluff, bright in season with yarrow and vetch and lupine (and poison oak!) announces Gull Harbor, a wilderness of forest and estuary lagoon and birds. A baymouth bar nearly closes off the harbor—only at low tide can the channel reasonably be hopped-waded. This is a good turnaround for a walk from the park.

A few breaks in the bluff permit shore houses but solitude is just about complete in the 1 mile to the DNR Marine Land Development Research and Development Station; docked research vessels may require the camera to be brought out. A few staircases descend from unseen houses. Again the camera, for a cluster of boathouses, cottages atop a 30-foot cliff, and a fleet of moored sailboats. Pretty.

Priest Point Park

The 254 acres of tall old firs and lush ferns, the deep ravines of Ellis and Mission Creeks, can content a pedestrian for hours. At the mouth of Mission Creek the Oblate priest, Father Pascal Ricard, built his mission to the Squaxin people in 1856. A snug duck-and-heron harbor and 1 mile of beach, views to ships docked in the Port of Olympia, complete a lazy day.

East Bay Drive, from Olympia, bisects this Olympia city park served by bus 20 to Boston Harbor. Forest uphill. Forest down to the beach. The park headquarters is a start for both. An alternative trailhead is Flora Vista Road at the park's far end from Olympia, but parking is not handy, so the sidewalk from the headquarters has to be walked. A forest path descends a gully to Priest Point. At a low enough tide Ellis Cove can be squished across on mudflats to the picnic area.

OLYMPIA: PERCIVAL LANDING PARK–TUMWATER FALLS PARK

Go off I-5 on Exit 105-B, turn right on Plum, then left on State to Water.

Olympia is a city for walking. Parks are linked 3 continuous miles from Budd Inlet up the Deschutes River to the top of Tumwater Falls. Limited parking at Water, large lots by Capitol Lake, a ton of parking along Deschutes Parkway.

Stroll from Percival Landing on the mile of shore boardwalk. Little boats. Big boats. Such ships as escaped the Ports of Tacoma and Seattle. Olympic Mountain views to Washington, The Brothers, and Constance. The 2 blocks along Water lead to Capitol Lake. Formerly, Budd Inlet did at low tide what comes naturally to these long skinny fingers of the South Sound—it became a mudflat. Gave state politics a distinctive aroma. To put a stop to old jokes and give the Capitol the odor of dignity, in 1949 a dam was built to impound a lake and a tidegate installed to let the Deschutes River do a deodorization. Partly ringed by lawns, partly cat-

State capitol from Priest Point Park

tails, partly tanglewood bluff, the lake provides a postcard foreground for the Capitol dome rising from green forest into clouds of gulls.

Proceed on sidewalk and waterside path over the dam-tidegate, where in season salmon and steelhead can be seen swimming upstream to spawn, and continue beside Deschutes Parkway. (To begin a walk here, go off I-5 on Exit 103.) Marathon Park (ample parking) has views of the Capitol and the skyline of downtown Olympia. Percival Creek flows from a green gulch. A walkway leads to Capitol Lake Interpretive Center, from which a causeway trail crosses the lake and passes under I-5 to Tumwater Historical Park, paths, picnic shelters, and a canoe launch.

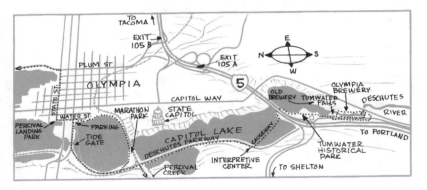

Tumwater Falls

Up Grant Street from the lake, which here narrows to the mouth of the river, is a handsome antique dwelling, a registered Historic Place, built in 1854 by Nathaniel Crosby III, Bing's grandfather. From the riverbank gaze to the imposing brickery of the original Olympia Brewery, built in 1905, converted to other enterprises upon the advent of state Prohibition in 1916. The new brewery, on the hill above, was opened upon Repeal in 1933.

Here, too, are the first looks at the lowermost cataracts of the Deschutes, called Tumwater Falls, partly retaining the Indian name, "Tumtum," for the throb of the heart suggested by the sound. Walk uphill along the river to Deschutes Parkway and the entry road to Olympia Brewery. Past Falls Terrace Restaurant enter Tumwater Falls Park, ¼ mile from Capitol Lake. (To drive to the park, leave I-5 on Exit 103 and follow signs to Deschutes Parkway and the park entrance.)

Soak up the history. The headquarters exhibit has a granite erratic from Hartstene Island; its petroglyph pictures mountains, sun, bow, arrow, a bear, and assorted animals. A panel of photos shows the falls in olden times and buildings that were here: Horton Pipe Factory (1872), the first power plant (1890), Ira Ward house (1860), George Gelbach Flour Mill (1883), Tumwater Falls Powerhouse (1904), and so on. A monument tells how Colonel Michael T. Simmons arrived in 1845 with thirty-two companions and established the first American settlement (which they called Newmarket) north of the Columbia River.

Soak up the scenery. Southernmost of Cascades rivers to enter Puget Sound, here the Deschutes got hung up on a stratum of hard rock precisely at tidewater; a series of foaming cataracts strung along a slot of spring-dripping, fern-and-moss-hung rock, drops a total 115 feet. In the ¼ mile of the gorge are trails along both sides, artfully placed in the clouds of spray billowing from plunge basins, smaller falls of tributary creeks cascading into landscapings of native shrubs. Sidepaths lead to rock outcrops scoured and potholed by the river, view platforms of the falls, and fish ladderways, where in season spawning salmon and steelhead can be watched battling up the torrent. So, walk up and down both sides of the gorge, crossing at lower and upper ends on bridges, in ¾ mile doing the whole park. But better plan on doing it twice or more. And don't hurry.

The imposing structures atop the cliff ought not be ignored. The large sign anounces daily visiting hours.

Eld Inlet

After Henderson comes Budd, then Eld, third in the southward sequence of finger inlets. Except at the head, Mud Bay, where saltgrass and mudflats merit poking about, the shore is mostly Privatized.

The Evergreen State College

Bus: 41 or 44

Go off I-5 on Exit 104, drive US 101 for 3 miles, and exit on Evergreen Parkway to the campus. Park just beyond the entry booth in Lot B or Lot C.

The 1000-acre campus, 3300 feet of beach, is a "wildness within" the more valuable to the state for the presence of young environmentalists who there absorb the feel of it through their pores while studying it in classrooms.

Cross the plaza to the library, go between it and the Activities Building, by the Recreation Center and Residence Halls, and cross Driftwood Road to Parking Lot F. Bear left to the far side, about ¾ mile from the start, to a sign, "Nature Trail." The path samples huge stumps from long-ago bullteam logging, alder bottoms and a gurgling creek, a pond, an old pasture, ferny-mossy maples, and handsome cedar and fir and hemlock.

At ¾ mile from Lot F is a T. The left leads a few yards to a baymouth bar enclosing a little lagoon. When the woods are bright with the flowers that bloom in the spring, this beach should be visited only by liberals.

The right goes ¼ mile in firs and madronas to Geoduck House, the marine ecology studies center, on Squaw Point. Sit on the lawn under a big fir, and look to the college's fleet in Snyder Cove and across to Young Cove and Flapjack Point and up to Black Hills and the Olympics.

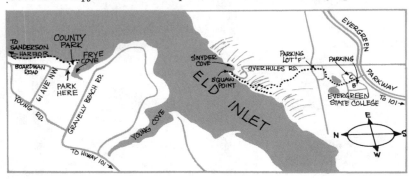

Frye Cove Park

Drive US 101 a scant 2.5 miles past the crossing of Eld Inlet and turn right on Steamboat Island Road. In 1 mile turn right on Gravelly Beach Road. In 2.2 miles turn left on Young Road. In 0.7 mile turn right on 61 Avenue NW and proceed 0.5 mile to Boardman Road. Turn right on Boardman and go 0.2 mile to the end.

A Thurston County sign says "Path to Beach. Welcome. Observe Park Rules." Take either the left or right fork to the beach. For the gem experience, walk south to the mouth of Frye Cove, uninhabited and lonesome, one of those charming estuaries appalling to boot but intriguing to gaze into, wondering what would be found around the sinuous corners, deep in forest, if one had a canoe. Firs lean over the water, framing the scene.

At a low-medium tide, head north under a steep forest that roofs the beach and often blocks it with logs and branches. A glorious maple extends 35 feet out over gravels and waters. A Douglas fir 5 feet in diameter grows out of the very beach! Duck into a green-dark alcove of overhanging alder to find springs dripping down a clay cliff hung with maidenhair fern. Climb patiently over seaweedy, barnacled logs or, at low tide, squish around them in boot-swallowing mud. Look out the inlet to its mouth at Cooper Point.

Though several houses are hidden up in the woods in the first 2 miles, scarcely so much as a trail betrays their presence. Beach-near houses then begin and continue the 1 mile to Sanderson Harbor.

TOTTEN INLET

The fourth of the finger inlets has much lonesome shore, many beach accesses familiar to local Privates, and a pervading deep suspicion that roving Publics might be oyster-rustlers. Get a canoe.

Arcadia Point

Drive US 101 past Kamilche 1 mile and turn right on Lynch Road, which joins Arcadia Road, which at 10 miles from 101 ends at Arcadia Point. A block before the end is a parking lot for "Squaxin Island Tribe Public Boat Ramp."

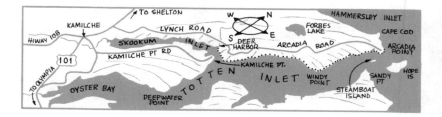

Sunrise and Mount Rainier from Arcadia Point

In the 1970s the older surveyor found a number of beach accesses to the finger inlets, published them, and suffered the wrath of oyster-farmers' attorneys threatening to bury him under the majesty of the law. That's no fun. Those accesses have been temporarily given up. However, at the tip of the peninsula between Totten and Hammersley Inlets, the Squaxins have provided a Public parking place by the beach.

Left a few feet is the light on Arcadia Point, where a moatlike yacht basin prevents exploration into Hammersley Inlet. The walk is right, southerly along Totten Inlet. In ⅓ mile is a till point pocked by bird caves; at middle tides the channel through the mudflat cove beyond the point can be walked across. Above the grassy baymouth bar are houses but soon the way is wild, though at intervals the top of the 100-foot bluff is cleared. Old, unused concrete bulkheads, old unused roads to the beach, and remains of a boathouse-on-pilings overwhelmed by a clay slump are passed. The sliding bluff forest sometimes pushes out on the beach, forcing mean struggles through weedy, barnacled logs. Steamboat Island is passed. A double-trunked maple leans 40 feet over the beach. Creeklets dribble out of green-delicious gulches. Sands are tracked by deer and raccoon.

Only a couple of houses are encountered beside the beach in the 2¼ miles to Windy Point. Views are long down Totten Inlet and to its mostly wild far shore and to the Black Hills. Though not surveyed, the way appears open and pleasant and little-inhabited another scant 4 miles to the mouth of Skookum Inlet and Deer Harbor.

HAMMERSLEY INLET

The last of the finger seas, river-narrow most of its length, a fairyland of odd little capes and amusing little coves, is the best of the lot, so good, so great, the whole deserves to be a state park. Residential love has not yet seriously impacted "the wildness within." However, the Public foot-traveler here discovers his/her limits. Dreams grow of rowboats, canoes, kayaks, rubber rafts—any craft quiet enough and portable enough to carry persons respectfully through the wildness.

On the tip of "Hammersley Point," at the inlet mouth, is an abandoned farm. Gnarled fruit trees. The aroma of mint stirred up by boots. Views northward along Pickering Passage to the totally forested Squaxin Island. Across the inlet mouth, mansions and yachts of Arcadia Point and, beyond, Hope Island, mostly wild, recently acquired by State Parks to serve stinkpotters, and picture-pretty Steamboat Island at the mouth of Squaxin Passage and Totten Inlet.

Look the other way! Just down Hammersley are "the narrows" across which George Washington might easily hurl a silver dollar. The far shore is guarded by the forested bluff of Cape Cod, and the near shore by the bare-till cliffs of arête-skinny Cape Horn. Envision paddling. Because you can't really *walk* much. (When the tide is boiling past Cape Horn, you can't really paddle too much through the whirlpools.)

Walker Park

Drive Highway 3 to the south end of Shelton and turn right on Arcadia Road. In 2.5 miles turn left on Walker Park Road and go 0.3 mile.

Walking west to Eagle Point is made impractical by beach-invading bulkheads. The less-populated shore east is open enough 3 miles to Skookum Point and 1 mile beyond to Channel Point at the mouth of Mill Channel, the estuary of Mill Creek, a finalist in the competition for the South Sound's Champion of Charm.

Past the foot-stopping channel are the most sublime 2 miles of this inlet and possibly the entire "sea in the forest." The shore all the way to Cape Cod appears pristine and so does the facing shore to Cape Horn. But you can't get there from here. (Kayak, anyone?)

From the shade of big firs in this Mason County park, the prospect is

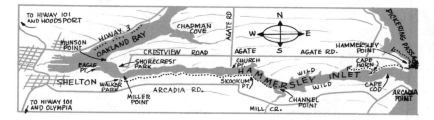

pleasing westward to Shelton and Oakland Bay. Ships carry lumber to Seattle, logs to Japan.

Shorecrest Park

Drive Highway 3 north from Shelton to Deer Creek, turn right on Agate Road 3.8 miles to Agate, turn right on Crestview a long 2 miles, then left on East Parkway Boulevard 0.5 mile, and finally right on East Shorecrest Parkway.

The views on this shore are superior. The tiny but luscious Mason County park is walled in by "No Trespassing" signs. Though the bank of iron-stained glacial drift is too low to keep houses away, most are tucked discreetly in the dry-country rainshadow woods of fir and madrona. The trees lean picturesquely over the beach. From the bank hang festoons of poison oak, shiny green (Oregon grape–like) in summer, shades of red in fall.

Hammersley Inlet from Shorecrest Park

The park itself gives an excellent view of steaming-clunking-humming lumber mills and beautiful downtown Shelton, famed far and wide as the native land of Bob and Ira Spring. Closer, better views are east ½ mile from Munson Point. Continue 2½ miles to Chapman Cove for long views up Oakland Bay.

In the other direction the shore quickly rounds the low gravel cliff of Miller Point, the beach easy-walking sand and pebbles under arching firs and madronas, by scattered houses. Across the cozy inlet, barely ¼ mile wide, a seeming lake in the woods, are houses and yards and dogs barking and children playing. The beach proceeds 3 miles to Church Point light and street-end parking, an alternative start.

CASE INLET

The Whulge Pilgrim journeys here to pay homage to the waters that curl so far north as nearly to join Hood Canal and make Kitsap Peninsula an island. Candidly, paying the homage is the only reason a person from Puget Sound City would spend so much time driving here for a day's walk. There's no such thing as a bad beach, but as is true of martinis and sex, some are better.

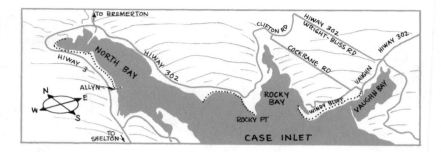

Allyn Park

Here is the Momentous Spot, the waters of Puget Sound's North Bay just 2 miles from Hood Canal's Lynch Cove. (In the era of World War I, Father and Mother Spring used to get a farmer to portage their canoe from Lynch Cove to North Bay.) Drive Highway 3 from Olympia or Bremerton, or Highway 16, 302, and 3 from Tacoma, to the Port of Allyn dock and the little City of Allyn park.

In 1½ miles north through guck and clams and the rich reek of salt rot, a holy vagabond attains the saltgrass marsh-meadows of the bay head. Recite the mantra and start back to Bellingham.

Rocky Bay

On the west side of North Bay, at the mouth, is walking less momentous but also less ooky and more scenic. On Highway 302 at 0.2 mile north of the right-angle turn at Rocky Point, park on a broad shoulder.

Drop the several feet to the beach and walk north ½ mile for views to Allyn and the bay head. Then walk south ½ mile to Rocky Point for views down Case Inlet to Reach and Stretch Islands and around the corner into cute little Rocky Bay.

Vaughn Bay

The bay next door, still another of the cozy estuaries abounding in the South Sound. At 1.2 miles west of Key Center on Highway 302, go straight ahead on Hall Road 0.5 mile to the Public boat-launch at Vaughn.

An admirable baymouth bar (many houses, sorry about that). Naked gravels of Windy Bluff. The spit pushing into Rocky Bay.

MAINLAND: SEATTLE TO EVERETT

~~~~~~

The Whulge Trail starts in Seattle on the central waterfront from Skid Road (or as tin-eared Easterners misspeak, "skidrow") to Smith Cove—the Gold Rush and Coal Rush and Silk Rush waterfront, the tall ship and mosquito fleet waterfront, now become the play waterfront and the city's chief history feast. Next north is Magnolia Bluff, the longest stretch of natural (mainly) beach between Tacoma and Everett, climaxing in the spit of West Point, the treasure of Puget Sound City, a metropolis whose claims to soul are brought in question by use of its supreme temple of Nature as a crapper.

The rest of the route as far as Everett is the all-tides walkway provided a century ago by James J. Hill, the Empire Builder. Not that the Great Northern Railway (now the Burlington-Northern) was intended for hoboes, tramps, and bums. In some perverse legal sense, the tracks technically are private property. Practically speaking, from their beginnings in the nineteenth century American railroads have been de facto Public,* and to render them securely Private would require more fencing and policing than ever could be justified to save the occasional pedestrian from getting hamburgered. (The cost of the lawyering that would be needed to censor publications that acknowledge the existence of railroad tracks also would be considerable and would raise up the specter of revestment of corrupt railroad grants. In any event, the railroad companies are getting out of that business as fast as they can and surviving rail lines are sure to be taken into Public ownership by the middle of the next century.) For liability reasons, the railroad never will confess they couldn't care less if you walk the tracks. When mobs of addled youth are reeling along the rails, the police may come a-chasing, even arresting. Should you ever be told to "Scat!"—SCAT. Keep in mind that you need not be stoned or deaf to get squashed; when winter wind is blowing by the ears and storm surf pounding, a train may creep right up behind you. Unless, of course, you're on the parallel lane of the Whulge Trail, down on the beach.

The "railroad beach" isn't all that great—mainly because there isn't all that much of it. An environmental impact statement for construction of the Great Northern Railway along the shore from Ballard to Everett would bear comparison with those for the barbarian invasion of the Roman Empire and the burning of the Alexandria Library. In the 1890s, of course, what we now call "impact" was hailed as "progress." The

---

*See the publisher's note on private property on page 11.

Seattle skyline from Waterfront Park

beachwalker of today belatedly registers a complaint that the handsome seawall of granite blocks was erected very close to the line of mean low tide. Saving where a spit or delta pushes out in the water, there is no beach whatsoever except at quite low water. Pristine beaches of the North Sound generally have a walkable lane in calm weather at any level of the tide below 9 feet or so. On the Jim Hill Trail, the lane doesn't open until the level drops below 5 or 3 feet.

To look at the bright side, the Rail Trail is never closed. At the highest tides, in the most violent storms, the path atop the seawall is open. The best time to be here, in fact, is when ocean-size surf is booming against the wall, washing up onto the tracks, hurling spindrift into the bluff forest.

If the Jim Hill Trail is open in the worst of weather, it also is free of insult and threat in the best. On those balmy summer Sundays when people who live on the beach south of Seattle are exercising what they believe to be their property rights, nobody (well, hardly nobody) disturbs the peace of the track-walkers.

The bluff is as characteristic of the Whulge Trail North as the railroad. The abrupt lift of landscape 200–400 feet above the shore constantly slumps off chunks. Extending nearly the full length of the trail is thus a strip wilderness, houses mostly at the top and pretty much out of sight, the steep, wooded, brush-tangled slope harboring a thriving population of birds and small beasts, the water-side walker "away from it all" for hours at a time while right in the middle of it all, strolling along in the heart of Whulge City.

So much for the land side, the bluff side of the Jim Hill Wilderness. As for the water, it's just your standard, routine Whulge. Waves on the beach, shorebirds on the sands and waterfowl swimming and gulls and crows keeping watch for tasty bites, a panorama across the waters to islands, Kitsap Peninsula, and the Olympics, the parade of tugs and log rafts and barges and freighters and ferries and fishing boats and playboats, and memories of the water traffic that was, the old pilings, remnants of docks last used half a century ago, ghosts of the mourned mosquito fleet.

The Privatizers who are able to pay up to $3000 a linear foot for beach frontage and not be crushed by correspondingly heavy property taxes feel that wealth hath given them privileges—specifically, the right to bar the Public from the water—indeed, that with their wealth they have *bought* the water. But the way of life between the Cascades and Olympics has been shaped more by the Whulge than any other element, even the rain. To adapt the dictum of Mr. Bumble, "If the law says the people can be walled off from the Whulge, the law, sir, is *a ass!*" Walking beside the Whulge is as inalienable a right as turning the eyes up to the heavens. Thanks to the railroad between Seattle and Everett, the Public has the freedom of both heavens and the Whulge. Thanks be that elsewhere on the Whulge, since 1971 and 1987 the Public Trust Doctrine and other tenets of the common law are beginning to restore Public rights stolen away over the years by implementation of the Private Greed Doctrine. Meanwhile we murmur an equivocal prayer that the thermostat of the flames eternally roasting Mr. Hill is not turned up to the maximum.

For a day-by-day step-by-step celebration of the Whulge Trail, look in a library for *Walking the Beach to Bellingham,* not a guidebook but the older surveyor's memoir.

USGS maps: Seattle South, Seattle North, Shilshole Bay, Edmonds West, Edmonds East, Mukilteo, Everett

MYRTLE EDWARDS PARK–ELLIOTT BAY PARK

Bus: A hatful of lines to close-by streets—plus the Waterfront Trolley

For Myrtle Edwards Park, drive to Broad Street at the north end of Alaskan Way; for Elliott Bay Park, drive 16 Avenue W from Elliott Avenue via W Galer.

South from Broad Street to King Street Station, 1½ miles

Seattle's central waterfront has undergone many a transformation since Henry Yesler built his sawmill, the logs supplied by oxen dragging them along a skid road, and his wharf, which brought loggers and fishermen and lonesome settlers from all around the Whulge by steamer, by sailboat, by rowboat, by canoe. Elliott Bay's excellent shelter from southerly blows and the closeness of solid land to deep water quickly made it the premier port of the region, and so it remained through the Coal Rush and the Gold Rush and World War II. However, larger ships and cargos began to demand the spacious flatness of "made" land on the Duwamish River. The central waterfront became an amiable slum, most of the pier buildings empty, few of the slips ever seeing a ship. Even in decay, however, it refused to be elbowed aside in the affection of the populace (and of the tourists) by such artifices as the Seattle Center. After musing a good long while, the Movers & Shakers saw there was as much money to be made from play as work. The central waterfront was transformed for fun. One

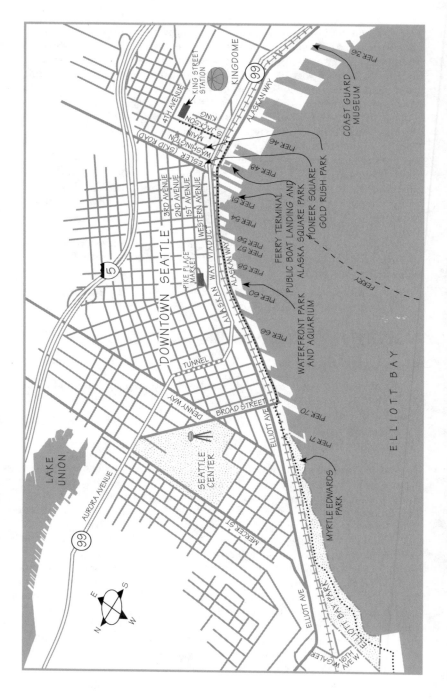

can hope that Alaskan Way (nèe Railroad Avenue) is not entirely converted to boutiques and eateries. What the hucksters call "dilapidation," others of us value as history. The old settler considers industrial grime to be the essence of waterfront. Office buildings, hotels, condos, and even cruise ships (the *Love Boat?*) are no substitute for the workaday traffic that reminds why Seattle came to be here in the first place.

This is not a beach walk. The beach, long since buried, was inland, at the foot of the bluff. This is a history walk, a scenery walk, a fish-and-chips-and-curios walk, the best lowdown, downtown waterfront walk in the West. A veritable five-star tourist trap, and that is not meant in a bad way.

Plaques along the way note historic spots, such as the first *maru* from Japan, marking the advent of Seattle as a world port; arrival of the "ton of gold" from Alaska; and the landing used by sailors of the Great White Fleet. Thirteen battleships of the Atlantic Fleet anchored in Elliott Bay for 4 days in 1908. The ships lit up the sky at night with a searchlight show. The Alaska Building was draped in more than 500 flags. On the last day of the celebration, May 26, a military parade through Seattle was 3 miles long.

The walk can begin at either end and dozens of middles; if leg energy runs low, the return from Pier 48 to Pier 70 can be done sitting down, on the green-and-cream waterfront trolley, old-timey and no more obnoxiously quaint than the cablecars of San Francisco. To cite some attractions:

- Piers 58 to 60 are the city's pride, the Waterfront Park and Aquarium. The one has benches for viewing water traffic and sipping clam nectar. The other has a model tidal basin, fish ladder, underwater viewing room, and examples of marine life indigenous to local waters. Across Alaskan Way the stairway and elevator lift a person to the Pike Place Market.

- Pier 57 has Water Link, a maritime interpretive center open in summer, and the Gray Line *Sightseer,* which tours the waterfront and continues around West Point and into Shilshole Bay to the Ballard Locks.

- Pier 56 is headquarters of Seattle Harbor Tours, operator of the *Goodtime* fleet, "mosquitoes" that tour the harbor, including the Duwamish Waterways, permitting close-up looks at the working waterfront, and voyage to Blake Island State Park. There, at Tillicum Village, descendants of the Original (12,000 years ago) Settlers serve baked salmon and display examples of traditional arts and crafts. Moreover, the 4-mile circuit of the island beach and the dozen-odd miles of island trails are the best beach-and-forest hiking so near Seattle. The trip is praised elsewhere in these pages.

- Pier 54 (in an older numbering, Pier 3) is Ivar's Acres of Clams, which rates singling out among the scores of eateries because it occupies a remnant of the Galbraith Dock, which was the chief base of the mosquito fleet during its final decades. In summer the sternwheeler *Emerald Princess* sets out from here on tours of the waterfront. Also here is Ye Olde Curiosity Shop, famous for scrimshaw, Hong Kong totem poles, and mummies.

- Pier 51 is the Washington State Ferries Terminal, better known as what's left of the historic Colman Dock. The green-and-white Washington ferries will take you over the waters to Bainbridge Island or beyond it to Bremerton. Unlike the ghastly expense of automobile passage, pedestrian fares are really cheap, the biggest bargain in Seattle. Don't miss the Tsutakawa fountain at the street entrance to the terminal.

- The ferries and the modern mosquitoes give the best perspective on the skyline of downtown Seattle. Not entirely submerged by its giant new neighbors is the Alaska Building, its name giving away its age. At fourteen stories, this was the city's first "skyscraper" and its first steel-reinforced structure. The Smith Tower, formally unveiled on the Fourth of July of 1914, was hailed as the "Queen City's noblest monument of steel," the tallest building outside New York City. With its 1929 companion, the Northern Life Tower, it dominated the downtown sky until the 1970s brought the Sea-First Building, whose summit stands 714 feet above sea level, and the mid-1980s brought the tallest building west of Chicago and north of Houston, 76 stories, topping out at 1409 feet above sea level. Designed to withstand most earthquakes and nearly

Seattle fireboat

all winds, Mt. Selig (Columbia Center) goes as high as a person can get afoot in King County west of Cougar Mountain (1595 feet).

- Alaska Square Park is a prettied-up green spot.

- Pier 48 used to be the terminal of the blue-and-white Alaska ferries until Bellingham bribed them away. Until then it was possible to walk aboard here with a sleeping bag and rucksackful of groceries and take deck passage to Haines. As some consolation for the loss, in 1994 the *Queen of Burnaby* (British Columbia Ferries will give it a new name) will begin car-ferry and foot-passenger service to Victoria, reviving part (not all) of the traditions of the pre–World War II *Princess* line of ribald song and story. The Working Waterfront Viewpoint is here, equipped with periscopes. Across the railroad tracks is the Underground Antique Mall.

- The Washington Street Public Boat Landing has been that for generations and still is. During Fleet Week in the 1920s and 1930s, the liberty parties from the battlewagons and cruisers debarked here. Seattle had the reputation as "the best liberty town on the Coast" and many bluejackets, swept up in the Shore Patrol dragnet, here embarked semiconscious and under restraint of the Navy's "jimmylegs."

- Pier 46, now a fenced-off container-ship terminal, was the site of the King Street coal bunkers and dock, where for many years after 1878 the coals from Newcastle (and Renton and Franklin and Black Diamond) were transferred from the Seattle & Walla Walla (later, after several changes in name, the Pacific Coast Coal Company Railroad) to sailing ships, then steamers, for transport to San Francisco, China, Australia, and South Africa.

- Pier 36, another container terminal, has the Coast Guard Visual Traffic Center and Coast Guard Museum, displaying ship models and marine memorabilia (free parking, open 1:00–5:00 P.M. weekends, Wednesdays, and holidays).

- Turning inland from the waterfront on Jackson, King, Yesler, or Main takes the walker across Alaskan Way, under the highway viaduct, to Pioneer Square, Klondike Gold Rush National Historic Park, benches, bricks, and trees of Occidental and Pioneer Place Parks, guided tours of Underground Seattle, and bistros and shoppes and one of the greatest bookstores in the West.

- End (or begin) in the King Street Station on South Jackson Street. (The close-by Union Station survives structurally but not railroad-functionally.) Within the echoing vaults listen for conspiratorial whispers of ghosts plotting how to bribe the Congresses of Heaven and Hell into giving them cloud grants (alternate sections in a 40-mile strip either side of the tracks) for the Great Heaven Railroad, the Northern Hell, and the Union Eternal. Wondering how the trains arrive here from the north? In June 1893 the first Great Northern passenger train arrived—via Railroad Avenue—that is, the waterfront. What with ships loading and unloading, the congestion was fierce. A bypass tunnel 5141.5 feet long, 25.8 feet high, and 30 feet wide (the widest tunnel in the world, then!) was completed in 1904 under 4 Avenue, the tracks leading into the Union Depot, opened in May 1904. Walk east from King Street Station and look down from the street to the tunnel mouth.

North from Broad Street to Smith Cove, 1½ miles

A large metered area extending to Bay Street permits parking long enough for a leisurely walk north to Smith Cove and back. The 1200-foot length of Myrtle Edwards Park (City of Seattle) connects to 4000-foot-long Elliott Bay Park (Port of Seattle).

In the whole of its green-lawn mile through the two parks, the path is close by the seawall; at low tide the skinny remainder of beach can be walked instead. Trees offer stretches of shady strolling. Train-watching (adjacent tracks are fenced off) is superb as are ferry-watching and general ship-watching. Also available for watching are ducks, gulls, crows, Elliott Bay, and the Olympics. Keep elbows sharp for joggers. A walking stick gets respect from sneering bikers who muscle into the foot-only lanes. The 200 tons of granite and concrete arranged in a sculpture have caused remark. So, too, notably among residents of Queen Anne Hill who thereby lost their views, has the monster grain terminal at Pier 86, next to which a fishing pier juts 100 feet from shore.

The path ends at Pier 89 on Smith Cove. A large parking lot (free) on 16 Avenue W (¼ mile off Elliott Avenue via W Galer Street) permits the walk to be done from this end.

SMITH COVE PARK

Bus: 19, 24, or 33

Exit from 15 Avenue W onto 14 Avenue W, signed "Elliott Bay Marina–Smith Cove Park." Cross Magnolia Bridge, pass the Pier 91 exit, turn off right to go under the bridge to 23 Avenue W and the park.

The piers of Smith Cove block shore-walking to and from Elliott Bay Park. Smith Cove Park is a nice spot to sit and look: to Alki Point, Blake and Vashon Islands, Restoration Point on Bainbridge Island, the Green and Gold (Blue) Mountains on the Kitsap Peninsula. Below the riprap is beach, and fairly natural at that.

Smith Cove Park to West Point, 3½ miles

The first scheduled walk by The Mountaineers, weeks after the founding of the club and months before its first ascent of a mountain (Si) was from Smith Cove to West Point Lighthouse. Retracing those footsteps of

1907 puts the sensitive walker in a historical mood, as does the connection to the preceding 4000–5000 years when the postglacier shoreline hereabouts had stabilized and the Original Inhabitants began pulling canoes up on shore to dig clams.

In the era when chesty engineers were sluicing away chunks of Beacon Hill and the entirety of Denny Hill, the expectation was that much of Elliott Bay could be made into dry land. For the best part of a century people of Seattle assumed the resulting plats—unfilled, under water—were the amusing legacy of the greedhead lunacy typical of pioneers.

Eventually the city decided the time had come to end the joke and appropriate a few dollars to buy out the grandchildren of the frontier fools. Lo! The passing years had sharpened the skills of engineers and lawyers and the greed of the grandchildren. As prominent citizens of great fortune and frequent contributors to worthy causes, they might have been expected to take a philanthropical stance. Instead, they sold to an entrepreneur who in the mid-1980s proposed to develop the underwater plats for a marina. The State Wildlife Department assessed the plan: "There are few areas where a marina could hold greater potential for fish and wildlife losses.... It is in direct conflict with the State Environmental Policy Act and the Shorelines Management Act." The Muckleshoots complained that nineteenth-century treaties had given them rights: "We're supposed to be able to fish there in perpetuity." The Washington Environmental Council raised a storm. The mayor's Environmental Advisory Committee shouted, "No!" But the city's Land Use Division director felt the marina's

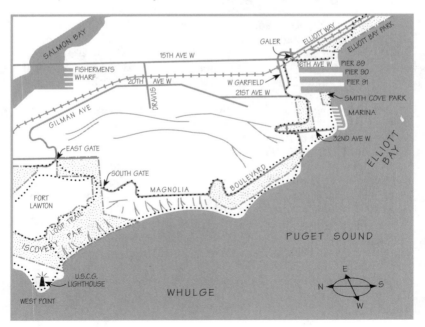

Smith Cove Park and shipyard

restaurant would be a touristy spot for a drinky-poo with a view. In 1992 the $43 million Elliott Bay Marina opened 1200 slips for stinkpots.

The marina is not the unmitigated disaster it might have been. Benella Caminiti and supporters loudly demanded and got public access to the shore. The way through the marina for pedestrians traveling between Smith Cove Park and West Point is a ½-mile boardwalk. Public view-seekers can drive to the marina from 15 Avenue W via a ramp off the viaduct to Magnolia Bluff. Of the docks extending out from the walkway, G Dock is open to the public, to let them gasp at the power yachts, larger than the *Mayflower* and suitable for rich folks' trips around the world. At the end, a small craft is stationed. Free and on request, an attendant transports you out to the observation platform on the breakwater. Views! Open 9:00 A.M. to dusk. Wheelchair access!

To continue to West Point, descend from the marina boardwalk onto the beach and start enjoying views and the Main Street procession of ships and ferries and other craft to and from the downtown waterfront and the Duwamish Waterways. Other views are to Four Mile Rock and across the mouth of Elliott Bay to Alki Point. Look up the vertical till bluff to the line of madronas (Wilkes thought they were magnolias). Gamblers Row, where Perkins Lane follows slump terraces across the face of the bluff and where the *vita* is so *dolce* that residents are willing to risk losing homes in a slippery spell, intrigues the passerby. Old pilings at the bluff foot and litters of boards on the cliff speak of gambles lost over the decades.

The way swings from westerly to northwesterly to northerly, Seattle and its towers are lost around the corner, and the view now is over the water to Bainbridge Island and the Olympics. At low tide the beach is a tideflat so broad that the walker who follows close by the waves is so far from the bluff he/she is scarcely aware of houses tucked in the trees. One is amused by the sign "End of Public Beach," giving notice that from here to Smith Cove people clutch antique pieces of paper. Silly paper! Silly people! Silly foxes. In 1992 a roving Canadian who had snapped up some of these nineteenth-century scraps of paper proposed to build nine luxury houses on stilts behind a breakwater, an 1800-foot channel to let stinkpots through the shallows, and a 1200-foot bridge to connect houses to the bluff.

At the "End of Public Beach" begins Discovery Park.*

DISCOVERY PARK

Bus: 19 to South Gate; 24 or 33 to East Gate

Drive west from 15 Avenue NW on Dravus, north on 20 Avenue NW, which becomes Gilman Avenue, which becomes Government Way, to the East Gate. Pick up a map at the visitor center and (if driving) proceed to the North Gate parking area, very large and central.

Seattle's largest park covers 534 acres above high tide, several hundred more in state tidelands assigned to the city for park use, a good bit more to be obtained from the military when it completes its evacuation, and certain other tracts that may be slow in coming but will come because they must. The 1972 master plan is quite clear that this will not be a headquarters for aerobics/kinetics. "The primary goal of this park in the role of the city is dictated by its incomparable site. That role should be to provide an open space of quiet and tranquility for the citizens of this city—a sanctuary where they might escape the turmoil of the city and enjoy the rejuvenation which quiet and solitude and an intimate contact with nature can bring."

A wildlife sanctuary ringed around by megalopolis. Seattle's finest beach, noblest wave-cut bluffs, and what *was* the most glorious sandspit of Inner Whulge and someday will be again.

Since establishment in 1972, the park has been in an ongoing process of un-development. Many structures of military vintage are being removed. Old roads are being demolished—or left to the devices of moss and grass that visitors may witness the patient reclamation by Nature. The exotic species of plants imported over the past are being weeded out, native species re-introduced.

Tacoma's Point Defiance Park, noted for generations as one of North America's greatest city parks, has been joined on the honors list by Seattle's Discovery Park. To sort out "the infinite riches in little room," the follow-

---

*See the publisher's note on private property on page 11.

ing treatment proceeds from (1) historical, to (2) upland trails, and (3) the beach, West Point.

Indian Cultural Center (Daybreak Star Arts Center)

The military began its evacuation in 1972 after three-quarters of a century in residence. Seattle's sewers arrived shortly after the soldiers; this, too, will pass. The West Point Lighthouse, since 1872 marking the tip of the magnificent spit, will be encouraged to remain, to recall the tall ships it used to guide through the night, and the steamers, and even a few canoes. The second-growth forest reminds of the tidewater loggers of the 1860s. The park's name evokes the voyage of Captain George Vancouver, in 1792, in HMS *Discovery.*

The earliest settlers arrived ten or a dozen millennia ago. David Buerge, in *Naming the Land,* says there were eight or nine peoples in the Seattle area, or eight or nine communities of the same people, the same extended family, speaking a common language, Lushootseed, and sharing a single "nationality," as do the Scots, Welsh, Cornish, and English who for the last several centuries or so (but not *before*) have been considered by geographers (if not always by themselves) jointly British.

The Duwamish lived in Seattle and Renton and along the river; the Suquamish branch of the family produced the most famous local leader, Sealth. The largest village, Dziszilalich, was at Pioneer Square.

As for other branches of the family, Lake Washington was the home of the Hatchuabsh, the "big lake people"; Lake Sammamish, of the Hathatchuabsh, the "second lake people," and also the Issquoabsh; and Lake Union, the H-atschubsh, the "small lake people."

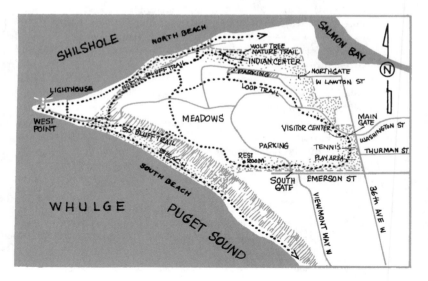

Known to their neighbors, who feared them, as the "people of the moon," the Snoqualmies lived at Fall City and Carnation, from where they hunted, traded, and raided.

The major saltwater people, another part of the Duwamish extended family, were the Shilsholasbsh or Sheel-shol-ashbush, meaning "threading the bend" (canoeing to Lake Union). Their home extended from Smith Cove to Mukilteo, north of which lived the Snohomish. The largest village was at Salmon Bay, to catch salmon headed for Lake Union. Campsites lay along the shore to the north; Whulge walkers will guess them. The saltmarsh of south Edmonds, cut off by a baymouth bar, likely held a second major village.

The Shilshole people seem to have suffered a great catastrophe along about 1800, perhaps an extraordinarily destructive visit by the dreaded Northern Raiders. Subsequently, of course, they suffered the onslaught of European children's diseases, here intensified to plagues. Early European visitors saw three longhouses at Salmon Bay. By 1853 the population was reduced to a dozen families; by the late 1880s, two families. "Indian Charlie" (Hwulch'teed) lived in a cedar shack on the site 50 years, to the turn of the century. He was the last of his people. The U.S. Army Corps of Engineers dredged his homesite for the Ship Canal.

The worst catastrophe befalling the Original Residents was Territorial Governor Stevens, who in the 1850s "negotiated," at U.S. Army gunpoint, a series of treaties that imposed upon the millennia-old local culture the alien European concept of property ownership. The catastrophe was compounded and enlarged over the years by the Original Residents' lack of attorneys. In 1974 federal judge George H. Boldt compensated for the deficiency by ruling (the "Boldt Decision") that the long-ignored treaties were binding upon the United States and the State of Washington and that the Originals therefore could exercise their treaty rights without being hauled off to jail by armed officers of the State Game Department. But in a follow-up decision, in 1979, Judge Boldt ruled that five of the Original Peoples (Duwamish, Snohomish, Steilacoom, Samish, and Snoqualmie) did not exist, never had, and thus had no treaty rights. In 1993 the Originals' attorneys filed suit, citing Boldt's death certificate (1984) that in 1978 he had fallen victim to Alzheimer's disease and in 1979 was mentally incompetent.

Upland Trails

The upland is sampled by more than 7 miles of trails. The 2.8-mile *Loop Trail* approximately circles the park periphery, passing all park entrances and Metro bus stops, connecting to all paths.

From the North Gate parking area ascend the hill on any of several paths ¼ mile to intersect the loop. In the counterclockwise direction it soon passes the sidepath to the North Bluff, views north over Puget Sound, and the North Beach Trail and the access to the Indian Cultural Center.

West Point Lighthouse from Discovery Park

Crossing the service road (route of stinky trucks) to West Point, it passes the South Beach Trail and at South Bluff, atop the famous sand cliffs, provides glorious Sound views. Inland is the South Meadow, whose dunes date from a drier climate of the past.

Up and down through woods and past old Army buildings, the Loop Trail self-completes, on the way sampling the bluffs, as much as 250 feet high, the meadows which top out at 360 feet above sea level, and the mixed-species second-growth forests, and giving access to the structured open spaces, including the Fort Lawton Parade Ground in the park's Historic District and the Indian Cultural Center.

Through the generations of bivouacking the soldiers largely converted the vegetation to species from the East, Europe, Macedonia, and the domains of Cyrus the Great. Citizen volunteers of Friends of Discovery Park are patiently eliminating foreigners and making the ecosystem safe for natives. The trail and park are getting better and better, year by year.

The ½-mile *Wolf Tree Nature Trail* sets out from North Parking and circles through mixed forest and swamp, along the sidehill, and over Sheuerman Creek; the latter is named for the Christian who bought the land in 1887 and with his Original wife, Rebecca, lived in a log cabin with their ten children. We learn this from the pamphlet available at the trailhead, and much more, including explanations of sights along the trail: "dog hair stand," "witches broom," and "wolf tree."

From the north arm of the Loop Trail a sidepath leads to North Bluff and the Shilshole Overlook of Shilshole Bay, Bainbridge Island, the Olympics, and Mt. Baker. The ½-mile *North Beach Trail* descends 150 steps carved in the bluff to a precious scrap of totally natural beach (all that's left hereabouts) between the Privatized shore of Lawton Woods to the north and, to the south, Godzilla Land.

The ½-mile *West Point Trail* descends 137 carved steps from the North Bluff to an end at the West Point service road just across from the South Beach Trail. The Hmongs from the hills of Laos rehabilitated this old trail in 1982, building bridges and wooden stairways and surfacing the trail to a safe and lovable path in any season. The bluff terrain is steep but the trail permits relaxed enjoyment of the superb forest, which includes enormous bigleaf maples at least 130 years old, their bark draped with moss, branches hung with licorice fern. Old! Green! Serene!

The especially nice feature of the ½-mile *South Beach Trail* is that it lets a person drop from the Loop Trail to the beach free from the reeking and rumbling trucks of the Metro service road. The start is from the Loop Trail near the South Bluff promontory. Views are grand over the water to the Olympics. Watch for canine tracks; the park is Old Coyote's favorite hangout this side of the Issaquah Alps.

West Point

The storm southerlies blow free from a long, long reach of the Whulge. They impel longshore currents that take on a full load of sand from the cliffs of Magnolia Bluff. For many a millennium, they have unloaded at West Point, building a spit that hasn't a rival this side of the Strait of Juan de Fuca.

It is, no contest, the Number One spit of the Inner Whulge, and arguably of the entire Whulge, because of its location in the middle of Whulge City, at the crossroads of Main Street where ships from far seas turn this way into Elliott Bay, that way toward Bremerton, or continue south to Tacoma and other ports; where ferries shuttle from the bay and from Fauntleroy Cove to four landings across the waters; and where fishing boats, tugs and barges, and playboats ceaselessly go every which way. This is the epitome of "the wildness within," where city and Whulge are One, "not man apart."

Until 1966 West Point was disturbed to a relatively minor extent by a century of the West Point Lighthouse, two-thirds of a century of Fort Lawton, and nearly that long of a raw-sewage outlet rammed through by the young city's Quintessential Engineer, R. H. Thomson, the same bully who deconstructed Denny Hill. Then came that most Worthy Cause, Metro, which filthied West Point with a sewage plant. Because the Army had been there so long, blocking easy Public visitation, comparatively few people stood up to defend the spit. At present, the hiker must avert his/her gaze from the god-awful structures squatting where the tidal lagoon used to be and hold his/her nose while walking past to the clean winds at the lighthouse.

This was desecration enough, but then Metro proposed to install a secondary-treatment facility that would make 1987 look like the good old days. To its everlasting credit, the City of Seattle, led by its then-mayor, supported by the Friends of Discovery Park, cried "It must not happen! Metro must get off the point!" Members of the Metro Council protested, "It's Seattle's park! Let Seattle pay for it!" This sort of vision, able to make out objects on the tip of the nose but no farther, would pronounce Mount Rainier to be "Tacoma's volcano."

A public Hall of Shame is contemplated, a place where the great-great-grandchildren of the eco-criminals will be reminded of the taint in their blood. R. H. Thomson will be there, for Denny Hill and the West Point sewer. The Metro Council will be there. The heirs of the pioneers who perpetrated the Elliott Bay Marina (not to forget their attorneys-at-"law").

Seattle ultimately will prevail. King County—and all the provinces of the Whulge—will have their West Point. Man's blasphemies will be removed, Nature will be permitted to restore a complete and natural beach—the waves throwing up a driftwood line, the winds blowing up a dune line, the waters filling up a lagoon marsh, and the reeds growing and the blackbirds scolding birdwatchers. All will be as it was before and folks will come from the world around to praise Seattle for its soul. The grandchildren of the Metro Councilors will apologize for their grandfathers and grandmothers.

The chorus of denunciation failed to daunt the Metro Council but did sensitize it to the need to perform some publicly braggable act of penance. The opportunity that presented itself was the unearthment by archeologist Lynn Larson of millennia of activity on I'ka'dztcu ("thrust far out"). In the words of *Post-Intelligencer* writer Solvig Torvik, "a massive, 35-acre concrete complex has been superimposed on the remnants left by people long vanished.... While some 200,000 trees and bushes will be planted to hide this unlovely technological wonder, all that's left of the natural environment is a thin fringe of grass waving in the breeze along a cramped strip of beach. Nevertheless, some of the history ... has been preserved.... It cost Metro 1 month and $35 million to delay construction while Larson and her crew scrambled to salvage artifacts." So pin a medal on Metro, right?

For now, until West Point can be repaired by a wiser, kinder community, walkers will visit the scene of Metro devastation in order to look the Enemy in the face that they may know Him when He seeks to intrude His evil elsewhere.

The tip of West Point itself must be visited. Whether via the sewage-truck road or the West Point Trail or South Beach Trail, descend from the bluff and hold your nose to pass the engineers' triumph. At ¼ mile past the stinkery is the lighthouse. Stand on the tip of the spit in a loud, clean wind and gaze into the present to see the past.

Shield eyes and nose while returning past the scene of the former dunes and lagoon to the foot of the bluff. The "amelioration" en route is as heart-rending as the cosmetics the embalmer paints on the corpse of a beloved friend.

However, at low tide there is greatness to be known, a mystical experience. The bluff is a tall wilderness of trees and bushes, the greenery broken on high by the famous sand cliffs, and at the bluff base by vertical walls of blue clay. The sign to the south, "End of Public Beach," is pure nineteenth century living on into the twentieth, certain to die in the twenty-first.

The way north from West Point is cruel. In the process of "amelioration," the riprap wall which destroyed the beach will be ripped out. The inland where once was lagoon and meadow will be partly refashioned into the semilikeness of pristine shore. At the north end of the Metro devastation is a little bit of the pristine, unameliorated past to demonstrate what has been foolishly, needlessly thrown away as a sop to the engineers' hubris. At low tide enough beach is open to walk for a look into Shilshole Bay.

North Gate to Chittenden Locks, 2½ miles

Discovery Park is Seattle's best, its largest, finest "wildness within," the area's premier shore park. The "Jim Hill Wilderness" begins not far to the north and extends to Everett. Between the two a connecting link is wanted, both for wildlife travel and for people feet.

The Friends of Discovery Park are seeking funds to acquire lots sub-

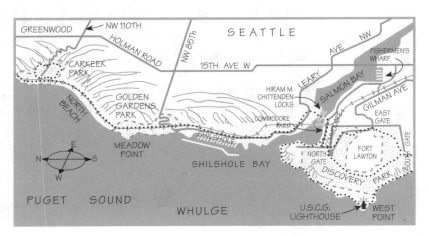

ject to possible development and thus complete the Public ownership of the Kiwanis Ravine, half of which is already a park. Two streams flow down the deep slash in the bluff, habitat of eighty or more native plants and some fifty-six species of birds; a dozen heron nests are Seattle's last significant heronry. The ravine can be sampled from 40 Avenue, which descends from North Gate to Commodore.

Commodore Park is a jimdandy. Look out saltwater Salmon Bay past railroad bridge and jetties to Shilshole Bay and Puget Sound. On a sunny day admire the queue of vessels waiting to go through the Big Lock or the Little Lock into freshwater Salmon Bay. In the season when the fish are coming in to spawn, see the fishermen cursing the sea lions as they feast.

Follow the promenade path through the park to the pedestrian walkway over Chittenden Locks. Pause to examine the fish ladder that salmon and trout which escape the hunger of the sea lions ascend on their way to spawning grounds in the Lake Washington basin. A below-ground viewing gallery gives the best close looks at big fish available outside a fish market. (After studying the fish you may wish to study fishing boats. For a sidetrip, walk east on Commodore 1 mile to the fleet based at Salmon Bay Terminal, "Fishermen's Wharf.")

Chittenden Locks in Ballard

Hiram M. Chittenden Locks ("Ballard Locks") are the key component of a navigation system dedicated in 1917. A channel was dredged from Puget Sound through Shilshole Bay to Salmon Bay, joining this body of water via the Fremont Cut to Lake Union, and that body via the Montlake Cut to Lake Washington. The latter was lowered from the natural elevation above sea level of 29–33 feet to the level of Lake Union, 21 feet, and Salmon Bay was raised by the dam at the locks. Lake Washington, which formerly emptied via the Black River to the Duwamish River, thence to Elliott Bay, now drains through the Lake Washington Ship Canal to Shilshole Bay. The Black River virtually ceased to be. The Cedar River, which flowed into the Black and thus the Duwamish, was diverted into Lake Washington, which it thus furnishes a constant source of flushing water from the mountains, the uncelebrated other half of the clean-up-the-lake success story for which Metro always takes full credit. Awareness of all this fooling around with Mother Nature adds interest to watching ships and boats being lowered or raised through the locks. (Footnote: The Ship Canal never made Lake Washington, as Movers & Shakers claimed would happen, a great seaport.)

Adjoining the locks are the 7 acres of Carl English Botanical Gardens, displaying plants from lands all over the world.

GOLDEN GARDENS PARK

Bus: 46

Drive from Ballard past the Chittenden Locks and Shilshole Marina.

Meadow Point is Seattle's sole surviving "complete" spit, much molested to be sure, yet still retaining a recognizable driftwood line, and dune line, and even a bit of lagoon. (Egged on by Friends of Golden Gardens Park, Seattle plans rehabilitation of those natural features, paid for by Metro as part of its mandatory "amelioration" for its West Point devastation of natural features.) The point was spared from swimming pools and sewage plants, golly knows how. An attempt was made to erect a fish tank but that was diverted to the Seattle waterfront; the chief signs of human presence north of the marina and parking lot are the tracks of bare feet in the sand. The 95-acre park dates from 1923; the bathing beach was popular long before that, since 1907 as part of a private development.

The park is the start of the Jim Hill Wilderness, whose Great Northern (now Burlington-Northern) Railway follows the shore from here to Everett. The tracks can be walked 1 mile in the other direction to Chittenden Locks, should one wish to goggle at millions of dollars' worth of playboats behind a monstrous jetty, contribution to the beauty of the waterfront by the Port of Seattle, which also prizes Sea-Tac International Airport over any interest in quality of life under the umbrella of jet violence.*

---

*See the publisher's note on private property on page 11.

North from Meadow Point to Carkeek Park, 2 miles

The low bank above the tracks is solidly housed through the Blue Ridge community and the North Beach area. There is a "however" here, at 1 mile from Meadow Point.

North Beach*

Bus: 18 to Triton Drive

Drive Seaview to NW 85 Street, turn left to 24 Avenue N, left to NW 98 Street, and left toward the water. Go southwest on Triton Drive about a block (passing fenced-in Blue Ridge Park), and turn right on Esplanade. In a couple of blocks pass fenced-in North Beach Club and continue on Esplanade to the end. No parking, so back up to a point of opportunity.

At the end of Esplanade is a Metro pump station. Walk through to the railroad tracks and away you go.

On fine spring Sundays the choir of the Asbury Methodist Episcopal Church used to walk here between services to go wading. The beach was a picnickers' favorite before Golden Gardens was a park. The mosquito fleet called at the dock. After World War II the war-wealthied walled off the water; shrubs and lawns and fences blocked trails that had been Public. But there still were sneak-through routes and the 1989 voter-approved open-space bond issue included lands in the vicinity of old North Beach.

Onward North. Beyond the shallow valley of North Beach, the bluff rears up 200 feet, tall and steep and unstable. In winter the Seattle papers used to regularly report, "Slide over the tracks at North Beach." A sensor wire was installed at the bluff foot; now, when a chunk of bluff slides, a light blinks on somewhere and the trains are radioed to watch out.

The walker looks west over wild waters where people are fewer than birds, man's vessels scarcely more numerous than whales and seals and sea lions. The walker looks east into the wild green wall of the wave-cut bluff where wild critters lurk.

To Start the Walk from the North. The advantage of starting this stretch of beach from the north is the walker can turn around at piling stubs of the ancient dock on Meadow Point and not ever have to see the stinkpot fleet or the bronze Norwegian.

CARKEEK PARK

Bus: 28 or 29 to NW 100 Place

Drive Holman Road to Greenwood Avenue and turn left to NW 110 Street, which becomes Carkeek Park Drive.

Along about 1880, soon after the giant cedars were felled, skidded to the beach, and rafted to shingle mills in Ballard, a Bavarian-born baker and confectioner, A. W. Piper, cleared land for a farm. He died in 1904,

---

*See the publisher's note on private property on page 11.

and in 1927 the land was bought by Seattle to replace the original Carkeek Park (gift of the Carkeek family), which had been patriotically donated to the U.S. Navy for the Sand Point Naval Air Station. In 1981 volunteers of the Carkeek Watershed Community Action Project (CWCAP) experienced a spasm of nostalgia for Bavarian apple pies. Hacking away ivy and hellberries and brush, they found gnarled, mossy survivors of Piper's orchard—some thirty apple trees, two pear, two cherry, and a huge sweet chestnut. The volunteers sat in the grass sampling archaic varieties of apples, appreciated, as one put it, "by the same kind of people with a taste for baroque music."

Piper farmed the plateau upland and the valley bottom. Near the mouth of Piper's Creek, on the south side, a brickyard made blue glacial clay into the basic building block of pre-concrete America. In the era of World War I, the older surveyor's mother and friends used to walk after Sunday school north from Ballard along the Great Northern tracks to "the brickyard."

The 1930s brought the Civilian Conservation Corps and the first development, including trails. However, when the older surveyor made his initial visit in the fall of 1937, hiking with Troop 324 from the Scout Lodge next to Ronald School to attend the overnight Camporall of the North Shore District, the park was mainly under Nature's management. It remains so today, one of the two largest wildlands on the Whulge between Ballard and Everett.

The park of today—the 193 upland acres of bluff and canyon and the 23 acres of Piper's Creek tideland delta—was shaped to present form in 1953 and 1976. In the latter year the Viking Council of the Boy Scouts developed the major trail, 1.3 miles from the railroad tracks up Piper's Creek, ascending the canyon floor in lush mixed forest, passing a dozen basalt-boulder "energy dissipators." Crossing and recrossing the sandy creek, the trail climbs the narrowing canyon, at last leaving it to ascend steeply to a small parking area at the street-end of 6 Avenue NW, which leads to a bus stop on NW 100 Place close to Holman Road NW.

For a loop return, find one of the several paths climbing into wildwoods south of the canyon and wander along the hillside to a bluff 175 steep feet above the tracks and beach, giving fine views over the water and south to Meadow Point.

In the 1980s came the CWCAP, a citizen group working with public agencies to "turn Carkeek into a model urban watershed, purged of fecal pollution and abandoned rusted bedsteads." Recovering Piper's orchard has been one project. Another is the Salmon-to-Sound Trail, to restore the coho salmon run to Venema Creek and Mohlendorph Creek, which empty into Piper's Creek downstream of the Worthy Cause stinkplant. (A 1980 plant of coho fry had limited success. A 1984 plant of chum fry brought, in November 1987, a spectacular return of mature chum salmon. A fry class planted during the Earth Days of 1989 and 1990 brought a spectacular return in the Christmas season of 1993.) At a scant ½ mile from the mouth of Piper's Creek, the route diverges from the Piper's Creek

Trail to ascend Venema Creek to the spawning grounds—used, too, by native cutthroat trout.

One reason the water quality here is excellent is that parts of the West Fork Venema forest appear to be virgin, trees up to 4 feet in diameter and no sawn stumps.

The CWCAP also is properly proud of its Viewlands Botanical Trail, looping around Viewlands Creek and upper Piper's Creek. Exotic plants are being cleared out, natives planted, and a teaching path established for use by Seattle schools.

As the map in these pages suggests, there are other paths in the park, at least 8 miles.

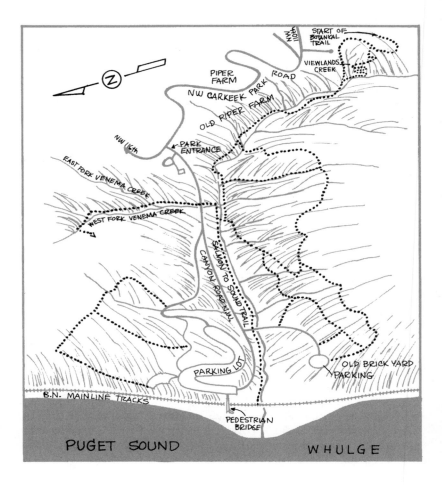

North from Carkeek Park to Richmond Beach Park, 4½ miles

The bluff wildland and wildlife refuge is a near-constant presence. Beside the high-tide lane atop the seawall are alders and maples, flowers in season, frogs croaking in marshy ditches, creeks tumbling down little gorges. One scarcely believes houses are at blufftop.

North ½ mile from Carkeek Park is Whiskey Cove, hardly distinguishable as a cove but used during Prohibition as a landing by the small, superswift, black boats of smugglers running a load of the good stuff in from Canada. A bit of sandy beach (low tide only) latterly has attracted throngs of nude bodies. The neighbors have reacted in two ways. Some got out their binoculars and beat through the bushes to viewpoints on the bluff. Others called their ministers who called the police. Railroad dicks, having meticulously studied the scene and fully documented the nudity with telephoto close-ups, sprang out of the brush to enforce the "dress and depart" code. In all his visits over the years, the older surveyor never has seen a nude body at the cove except his own, and that was because as a boy he didn't own a bathing suit. Nor has he ever seen a railroad dick, there or anywhere.

At 1 mile from the park is a canyon in clay and sand; generations of local kids have worked away at eroding the deposit while trying to break their necks climbing the vertical walls.

Highlands Point

At 2 miles from Carkeek Park (and all this way no houses by the beach) is Highlands Point and the wide valley of Boeing Creek, named for the logger–aircraft manufacturer who kept this section of forest as a rich folks' retreat; not until World War II was the ancient forest of the "Boeing Tract" logged to further enrich the rich. The newspapers delighted in nineteenth-century logging so near the city so late in history; only a few Publics mourned the loss of the equivalent of a dozen Seward Parks.

On the south side of Boeing Creek a road ascends the wild creek, in big trees that weren't worth logging (snagtops and wolves), to The Highlands, a residential park established in 1910 or so, the 100-odd castles fenced and policed to exclude stray hoboes and adventurous children on exploring trips. On the north side a road-trail gated to exclude vehicles ascends a greenbelt easement ½ mile to Innis Arden Way and Shoreline Park. The Friends of Shoreline Park are urging King County Parks to dedicate the surviving virgin forest as a permanent pocket wildland, low-impact re-creation only. No kinetics.

Onward North. North from Boeing Creek is more wild bluff. Keep a sharp eye for a path up a gulch to Innis Arden; in olden days this trail continued overland to Richmond Highlands.

To Start the Walk from the North. Walking just halfway, to Highlands Point/Boeing Creek, is a leisurely stroll; a cooling sidetrip up the creek to the big trees is appealing on a hot day.

RICHMOND BEACH PARK

Bus: 302 or 305

From Aurora Avenue at N 185 Street turn west on Richmond Beach Road and follow it down the steps of wave-cut bluffs, each representing a former level of the waves. When nearly at the water, one bluff remaining, turn left to the parking area.

The parking area is in the enormous "cirque" from which the Richmond Beach Sand and Gravel Company, starting in early 1900s, barged huge amounts of glacier dumpings. Until the 1940s local kids strapped barrel staves to shoes for sand-skiing races. The mining continued to World War II, during whose early weeks, on a blacked-out moonless night, the older surveyor was arrested by the Army on suspicion of being a Japanese saboteur intending to molest the gravel.

A skybridge crosses the tracks to what used to be a lofty sand hill. A diving board on the brink launched plunges into space, splashing in sand or water, depending on the tide.

In 1909 the Richmond Beach Shipbuilding Company built the steam fireboat *Duwamish* for the Seattle Fire Department. In the 1920s and 1930s shipwrecking replaced shipbuilding; wooden ships were stripped of metal fittings and set afire, the clouds of black smoke drawing throngs from throughout north Seattle. The last clipper ship built in America had

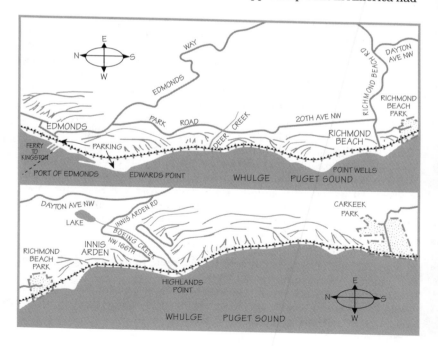

its funeral pyre here, and golly knows how many of the lumber schooners that used to carry Puget Sound trees around the globe, and countless mosquito steamers.

North from Richmond Beach Park to Edmonds Ferry Dock, 4 miles

The Whulge Trail proceeds from the park through the old community of Richmond Beach, past the site of the vanished steamer dock and the site of the Great Northern depot ripped out to be replaced by a Very Worthy Metro Sewer Plant, to Point Wells, known as the Potts Ranch until 1911 when Royal-Dutch Shell built storage tanks. The site was purchased the next year by Standard Oil of California for a distribution center (tanker terminal, asphalt refinery) which provided many jobs for the community, particularly during the 1930s when company assets were defended by hired gunmen against possible attack by the union's volunteer gunmen.

In its pristinity (the Potts Ranch era) Point Wells was a fit junior companion for the pristine West Point. The rail-walker who passes the Point Wells fortress fences is startled and bemused to discover, at the north boundary, nearly 2 miles from Richmond Beach Park, a bit of surviving spit. What's the name of the Worthy Cause that has spotted this as "one of the two best sites for a major new sewage-treatment plant"? One guess. Can the Terminator of West Point be rebuffed here? To paraphrase Robinson Jeffers, "It's only a little beach, but oh so beautiful."

In late 1993 Standard Oil (now known as Chevron) announced it was considering quitting Point Wells. Does Snohomish County Parks plan to buy and restore the spit? If not, why not?

Wild bluff resumes. Atop are the fence-guarded estates of Woodway Park, known only to the residents, daring children who trespass up the bluff, and TV audiences who have enjoyed the scene as decorated by pretty actresses and without the killer dogs posted at the brink to eat daring children. The shore here is amusing. When the wealthies built their castles on high, they came down a road 220 feet to their sea-level rail station and steamer dock. The carriage road had to be rebuilt every spring. The railroad eventually was relocated on a causeway well out to sea, beyond reach of the chunks of palatial estates, oft-reported in the press as the "Woodway Slide."

Except for the kempt-looking bluff rim, suggesting gardeners (and killer dogs) up there, the track-walker never would suspect houses, here or anywhere from Point Wells to Edmonds.

Edwards Point

Bus: Community Transit 110, 404, 141, 180, or 870

Drive south from Edmonds Ferry Dock on Sunset Avenue, turn right on Dayton and left on Admiral Way to the picnic tables and children's play area of Marina Beach Park.

At 3 miles from Richmond Beach Park, 1 mile short of Edmonds Ferry

Dock, is Edwards Point, the best destination for a walk from the south and the best start for a walk to the south. Union-Unocal had a tanker terminal here (storage tanks, small refinery) until 1990 but left a considerable portion of the natural beach undisturbed. The fate of the "Union Oil Marsh" remained unclear until mid-1993, when the City of Edmonds announced that 22.5 acres (*not* the entire 53 acres!) would have walkway-interpretive development on the north side, an excellent example of a half-good action by government, which sometimes throws a bone to the Public Deity but always gives the Privatizing Devil His due. To put on a happy face, the State Department of Ecology reports that the "... near 2000-foot ... asphalt path and charming wooden boardwalk provide viewers an intimate look at a unique urban wetland."

EDMONDS FERRY DOCK

Bus: Community Transit 147, 404, 416, or 870

Follow signs from I-5 to the Edmonds Ferry Dock. North of the dock is Sunset Beach Park, where cars may be parked 4 hours maximum. For a lengthier walk, park south of the dock in the vast Port of Edmonds lots.

At Edwards Point begins a 1-mile breach in the bluffs, a broad valley behind a baymouth bar, much of the pristine lagoon preserved as wildlife habitat. The site was a principal settlement of the Shilshole people, but not after 1891, when the town was incorporated, a year after arrival of the Great Northern Railroad. By 1909 the giant cedars of the valley bowl were feeding ten shingle mills. The last closed in 1951, yielding to the era of the stinkpot; marinas and et cetera are virtually continuous south from the ferry dock to Edwards Point, an excellent reason for walking to Richmond Beach not from the dock but from Edwards Point. The playboats are so proliferating, competing so bitterly for moorage space, an entertaining solution has been proposed: war. When the armada of Shilshole Bay razzed out to meet the fleet of Edmonds, thousands of walkers and birdwatchers would line the shore, cheering each sinking.

The dock itself is the city's most lovable feature. For a lunch stop and an incomparable viewpoint, take the voyage (foot-only passage is cheap) to Kingston on the Kitsap Peninsula and back. At least pause to watch the ferry ease into the slip, unload, and load. Time your visit for a storm and you may see the ferry take out the slip, in which case it must head south to Colman Dock in Seattle, making hundreds of commuters gleefully late for work.

Adjoining the dock on the north is Edmonds Underwater Park, sunken ships providing hangouts for marine life that scuba divers can look at but mustn't touch. Connecting to the underwater park is the above-water Sunset Beach Park, located at historic Brackett's Landing, named for the operator of the first mill. At low tide relics of old mills are revealed in the sand.

Edmonds Ferry Dock from waterfront beach access

North from Edmonds Ferry Dock to Picnic Point Park, 6 miles

Ever since Jim Hill provided the all-tides walkway, a favorite stretch of the Whulge Trail has been from Edmonds to Picnic Point, a full but not grueling day's roundtrip. Secondary accesses permit shorter beach hikes, each a delight.

The overwater views become distinctly and dramatically different. The north-of-Seattle shore and Bainbridge Island fade south in haze, the vista now across to the Kitsap Peninsula. But one sees out northwest between the peninsula and the white cliffs of Whidbey Island to the Admiralty Inlet route to the ocean. For the first time, and only briefly, there is a bit of water horizon.

Immediately north of Edmonds the bluff is a mere bank and houses line the railroad tracks. Then the wild wall rises again, cut by gulches and a sand canyon.

At about 3 miles the shore curves in to Browns Bay, in times prior to Privatization a favorite Boy Scout and fisherman hangout, now just a name on the map. In a lovely gulch is Lynnwood's sewage-treatment plant (the old story) and the first road (gated) to the beach since Edmonds.

At 4 miles a structure juts out on the water side of the tracks—historic (since 1930?) Haines Fishing Wharf. On slumping hillsides above is the village of Meadowdale, considerably reduced in size since the major slide of 1947. To the north ½ mile is fine broad sandy Meadowdale Beach at the mouth of Lunds Gulch.

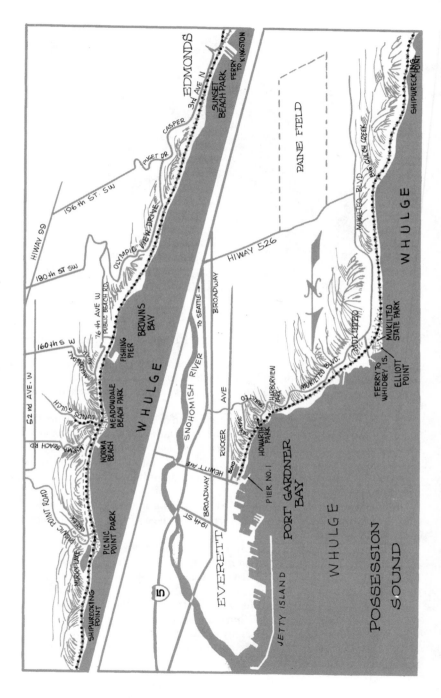

Meadowdale Beach Park

Bus: Community Transit 147 or 670

Go off I-5 on Exit 183, drive 164 Street SW 2 miles, turn right on 168 Street SW, cross Highway 99, and go ½ mile to 52 Avenue W. Turn right and follow signs on 160 Street SW, 56 Avenue W, and 156 Street SW to the park entrance.

For the Handicapped-Disabled entrance to the park, go off Olympic View Drive (the "Snake Trail," so sinuous and steep was it as a loggers' skid road) on 76 Avenue W, which becomes 75th, gated at the park entry. Parking at the gate for perhaps two cars and in all of Meadowdale's narrow streets only a half-dozen more. Cars with a Disabled Permit can drive from the gate to the parking at the bottom of Lunds Gulch.

The delta point thrusting far out in the waves, views up and down the Whulge, and the handsome creek rushing from Lunds Gulch and rippling over the beach were far-famed before there was a park. The serendipity of Lunds Gulch is that it is one of the two largest wildlands (Carkeek Park the other) along the Seattle–Everett shore. Even without a beach it would be a joy.

The main entrance, announced by a big wood arch, has a large parking lot, which because of Meadowdale's tenuous geography is the mandatory entry for mass use. The elevation here on the upland is 450 feet, an elevation to be kept in mind for the return from the beach at 0 feet. Good trail, sometimes very steep, partly staircase, winds down to the valley floor through massed alders, fern-hung maples, hemlocks nursed by huge cedar stumps notched for the fallers' springboards. A sign informs, "The early settlers used this trail to reach the Meadowdale train station. Because of its steepness, the local people called it the 'Chilkoot Trail'." A wide road-trail descends second-growth forest which is well along toward becoming semi-ancient, paralleling the creek's sandbars and waterfalls. At 1½ miles spot charred ruins of the Meadowdale Country Club clubhouse; no vestiges can be found of the golf course, which obviously was minute.

The ranger's residence and picnic facilities are here, where the (gated) road enters from Meadowdale. A tunnel under the railroad tracks safely conveys children and parents to the beach.

Onward North. Just around the corner, ½ mile north of Lunds Gulch, is (or perhaps, by now, was) another fishing wharf; this one at Norma Beach, long since closed, shows its age, seeming about to sag to the sands. Cars have little space to park but the Public feet easily can gain the beach via the railroad tracks.* However, it is an access best left to the locals. Alien cars are a nuisance.

A high sand cliff and a trail to the blufftop catch the eye; there's another way there (see below). Then, on a slump terrace above the beach,

---

*See the publisher's note on private property on page 11.

appears a row of homes (see below). Ghosts crowd the beach—lines of old pilings, remnants of docks, visions of the vessels of the mosquito fleet that steamed up and down the water road until the 1930s. More ghosts— concrete foundations of beach cabins. Are those mandolins we hear in the summer twilight? All this, 1 mile from Norma Beach, is none other than famous Picnic Point, a great sandy spit (actually, a cuspate hybrid) at the mouth of a superb valley, a creek rushing across the beach.

To Start the Walk from the North. For the roundtrip, Edmonds is the best start because Picnic Point is the climax. For partial walks, Picnic Point is the choice. Family short-trippers will be pleased to their teeth by a summer afternoon 1½ miles south to Lunds Gulch, 1 mile up the valley forest (20 degrees cooler inside) and thus back to the watermelon.

PICNIC POINT PARK

Bus: Community Transit 170, 147, or 670 along Beverly Park–Edmonds Road, then walk 2 miles to the beach

Take the Paine Field exit from I-5. Drive west to Highway 99 and turn south to Mukilteo Road, Highway 525. Turn northwest (right) to Beverly Park–Edmonds Road. Turn southwest (left) to a red blinker. Turn northwest (right) on Picnic Point Road and descend a forested, undeveloped, beautiful, wild, parkless gulch (passing the Alderwood Manor wastewater treatment plant, that the valley should not be a total loss) to the beach parking area.

I've wandered the wide world over,
And I'll tell you if man ever found
A place to be peaceful and quiet,
It's here on Puget Sound ...

No longer a slave of ambition,
I laugh at the world and its shams,
As I think of my happy condition,
Surrounded by acres of clams.

Every Whulge walker has a special spot where is heard in mind's ear Ivar Haglund singing *The Old Settler.* Picnic Point has been special for this surveyor's family since it arrived on Jim Hill's brandnew rails from North Dakota and for the photographer's family since it paddled a canoe from the Ark.

No sewage plant, no swimming pool, no aquarium or marina. Almost had a refinery until the Texas oilers were so frightened by the enraged citizenry they decided to turn a profit another way, building a city on the uplands, the value of the lots enhanced by existence of the park—the land leased (not sold!) to the county for a parking lot from which a skybridge crosses the tracks to the beach. Some "park."

But what a beach!

Despite lack of space for a trail system there is a nice bluff walk. Maps show Puget Sound Boulevard contouring the bluff face south to Norma Beach. But it doesn't make it all the way and hasn't since about 1960 (except for a temporary 1986 reopening for a local project).

Neither rain nor snow nor wind will keep the "old surveyor" at home. Pictured here at Picnic Point Park

Here on the ⅓-mile vanished section a hiker can sit in the woods, high above the beach, far below the blufftop, protected on every side from the twentieth century and, gazing over the waters, feel as remote from civilization as anywhere on the Whulge.

North from Picnic Point Park to Mukilteo State Park, 5 miles

The hiker who started the journey in Seattle now is aware of having come very far north. Indeed, the route here leaves Puget Sound for Possession Sound, across whose relatively narrow width is Whidbey Island. Still in view are the Olympics but now very close to north, above Camano Island, is the white volcano of Baker. At hike's start the Bainbridge Island ferry shuttled back and forth from Seattle to Winslow. Then came the shuttling of the Edmonds–Kingston ferry, which now retreats southward in the distance; to the north become more prominent the green-and-white vessels between Mukilteo and Columbia Beach, on Whidbey.

Just north of Picnic Point the tracks pass a murky lake dammed by a short railroad causeway; homes line the inland shore, leaders of flycasters festoon the telephone wires. At 1 mile is "Shipwrecking Point," a spit once used for stripping and burning wooden ships; a carcass and some rib cages remain.

In ¼ mile more is a substantial ravine and a trail. Houses of so-called Chenault Beach (named for the Flying Tiger famous in World War II, in hopes his fame would help sell lots, despite the tract having no beach) are seen atop the bluff. Decades after the Tiger had gone to a hero's grave the sewers came, houses began newly nearing the water, and there goes the neighborhood.

In 1 mile more (2¼ miles from Picnic Point) is a point with a very wide beach at low tide, the mouth of the wild valley of Big Gulch. Not a park. In fact, it once was degraded to an open ditch for flushing raw sewage from Paine Field Air Force Base. Cleaned up and looking nice, it now harbors a Worthy Cause—the Olympus Terrace Sewage Treatment Plant. No Public access from inland. Thus lonesome country. Until the 1980s the plant attendant saw deer and bear and weasels and seals, eagles perched in favorite snags, fleets of thousands upon thousands of brants and widgeons and other waterfowl swimming by. Construction of the treatment plant permitted land-developers to shift into high gear, and the locality is becoming steadily more human and less humane.

North ½ mile is the first close house in a long while, in a creek valley on a flat beside the tracks, access solely via the driveway. Shortly a road descends a slump terrace to within 50 feet of the tracks but is not recommended as a Public beach access, having very little parking. An interesting portion of this community is built outside the railroad tracks on a bulkheaded invasion of the beach; the dozen cottages have walk-in trail access only; the residents tend not to buy new refrigerators very often.

After this ½ mile of scattered dwellings, in the final 1¾ miles mankind retreats from the beach to the top of the bluff. The way features a tangled-green slot of a gorge, a great vertical cliff of white glacial till, another creek tumbling out of a gulch.

Rounding Elliott Point the railway swings inland and is fenced off through Mukilteo. The trail thus follows the beach to Mukilteo State Park. On the tip is Elliott Point Lighthouse, the first since West Point, a dandy. Adjacent is the ferry dock, suggesting a sidetrip over the water to Columbia Beach.

To Start from the North. The walking is as good from the north as from the south. Do it both ways. A joy forever.

MUKILTEO STATE PARK

Bus: Community Transit 170, 177, 409, or 880

Drive from I-5 via Highway 526/525 (Mukilteo Speedway).

The park is naught but a parking lot and a beach and non-stop ferry-watching. Who could ask for anything more?

North from Mukilteo State Park to Everett, 5 miles

Gazing from Mukilteo to the industrial sprawl of Port Gardner, the hiker may ask, "Who needs it?" But the wild bluff continues to guard the beach, and the assemblage of ravines is arguably the best on the entire Whulge Trail.

The shore, to here trending north, bends sharply eastward at Elliott Point. The view thus is across Possession Sound past little Gedney (Hat) Island to Saratoga Passage between Whidbey and Camano Islands and to Port Susan between the latter island and the mainland. No longer is there a procession of ships to and from the ocean and various ports of Puget Sound, but there is considerable traffic along Possession Sound to Everett.

Easterly for a scant 1 mile from the Mukilteo ferry dock the beach is blocked by an oil terminal and storage tanks. A road parallels the fence to a parking area at the far end, a better start for walking to Everett.

Mukilteo Lighthouse and Whidbey Island ferry

Passing a ravine, a trail-staircase up the bluff to a viewpoint, and then the most esthetic exposure of varved blue clay on the route, in 1 scant mile of continuous vertical cliff is the first of the exceptional wildland valleys, Powder Mill Gulch, a large creek, and a broad delta point.

In ½ mile is a nameless but admirable creek and in ¼ mile more is larger and superb Merrill and Ring Creek, whose prominent delta supports a driftwood line and dunes.

Harborview Park–Howarth Park

Bus: Everett Transit 8 and 10

The bluff lowers and houses creep near. The view of the harbor is superb from Harborview (Everett) Park, on Mukilteo Boulevard at Dover Street. On the north is a deep green ravine. On the beach was located Snohomish County's first steam sawmill and the bay's first townsite plat.

In a scant ½ mile more, 3 miles from the Mukilteo ferry dock, is the very excellent Howarth Park. Drive Mukilteo Boulevard to parking at the blufftop, or Olympic Boulevard, which descends to the floor of Pigeon Creek No. 2 at the beach level by the railroad.

Extending from Pigeon 2 south to a nameless ravine, the park has enough paths—on blufftop and in gulch depths and on sidehills, on wideview lawns and in wildwoods—for 2 miles of walking, scarcely any repetition. During Prohibition the forest sheltered a moonshine industry. Access to the beach is via a skybridge over the tracks. On the beach side a stairway winds around and down a wooden tower with the look of a donjon keep (actually, just stairs and restrooms).

A hop and a skip north is Forest Park, Everett's largest but barely touching the shore. Bald eagles obviously are nesting hereabouts. Too many to be tourists.

Onward North. The concluding 2 miles have a different appeal. Or to some tastes, none. Port Gardner is entered and Everett Junction reached. Here is Pigeon Creek No. 1, which in another location would have been a park but here was ravaged by trucks rumbling to and from the Port of Everett. In 1984 no fish had been seen in 20 years. Then commenced an "ecological voyage of discovery" by the children of Jackson Elementary School. By 1992 Pigeon Creek No. 1 had come back to life, one of the most successful projects of Snohomish County's Adopt-a-Stream Foundation.

From the junction the tracks lie between surprisingly wild bluff and the onetime site of a Weyerhaeuser pulpmill. Then comes Port of Everett Pier No. 1.

EVERETT PIER NO. 1

Bus: 23

Go off I-5 on Exit 192, and turn west on Broadway following signs "Everett Waterfront."

Pier No. 1 is the place to get inside the soul of Everett. Jim Hill's tracks skinny along between shore bluffs and the extinct pulpmills of the heirs of Frederick Weyerhaeuser, who founded his Northwest empire on 900,000 acres of the Northern Pacific Land Grant bought from his next-door neighbor in St. Paul, Jim Hill, for $6 an acre. On November 5, 1916, the steamer *Verona* pulled up to Pier No. 1 to unload passengers come for a free-speech rally. They were met on the pier by the city merchantry and mill bosses, sworn in as special deputies. Shots rang out. Before the *Verona* reversed engines, "Bloody Sunday" had cost the lives of two special deputies and seventeen Wobblies, a number of Wobblies were missing in action (drowned), and forty-seven of both parties were wounded. Everett has not erected a memorial to Milltown's most dramatic moment. Too many of today's leading citizens had family on the dock, shooting Wobblies. Too many others had family on the *Verona,* shooting special deputies.

North from Pier No. 1 to the Snohomish River, 3 miles

The walking route stays on the railroad past the Scott sulfite (white paper) pulpmill, whose stack gases are now so thoroughly scrubbed as to emit little but water vapor. The route then turns away from the tracks to West Marine View Drive.

Immediately north of the Scott complex is the U.S. Navy Home Port grandiosely planned for aircraft carriers, cruisers, destroyers, and frig-

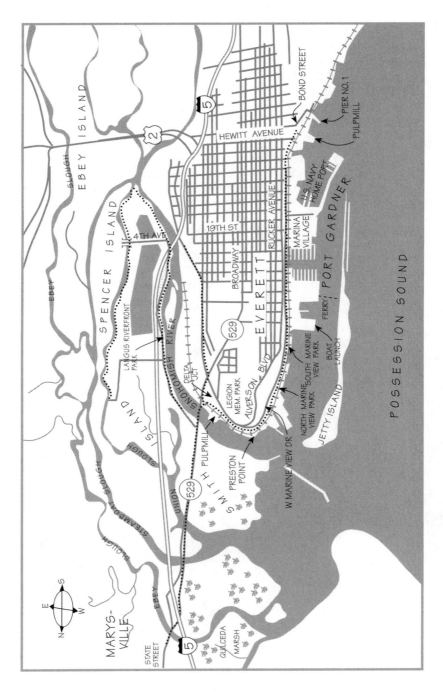

ates, a basic battle group that during Reagan's War was intended to be expanded to twenty ships. Critics in Congress (and the U.S. Navy) commented that carriers were as obsolete in 1988 as battleships in 1941. When the Evil Empire refused to play its designated role in the War Games, the Home Port was doomed, though final extinction is not expected until 1998.

Marina Village

At 1½ miles from Pier No. 1 is the big business for the tourist, Marina Village. At the entrance is a gabled, Tudor-style building constructed in 1927 as local headquarters for Weyerhaeuser, moved in 1928 from the location of the company's first sawmill, at the foot of Pacific Avenue, to the sawmill-pulpmill complex on the Snohomish River east of Highway 99, and in 1984 to this third location, where it serves as quarters for the Chamber of Commerce. Weyerhaeuser's pulpmills on the waterfront were dismantled in the early 1980s. The sawmill on the Snohomish River, built in 1915, was closed in 1979 and burnt in 1982. Mill E, built in 1971, was closed in 1984—Everett's last sawmill. Though Milltown retains small reprocessing mills and two pulpmills, it now mainly is Logtown—lakes of logs, seas of logs, oceans of logs floating in waterways, mountains of logs piled on reclaimed tideflats, waiting for shipment overseas.

Marina Village offers restaurants, inns, knickknack shoppes, and free parking. A walkway around the outer rim gives view of 2000-odd playboats in slips and a number of millions of logs in the bay. The *Snohomish River Queen* takes passengers on scenic cruises up the river to beautiful downtown Snohomish.

Fishing dock at Marina Village

Jetty Island

Now for something really excellent. Thursdays through Sundays, from July through September, a passenger ferry carries visitors from Marina Village to Jetty Island, built by the Rucker brothers in the 1890s to create "The New York Harbor of the West." The ferry (free) runs every half-hour or so.

Heaped up from dredging spoils, the artificial "spit" has got itself beaches and dunes and marine vegetation, just as if it were the real thing. The birds and sea creatures love it. So do the sea lions. The whole 2 miles, from Snohomish River to Home Port, are open to walking (allow 5 hours for a roundtrip). The route includes a nature trail that samples the life systems from lug worms to the dune grass where the voles hide.

The ferry is small and the island popular. It is advisable to make reservations with the Everett Park Department: (206) 259-0304. Rangers lead natural history walks twice a day.

Onward North. North from Marina Village at 10 Street, 1¾ miles from Pier No. 1, is the jutting fill of an enormous Port of Everett boat-launch; plentiful parking and a jolly good viewpoint of logs rafted in Port Gardner, protected by Jetty Island from stormy winds that blow, and the Olympics beyond.

The next ¾ mile along West Marine View Drive is on the shore walk-way (gardens, parking areas, and grand views) of Port Gardner Bay South View and North View Parks.

Where mills resume, West Marine View Drive climbs the bluff to join Alverson Boulevard. A mandatory sidetrip is the ½-mile walk up the viaduct to Legion Memorial Park and its blufftop viewpoint. Tremendous. Down Possession Sound to the pastel oil tanks of Mukilteo, over to little Gedney (Hat) Island and long Whidbey Island and the Olympics, to Camano Head and Port Susan, north over the Snohomish estuary to Wheeler, Frailey, Devils, Cultus, Baker.

Snohomish River*

Bus: 210

Drive West Marine View from Broadway (Highway 529).

From West Marine View Drive the route returns to the railroad for 1 mile, rounds Preston Point to banks of the Snohomish River, passes Weyerhaeuser's hissing rumbling steaming kraft (brown bag) pulpmill to Delta Junction, beside the twin bridges of old Highway 99 (now 529).

Scramble up the embankment to 529 for 2¼ miles of highway-shoulder walking to Marysville, featuring the best pedestrian-accessible exhibit of highway and railroad bridges north of the Puyallup River, nigh onto a century of civil engineering. In succession are crossed Snohomish River (views downstream to the kraft mill, source of the other Everett-identifying steam

---

*See the publisher's note on private property on page 11.

plume); Smith Island (wetlands in process of restoration); Union Slough; Spencer Island; Steamboat Slough; a large island on the Tulalip Indian Reservation; Ebey Slough (be careful before crossing to go left on 529); Marysville, and a final batch of ducks, boatworks, and mills.

SNOHOMISH ESTUARY

In major river deltas of the Whulge's eastern shore, the losses of primeval wetlands have been Nisqually, 28 percent; Puyallup, 100 percent; Duwamish, 99 percent; Stillaguamish, 64 percent; Skagit, 59 percent; Samish, 96 percent; and Snohomish, 74 percent. The estuary of the Snohomish, second-largest river, after the Skagit, to enter the Whulge, and the only estuary on the Pacific Coast within an urban area, embraces 1900 acres; in 1884 it was 12,000 acres. The lingering primeval nevertheless deserves the name, The Great Marsh. The sloughs and channels and island archipelago remind of the Mississippi. Yet though this urban wilderness, half-water, half-wetland, pleases humans, its first and last importance is as living space for wildlife.

Snohomish County owns 800 delta acres, the state another 200. The county intends to spend $2.5 million for further acquisition by the turn of the century. The initial goal of the Snohomish Wetlands Alliance—to buy Smith and Spencer Islands—has been achieved. It now seeks to buy the Quilceda Marsh and wetlands along Ebey Slough; to establish (in 1996?) a world-class interpretive center; to clean up a century of junk, restore wetlands, fix the scene to the liking of birds and beasts and quiet humans who come to pay respects.

Smith Island: Langus Riverfront Park

Bus: 210

From I-5 northbound, follow signs from Exit 195; southbound, from Exit 198. Go 1.5 miles on Marine View Drive to Broadway (Highway 529) and beyond the bridge over the Snohomish River turn right on Ross Avenue, signed "Langus Riverfront Park." Continue southeast 1.3 miles to the park.

The City of Everett park extends 1 mile along the west shore of Smith Island between the Snohomish River and I-5 (whose concrete covers 40 of its 96 acres).

The total riverfront, dike-path distance (1993) is some 4 miles: 1 mile (paved) in the park from restrooms and picnic tables and boat-launch; ½ mile downstream; a scant 1 mile upriver to the split-off of Union Slough and Steamboat Slough; and about 2 miles downstream along Union Slough to 20 Street NE.

See the waters that flow to the Whulge from Snoqualmie Pass and Dutch Miller Gap and Stevens Pass, the whole west-of-the–Cascade Crest

Langus Riverfront Park and the Snohomish River

section of the Alpine Lakes Wilderness and part of the Henry M. Jackson Wilderness. See the river creatures swimming and flying. See the *Snohomish River Queen,* Mark Twain in the pilot house, paddling from the Everett waterfront up the river to Snohomish.

Spencer Island: Restored Wetland

Access (1993) is via Langus Riverfront Park. Walk the dike trail around the south end of Smith Island and cross Union Slough to Spencer Island on the bridge at the end of 4 Avenue (closed to public vehicles).

Spencer Island, between Union Slough and Steamboat Slough, is now fully Public. The north end, managed by the State Wildlife Department, is a Habitat Management Area, where a waterfowl restoration project features new-built nesting islands—good news for duckbusters, duck-watchers, and ducks.

The south end, Snohomish County Parks the manager, is a no-guns, all-year wildlife refuge. The Spencer Island Restoration will breach the existing dikes at the south end of the island to return pastures to primeval tidal wetland; build a new woodwaste cross-levee between the renewed wetland and the rest of the island; and cleanse uplands of alien growth and replace with natives.

A trail is proposed to circle the island on dike-top paths, a loop of some 4 miles.

Don't rush here. Work is in progress. Prior to a visit call Snohomish County Parks to ask what's up: (206) 388-6616.

MAINLAND: SNOHOMISH ESTUARY TO FAIRHAVEN

At Priest Point the Snohomish estuary ends and beaches begin, first along Possession Sound, then Port Susan—whose good bluffs preserve the longest purely pristine mainland shore between Olympia and Bellingham.

Then, the crossing of the deltas. First, the Stillaguamish River. Next, the South Delta of the Skagit, Fir Island, between the South Fork and North Fork distributaries (the opposite of tributaries); in modern times this has been where the Skagit has emptied mountain water into Skagit Bay. The Middle Delta is bounded on the south by "captured" islands of the San Juan Archipelago, on the north by Pleasant Ridge "Island," and on the west by Swinomish Channel, which cuts off Fidalgo into islandhood and connects Skagit Bay and Padilla Bay; in the nineteenth century dikers halted most Skagit River overflows through this Middle Delta. The North Delta, from Pleasant Ridge to Elephant Mountain, hasn't seen the big river in ages; only seepage and dribbles empty to Padilla Bay and Samish Bay.

For the first edition of this book, the older surveyor walked virtually every foot of the delta front, hoping thereby to promote its formal establishment as a trail. The consequence was to the contrary. Paths where once the alien pedestrian was tolerated are now closed off by houses, fences, mean-it "No Trespassing" signs, and shotguns, even. Eventually the delta crossing will be opened to the Publics—will in fact be acknowledged as immutably Public.

Eventually, not immediately. Dikes are treated by the law as the property of the abutting owners, who have organized diking districts to build and maintain the dikes which have Privatized the primeval wetlands by destroying them. Only where a government agency (the State Wildlife Department) is the abutting owner can the dikes safely be walked by the Public. (For reasons why you don't want to try, read *Walking the Beach to Bellingham*. Barb-wire fences. Savage dogs. Birdshot whistling by the ears.) The diker Privates are not too proud to accept Public doughnuts, hot coffee, and sandbags—not to mention $338 million in Public funds (U.S. Army Corps of Engineers) to repair damage to ("Private!") dikes after the floods of 1990. In view of the Public subsidy, would it be unreasonable to ask, in return, walking easements on the dikes?

116

Snow geese and Mount Baker from the Skagit Wildlife Habitat Management Area

The crossing of the deltas is unique among Northwest pedestrian routes. Walkers are drawn initially by the fleets of waterfowl sailing, mobs of shorebirds hustling, raptors patrolling, songbirds chirping, in the varied habitats of open fields, freshwater, and saltwater, abundant feed supplied by Nature and humans. The Skagit Flats have the greatest naturally occurring population of bald eagles in the lower forty-eight and the largest concentration of wintering trumpeter swans, and are one of the best areas anywhere for watching birds hunting rodents and other birds.

So famous is the birding that walkers often neglect to mention the awesome panoramas over marshes and bays to islands and the Olympics, over fields of corn and cabbage and tulips and cows to the Cascades. Never are the mountains so tall as when viewed from the humbling horizontality where a person is so conspicuously vertical as almost to feel the urge to flop in the muck and wiggle.

History is very big here. Agriculture started even before the 1860s, when dikers began claiming (farmers and engineers insist on calling it "reclaiming," as if they were here first and Nature were the intruder) the riparian and tidal marshes. Hamlets founded in that era remain, antiques more or less hale, and everywhere are three-story farmhouses replete with chimneys and gingerbread. The nineteenth century lives! And dies: there also are derelict houses sagging in the silt, inhabited by the Addams Family, rotten boats moldering in sloughs, decaying pilings thrust out in bays, and names on old maps marking the sites of vanished villages.

Not to be scorned is the walking of delta roads; the barnwatching is the best, as well as the savoring of the ripe aroma of manure, as characteristic

117

of the delta as the pulpmill perfume of Everett. The initial survey followed the boundary dike between crops on one side and tidal marsh or tideflat on the other. That no longer is feasible—rationally speaking, it wasn't feasible *then*. However, remember that at lower-than-middling tides there is walkable marsh and sandflat *outside the dikes*. The farmer-gunner may insist these tidelands are Private. He is wrong.* But the rule is never to argue with a choleric, hollering man who is brandishing a shotgun.

The conclusion of the Whulge Trail is as unique as the delta. After sitting far back from saltwater in all its length from California, the Cascade Range juts west to the shore and from the loftiness of Chuckanut Mountain plummets to the beach. Except there's darn little beach. Just rock cliffs. Never fear. To the rescue of the hiker comes an old friend from the south, the familiar pair of shining steel rails leading onward from Samish Bay to Chuckanut Bay to Bellingham Bay and the triumphant denouement of the Whulge Trail. Fairhaven Historic District, that is.

USGS maps: Everett, Marysville, Tulalip, Stanwood, Juniper Beach, Utsalady, Conway, La Conner, Deception Pass, Bow, Anacortes, Bellingham South

TULALIP BAY

Go off I-5 on Exit 199, drive north on Marine Drive to 64 Street NW, and turn left 0.4 mile to a Y. Go right on Totem Beach Road 0.5 mile to the site of the Mission Beach Boathouse. North along Tulalip Bay, below St. Anne's Church, is Tulalip Bay Marina, the best place to park.

This is the "reservation" of the Tulalip "Tribes." There never was a Tulalip "People." Governor Stevens and the U.S. Army herded together here the Stillaguamish, Skykomish, Snoqualmie, and Sammamish peoples, all these consigned by the 1855 "Treaty" of Point Elliott to what for millennia had been a settlement of the Snohomish. Some of the folks forced to move here felt uncomfortable; the Snohomish, after all, were traditional enemies of the Snoqualmies, most of whom soon moved "home"—though they no longer had homes because they had no reservation and as of 1993 are not so much as recognized by the government as existing. The "Tribes" started off with 22,500 acres; only 12,000 acres remain in their hands, the rest (including just about every inch of waterfront) sold to European-Americans, who managed the "purchases" with whiskey, swindles, or simple bullying; historians note that though many a "Tulalip" was shot dead by whites, the murders attested to by federal agents and Christian missionaries, none of these nineteenth-century killers were brought to justice. (Lest an urge be felt to seek belated vengeance, note that these crimes were not committed by the folks who now "own" virtually the entire shore of the reservation, but by the great-

---

*See the publisher's note on private property on page 11.

grandfathers of the people from whom they bought their lots.) The Tulalip government has begun buying back some of the land but beach property is pricey. Recently the Tulalips refused to sell 46 acres to the Navy for its Everett Home Port. They patriotically offered to lease the land, but the Navy got sniffy and the deal likely will sink with the Home Port.

Tulalip Bay, as snug a harbor as there is on the Whulge, has history by the ton—of the European flavor back to Vancouver's anchorage here in 1792, of the Original Inhabitants way back to before ocean waters flowed into the post-glacial savannah valley to form the Whulge.

Two short walks are suggested to get in the mood. Stroll beach or road north along the shore from the marina to St. Anne's Church. A broad flat on a stubby peninsula, former site of a major Snohomish village, then of the Indian Agency Office, and until the 1940s of a longhouse where Chief George used to enthrall Boy Scout audiences with tales of olden days, now is the Tribal Family Center and Business Office. Tulalip Creek has been dammed for a salmon-rearing pond from which millions of juvenile salmon have been released since 1970.

For the second walk, go south along the shore 1 mile to the firehouse, cross the street to the site of the Mission Beach Boathouse, and drop to the beach for a lonesome under-the-bluff 1 mile north to "Mission Point," tip of the skinny peninsula that makes Tulalip Bay a bay. A long sandspit invites a low-tide sidetrip to the middle of the bay for views of the Tribal Family Center and fish farm and other Tulalip enterprises and the hamlets of Tulalip, Totem Beach, and Mission Beach. No Original Inhabitants are to be met on *this* stretch of their "reservation."

South from Tulalip Bay to Priest Point, 3 miles

The total Privatization of Priest Point presently requires the walk to begin on the north.

Save a scant 1 mile of road-walking by parking somewhere near the

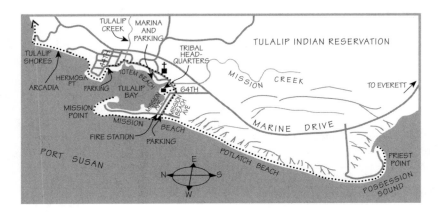

*St. Anne's Church on the Tulalip
Indian Reservation*

fire station. Across the road from the station is a turnout (probably no parking) atop the low bluff and a rude roadway down to pilings of the vanished Mission Beach Boathouse. Trail-access-only cottages of the on-the-actual-beach neighborhood of Mission Beach quickly end and for 1 mile the walking is lonesome under the naked, formidably vertical, 200-foot bluff. Staircases down from homes of Potlatch "Beach" begin, and continue 1 mile, but the houses stay up where they belong. The bluff finally yields to the spit of Priest Point, ¾ mile of hip-to-hip houses waiting for the C/4. Around the point a salvage-tug dock occupies the angle between river slough and bay beach; here was the outlet of the lagoon before it was filled.

Priest Point was site of a Catholic mission in 1858; the bell now is in St. Anne's Church, built in 1894. The view is grand over Possession Sound to Jetty Island, to pulpmill plumes, to oil tanks and ferry of Mukilteo, to ships at anchor and ships underway, to rotting old hulks—all in all, the best middle-distance perspective on Milltown. Also look to Gedney (Hat) and Whidbey Islands, to the Cascades from Three Fingers to Index. Hear the drone of Everett, suck in the rich aroma of pulp.

North from Tulalip Bay to Kayak Point Park, 8 miles

When a pageant is staged to choose Best Whulge Walk, this beauty will be a finalist. At a half-dozen spots roads have crept down the treacherous bluffs, but these are brief interruptions; there are three 1-mile wild stretches and three shorter ones and more than half the length is utterly lonesome. The only Public accesses are at the ends of the strip.

The way rounds Hermosa Point, views south to pulpmill plumes, to mountains from Si to Rainier to the Olympics. North of the point ¾ mile is the last piling-protected boathouse (of Arcadia) and the start of the first wild bit, 1¼ miles long. Beneath the noble bluff, up to 200 feet tall, largely sand slopes and blue-clay cliffs, the views south to Whidbey Island begin to yield to Camano Head, across the mouth of Port Susan.

A bulge is rounded, views of Tulalip Bay are lost, and homes of Tulalip

Shores occupy ¼ mile of a narrow sand flat. A scant ½ mile of empty beach leads to the wide valley and cute old community of Spee-Bi-Dah, onetime summer cottages clinging to forest hillsides above the green vale. In 1 mile more of wildness another bulge is rounded to another inhabited beach bench beneath an imposing 400-foot bluff. This ⅓ mile of Tulare Beach is followed by a ¼-mile wild bit, a lesser bulge, behind which is Sunny Shores, the houses mostly up on the crease in the bluff. Then comes 1 mile of wild beach—though with several trails down the 300-foot bluff from unseen houses. Now comes McKees Beach, a ½ mile of houses on a sandy-flat point. A final ⅓ mile of wild-bluff beach leads to Kayak Point Park.

To Start from the North End. That's a lengthy roundtrip, 16 miles, so most fans of Port Susan beaches prefer to start from the north and turn back at Spee-Bi-Dah or thereabouts, for a roundtrip of some 10 miles.

KAYAK POINT PARK

Go off I-5 on Exit 199 and proceed left on Marine Drive, following "Tulalip" signs (at 64 Street keep straight ahead) 13 miles to Kayak Point Park. Turn left 0.5 mile down to the beach parking lot.

Kayak Point Park is about as good as the Whulge gets. The history is long. Not to mention the 12,000 years or so of earlier chapters, in 1909 a developer sought to capitalize on that year's Alaska-Yukon-Pacific Exposition by offering sternwheeler tourist service from Seattle and the chance to buy 5-acre parcels for $750 each. Sons of one purchaser developed a resort, put two Eskimo kayaks on display, and thus the name. In the

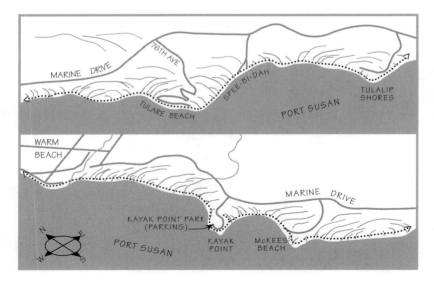

1960s an oil company bought up the land for a refinery, but aroused Port Susan citizens chased the oil tankers north to a more compliant (then) county, opening the way for Snohomish County to buy the land in 1972.

A short path from near the ranger station descends to the beach, passing an enormous Douglas fir. From the south-end shelter on the beach, the Bluff Trail follows the fence ¼ mile up to the blufftop campground. Combining wildwoods and saltwater, the 670-acre park, 3300 feet of beach, is notable for bald eagles that visit almost daily, mobs of great blue herons, bold coyote, and sea lions—the last commonly hang out just off the end of the park's 300-foot pier, which the park brochure imagines "extends into Puget Sound."

North from Kayak Point Park to Hat Slough, 6¼ miles

Realistically, the average walker will be fully contented by the first 2 miles. But the whole route must be at least written up because it witnesses the end of the "typical Whulge beach" and the beginning of something else entirely.

The spit flats accommodate several houses before the bluff rears up 180 feet. A sand cliff attests to a lake or delta of glacier times—the kids leap and roll and frolic. Views are over Port Susan to Camano Island and the Olympics.

A point is rounded to Warm Beach. The view opens north to the head of Port Susan, to the Stillaguamish delta, to Chuckanut Mountain. Very nice, but now, too, houses are cheek-by-jowl 1½ miles along the shore, parallel rows inland. Perhaps the only walker from Kayak Point to subject himself to the experience would be a person who in 1938 swam 50 yards here to fulfill a requirement to become a First Class Scout. The site then was enormously popular with the Public, so much so that often two

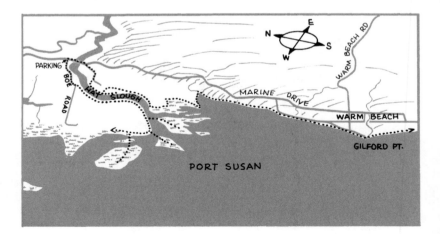

or more Scout troops were encamped at once plus dozens of families picnicking. After World War II it was Privatized to the max. The state's *Public Shore Guide* says there is a Public access at the end of South View Drive but the "bluff" signs erected there by the Privatizers deny it, express threats, and instruct the Public to "Use Kayak Point." Parking is limited (two cars). Take the bus: Community Transit 240.

Old pilings are passed: logging railroads used to dump logs here; the pilings were for booming the sticks into rafts to be towed to the mills. Views begin to Cultus and Twin Sisters and Baker. Habitations are left behind. So too is "dry land" as the bluff retreats far inland. The shingle beach yields to mudflat, delta saltmarsh, and tanglewood swamp. To a Whulge walker from the South, scarey stuff. But at medium tides the tidal channels can be hopped to reach the dike.

Dike! What is this? Fields and cows on one side, saltgrass on the other, the dike twists and turns 1 mile to Hat Slough, at this moment in geological/human history the chief distributary of the Stillaguamish River, which makes the head of Port Susan a semi-freshwater bay (and that's why, to the amazement of the older surveyor on a frigid winter day, it was partly frozen over). Emptying into Port Susan, this distributary connects to another, West Pass, that empties into Skagit Bay, the two providing boats a passage through; the passes also make Camano an island, here a clam-toss away.

In 1½ more miles beside or near the slough-river, passing horses, crabapple trees, cornfields, and a classic barn, the dike comes to Marine Drive a few steps south of the bridge over Hat Slough. Obviously the walk can begin from here, but probably won't.

SKAGIT WILDLIFE HABITAT MANAGEMENT AREA

Encompassing sloughs and islands, tideflats, swampy woods, marshes of saltgrass, cattails, and sedge-bulrush, and farm fields and dikes, the 12,761-acre Skagit Wildlife Habitat Management Area is the most important waterfowl habitat in Western Washington; wintering or nesting; twenty-six species of ducks are found here and three of geese, plus brant and whistling swan and sandhill crane. The 20,000–35,000 snow geese that winter are the superstars, but if a walker misses their show, he/she would not fail of other bird experiences, ranging from flitters in the bushes to great blue herons, clouds of sandpipers wheeling and diving in tight formation, and some of the 200 species of songbirds. Forget not the harbor seal, river otter, mink, deer, and beaver.

In olden days the delta was referred to as "Skagit Flats" and the duckbusters (including the older surveyor's father, uncle, and their friends) joined shooters across the West in very nearly exterminating many species on the Pacific Flyway. At last realizing they soon would have nothing left to shoot, they acceded more or less gracefully to a forced modification of their habits. In the 1930s the Washington State Game Department

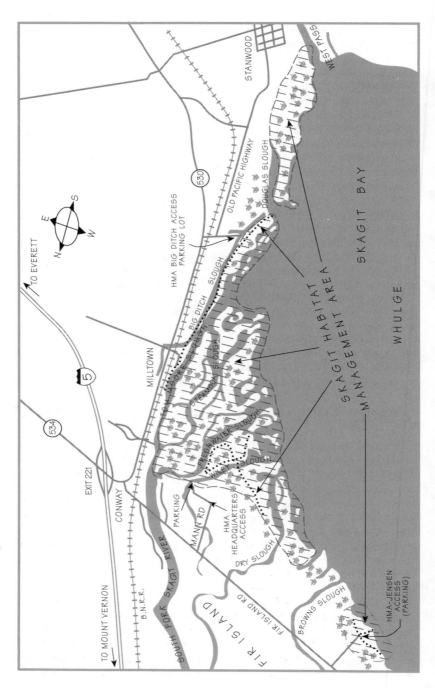

began buying lands for a system of "game ranges," renamed "wildlife recreation areas," then "habitat management areas"; the agency itself was renamed "State Wildlife Department" and began hiring biologists who do more than manage wildlife to maximize targets—they manage habitat to preserve the target species, plus the protected "non-game" species.

Thanks to the Wildlife Department's membership in diking districts, goodly samples of dikes are incontestably Public. These are the accesses described here. Enjoy.

Big Ditch Access

From the east edge of Stanwood, drive north on Highway 530. In 2.2 miles, where 530 drops from the hill to meet railroad tracks and Old Pacific Highway, turn left on the latter, then immediately right on the narrow road signed "Skagit Habitat Management Area, Big Ditch Access," leading 0.7 mile to the parking area. (Note: Don't forget to check beforehand to learn if you must have a conservation license, available at Headquarters Access. To park here a car may have to display either a hunting license or a conservation license.)

The Stillaguamish delta is polished off and the Skagit delta begun. Now the view is over Skagit Bay to the north end of Camano Island and to Whidbey Island, to peaklet-islands Ika and Goat, and to Mt. Erie on Fidalgo Island.

Cross Big Ditch Slough. On the far side go left on a spur dike ½ mile to the slough mouth; at low tide a person can sortie a mile or more out on the sandflat-mudflat, out amid the peep that whirl around the walker's head by the hundreds and scurry across the sand—peeping, peeping, peeping. *This* is the trip. To explore northward, turn right on the grassy dike between Big Ditch (a slough dug by farmers to lessen floodwater pressure on Fir Island dikes) on the right and cattails on the left. Out left is a 2-mile-long line of ancient pilings in the mudflats north of Tom Moore Slough. These mark a "training dike" built by the Army Engineers in 1911, part of a project to permit paddlewheel steamboats to navigate upstream to Mt. Vernon, as they did until after World War II.

In 1 mile of broad views over Skagit Bay to islands, over Skagit delta to mountains, is a delightful surprise. On stilts beside Tom Moore Slough is a village of "duck shacks" ingeniously constructed—largely in the 1930s and earlier—of driftwood and salvaged lumber. Each little house has its own perilous plank walkway from the dike, on the way passing a littler house; trips to these littler houses from the little houses, during the celebrations that follow the daytime birdbusting, can be treacherous on a dark and stormy night.

The grassy dike path yields to a semi-tunnel through hellberries, passing another village. Walk out to the bank of Tom Moore Slough; upstream at the toe of Milltown Island it is joined by Steamboat Slough, onetime route of the sternwheelers.

Snow geese in the Skagit Wildlife Habitat Management Area

Beyond the second village a final 1 mile of dike leads to the Habitat Management Area Milltown Access, but don't bother. Milltown Island, diked early in the century to keep out Tom Moore and Steamboat Sloughs, at last was abandoned by the farmer and bought by the State Wildlife Department. The pedestrian used to be able, in low tide and river run, to circle the island on dikes to Steamboat Slough—a scene removed from the modern world, safely still in the primeval. However, the dikes are busted and the bridge across Tom Moore Slough was permitted to collapse and access now is boat-only.

Headquarters Access

From Conway on I-5 drive Fir Island Road. Taking the east entry to Mann Road (the west entry also leads there), drive 2.2 miles to where Mann Road turns sharp right. Go left, signed "Skagit HMA Headquarters," 0.2 mile and turn left on the dike road to the large parking area. (Note: Don't forget to check beforehand to learn if you must have a conservation license, available at Headquarters Access. To park here a car may have to display either a hunting license or a conservation license.)

The walk is a loop, with sidetrips, around a nameless island between Wiley and Freshwater Sloughs. From the parking area walk the dike downstream along Freshwater Slough, tanglewood swamp left and drainage ditch right, at a couple points crossed by footlogs permitting roving in the fields. The dike bends right and in 1 mile crosses the marsh island to Wiley Slough. Here is an intersection. To the right is the dike leading back 1 mile to the parking lot, completing the basic 2-mile loop.

For the full treatment, first go left. Pass a causeway right, over Wiley

Slough. (For a sidetrip off the sidetrip, take the causeway and proceed ½ mile, until halted by a mean-it fence.) Hundreds of weathered tree roots in the marsh speak of past floods. As do rotten rowboats sunk in the reeds. The dike ends in ½ mile at the mouth of Freshwater Slough, a supreme viewpoint over the waters or sandflats. Seeking a mystical experience? On a crystalline winter day when the sun is bright and the breezes brisk, watch for a low low tide and roam far out on the wet sands mirroring the sky, amid thousands of whirling, diving, running, peeping sandpipers.

The original intent of the land (and water) acquisition by the (then) State Game Department was to provide public hunting. However, the sport has gone steadily downhill since the 1930s, when the shooting was so good that continuation at that rate another decade would have seen entire species eliminated from the delta. Conservation has helped spoil the fun. So has overpopulation by shooters. A few birdbusters persist in believing the basic fault is the birdwatchers, who now far outnumber the busters. They are accused of frightening birds away with the tromp-tromp of their feet on the dikes and the click-click-whir of cameras. However, considerable credit for the bad hunting must be given to smarter birds. For the smashing finale of a walk during hunting season, wait until 15 minutes after the close of legal shooting hours and see the thousands of fowl fly in from the bay where they have safely been sitting out the day, watching the clock.

North Fork Access

From Conway on I-5 drive Fir Island Road to just south of the bridge over the North Fork and turn west on Rawlins Road, perhaps signed "HMA North Fork Access" or maybe only "Blake's Skagit Resort." In 1.7 miles the road ends at the dike. Park on the shoulder. (Note: Don't forget to check beforehand to learn if you must have a conservation license, available at Headquarters Access. To park here a car may have to display either a hunting license or a conservation license.)

Over the ages the Skagit River has flowed over every portion of its delta, emptying at various times into Samish Bay and Padilla Bay. Presently, Skagit Bay is the choice. In getting there the river splits into two distributaries. The South Fork splits again, and again, into a maze of sloughs only a boater can know. The North Fork, on the other hand, maintains its unity nearly to the mouth, encouraged to do so by "closing dikes" which have closed off former distributary sloughs. The North Fork Access has the most treasures to offer the explorer afoot.

Outside the Dikes from North Fork Access South to Headquarters Access, 5 miles

The first 1½ miles south from North Fork Access are Public; at a very high tide, that's all the walking there's going to be from here. But good!

The path burrows through dike-top thickets of baldhip roses, the hips appearing in winter to be millions of cherry tomatoes. Two spur dikes permit sidetrips up to ¼ mile out in the water—or marshes. Beyond ½ mile of very Private dike (the farmer has leased hunting rights to a Private club whose members hate Public shooters and are absolutely choleric about birdwatchers and, remember, these red-faced Privatizers are heavily armed), the Habitat Management Area Jensen Access lets Public feet on the dike.

On a lonesome winter weekday the older surveyor climbed from parking lot to diketop—and a white cloud rose from the waters lapping the dike—thousands of snow geese. It was high tide. On another day, another high tide, Photographer and Mrs. Photographer carried their canoe over the dike to the water. Hours later they paddled in from the bay, amid the fleets of snow geese and friends—and a half-mile from the dike ran out of water.

What the Privates don't like the Publics to know is that though the dikes themselves and the enclosed land may (or may not) legally be Private, the land/water outside the dikes is open to Public boats and feet. Were Privates to shoot a birdwatcher here, it would be murder in at least the second degree. Some expertise is required to walk happily and safely outside the dikes. The stage of the tide must be watched; the lower the better. Where sandflat is exposed, go as free as the peep. In the saltmarsh, hop from tussock to tussock. Leap the muck-floored channels—or wear hip boots and just get down in there and slush across. Once the technique is mastered, a person readily can detour past the ½ mile of Private dike to Jensen Access and the scant 3 miles more to the Public dike of the Headquarters Access.

North Fork Mouth, 1¼ miles

Unlike the many-sloughed South Fork, the North Fork hugely flows to the bay in a single surge. And here the flatness of delta bumps against hard rock and startling eminences of peaklets of the San Juan Islands.

Walk the dike ¼ mile north to the North Fork—broad, deep, swift, impressive, spooky. Turn downstream through a sand-floored alder forest to meadows. Across the river are cliffs (startling, here in Flatland) of "Fish Town Island," a San Juan peaklet that truly was an island before the delta annexed it. In ½ mile on the bank is an indistinct Y. Take the right, continuing along the bank in grass hummocks and bulrushes. Across the river are clifftop cow pastures, then the bizarre village of Fish Town. (Fully described in *Walking the Beach to Bellingham,* the route through the hamlet was given in *Footsore 3* [Seattle: The Mountaineers Books, 1988] but has been deleted here out of consideration for the villagers, some of whom are proudly bizarre but dislike tourist cameras.)

At ½ mile from the Y the river at last splits. Bend left a final ½ mile to the mouth of the south distributary. A veteran of the glaciers where the Skagit is born is likely to have an epiphany here, at last knowing the great stream from end to end. Gaze over the calm waters of Skagit Bay. Where has the river gone? Out there, out there. Where Ika Island–Mountain rises 450 feet abrupt as a cinder cone.

Watch the tide! On his first visit the older surveyor forgot and shortly after his epiphany had a panic attack.

Craft Island, 1 mile

Walk from the dike on an obvious path out through the sea-meadows ½ mile to join the path from the river. Continue left a scant ½ mile in wet-foot meadows to Craft Island. Clamber up a bit of rock and spend hours (but watch the tides, in order not to spend a whole lot more hours) poking around green benches of moss and lichen and grass, in masses of ferns, miniature forests of cedar and juniper, fir and

Craft Island trail

madrona, thickets of snowberry and rose. The algae-colorful conglomerate walls are sculpted by tides into works of art that would grace any gallery. In spring it's all flower garden.

Though only 75 feet high, amid such flatness of delta and water the "mountain" seems enormously taller. The view is from Rainier to Canada, the Olympics to Baker, and all around to green delta and island-dotted waters. On one survey, some thirty herons were spotted perched on logs, pretending to be part of the woodwork. Beware of gulls dropping clams on the island to break them open; the shell fragments show it's a popular sport here.

SWINOMISH CHANNEL

The Skagit, in pushing its delta westward into the San Juan Islands, totally captured the easternmost, those which now stick up like pimples from the flats. It "got" Fidalgo Island, or just about. However, a slough navigable at high tide by boats between Skagit Bay and Padilla Bay still could be crossed with almost dry feet at low tide. Dredging began and continues and thus, by virtue of the Swinomish "Channel," Fidalgo remains an island, just barely. For the first edition of *Footsore 3* the surveyor walked the length of the Swinomish from bay to bay. The Port of

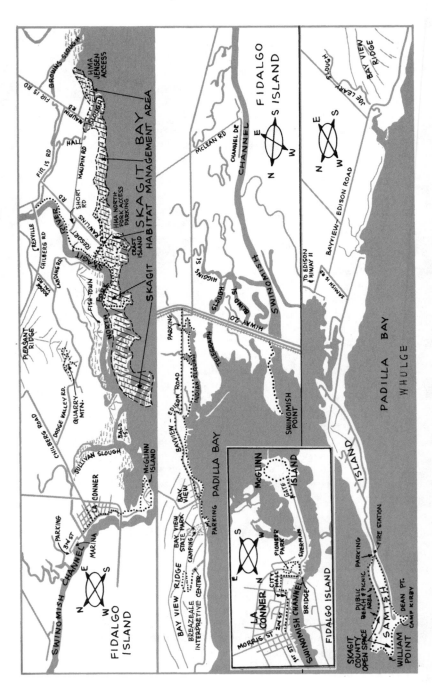

Skagit County Marina he enjoyed, sort of, envisioning a time when the fleet of its funboats which terrorize the San Juan Archipelago might go up against the armadas of Everett, Edmonds, Shilshole Bay, and Elliott Bay in a melee at whose end, as in the denouement of a Russian play, "everybody die." However, whereas in the late 1970s the surveyor walked north in birds birds birds to the junction of Higgins, Telegraph, and Blind Sloughs, a decade later it was houses houses houses, and not down behind the dike but right on top.

La Conner

Drive from I-5 or Highway 20 to La Conner.

La Conner is a town worth a walk. Situated where the San Juan Islands "come ashore" in the Skagit delta, beside Swinomish Channel which makes Fidalgo an island, the old fishing-farming-trading village become artist colony and tourist eatery has geographical and historical and cultural interest.

From the Magnus Anderson log cabin, built in 1869 on the North Fork Skagit and moved here in 1952, walk south on First by shoppes and old houses and museums, by fishing boats and playboats and tugs towing log rafts, in views over to the Swinomish Reservation, to which Governor Stevens assigned the Skagit and "South" (who they?) Indians. Where First enters an industrial concern, jog left on Commercial, then right on Second, by the City Hall (1866) and the La Conner House (1878). At Moore Clark's business turn left on (unsigned) Caldonia, then go straight on Third to Sherman, then right at the foot of "Pioneer Park Mountain." Leave the street and climb the trail into the forested park dedicated "In memory of Louisa A. Conner, for whom La Conner was named in 1870." Pass the High Orange Bridge to Fidalgo Island and drop back to Sherman at Schenk Seafoods, a scant 1 mile from Morris Street. Return north along the channel, admiring the workboats, looking over the waters to the stinkpots slobbering up a onetime marsh on Fidalgo, pausing to appreciate the arts and crafts of the Fish Towners who display their work here and to have a progressive lunch at the string of fooderies.

East of town on Chilberg Road is the world-famed Tillinghast Nursery, seed-and-cutting supplier to the world. North from Chilberg on Best Road are Skagit Rose Farms, the county's largest array of dried flowers and wet ones, too, in pots, baskets, swags. Watch the papers for announcement of the climax of the flowering, when the delta is aflame with color.

McGlinn Island*

Drive south of La Conner about 1 mile to the end of county road at an abandoned quarry.

---

*See the publisher's note on private property on page 11.

A tideflat neck dried up by dike-and-fill hitches "Pioneer Mountain Island" to "McGlinn Island Mountain." Though the quarry is gated, the gates are rusted open and the "No Trespassing" signs are faded. Should the "tolerated trespassing" have ended when you arrive, go away and raise hell with Skagit County. This gem of the delta has been a de facto Public park for a century and a quarter; to call it "Private" is to mock the Public Trust.

The "mountain" is small (¼ by ½ mile) and towers merely 125 (quite vertical) feet above saltwater and marshes. The interlacing paths require no guidance. Poke around and find a little sandy-beached cove at the mouth of Swinomish Channel. Other paths open to grassy brinks of 100-foot cliffs dropping sheer to the water. Look beyond the jetties guarding the channel entrance and the enormous rafts of logs to the 450-foot peak of Ika Island, and to Goat and Bald and Craft Islands, and over Skagit Bay and delta to Three Fingers and Pilchuck. From another spot, see the white cone of Baker. Note large granite erratics dropped by the glacier which gouged the cliff-walled outlet of Swinomish Channel.

Swinomish Point*

Exit Highway 20 just before the bridge to Fidalgo Island, at the sign "Swinomish Point Boat Launch." Parking is under the bridge.

Clouds of dunlins dipping beaks in mud, fleets of ducks sailing, "Christmas trees" of Marsh Point oil refineries, a stunning panorama of San Juan Islands from Fidalgo (Mt. Erie) to Hat to Guemes to Cypress to Orcas (Mt. Constitution) to Samish to Lummi, Chuckanut Mountain, Baker and Shuksan, and peaks in Canada. All from a peninsula of sand dredged from the Swinomish Channel, thrusting far out in Padilla Bay.

Before the turn left to the parking area, note a gated road straight ahead over the railroad tracks. Walk across the tracks and follow the road left past an abandoned gravel-sorting plant. At a dilapidated green shed head right (north) into the spoils-dumping area. The sands are sorted by winds and driven by winds, though prevented by workwheels and funwheels from perfecting classic dunes. Seagrasses have established themselves. And birds! Signs proclaim a wildlife refuge. In a scant 1 mile the medium-tide walking ends at low mounds of what recently was bay bottom. At low tide the route extends far out on the undredged bay bottom.

PADILLA BAY NATIONAL ESTUARINE RESEARCH RESERVE

Drive Highway 20 west from I-5 (Exit 230) and turn north on Bay View–Edison Road past Bay View State Park to the Breazeale Center.

---

*See the publisher's note on private property on page 11.

For nigh onto 13,000 years the Skagit River has been extending its delta out through its onetime fiord, which originally extended 20 miles into the Cascades. Left to itself another millennium or so, it would have finished filling Padilla Bay, as it very nearly did before the main outlet shifted south to Skagit Bay. In 1859 European-American settlers arrived to take up the assault on the bay and by the 1890s had diked off most of the semi-land of the saltmarsh, establishing the artificial shores of today's bay. Over the years this "unused" remainder kept schemers busy proposing oyster-ranching, a nuclear plant, a log-export complex, more oil refineries, a magnesium smelter, a lime plant, a concrete plant, filling the whole thing to grow turnips to make gasohol. The ultimate foolery was a frontiersman-idiot notion to create a "Venice" of 30,000 people living on 90 miles of artificial peninsulas built of the spoils from dredging the channels that would lead stinkpots to front yards. "Even the Army Corps of Engineers had a hard time keeping a straight face...." (The hiker is hereby commanded to hie to a library for the Summer 1987 issue of *Living Wilderness* and read "Fecund Mysteries," by Phillip Johnson.) Starting in 1963 the Orion Corporation bought up much of the bay bottom (yes, Virginia, that is possible under our laws!) and has been pressing its reductio ad absurdum claims. Early in 1988 the state Supreme Court ruled against Orion's attempt to extort an inflated price for the bay from the public agencies seeking to buy it. In 1993 Orion accepted a booty of $3.6 million

Interpretive sign beside Padilla Bay Shore Trail

and went away unmourned, shameless to the end. (Corporations have the rights of a human, but not the conscience.)

The opposition to the Orion scheme was organized by Edna Breazeale, who had lived on Padilla Bay since 1901. Having aroused the Public and donated the family farm, in 1982, at the age of 87, she was the star of the ceremonies dedicating the Padilla Bay National Estuarine Research Reserve. By the time of her death in 1987 her dream was coming true, her home was treasured across the state and nation.

The 4000-acre reserve Edna Breazeale knew has been quadrupled by acquisition of the 8004 acres Orion had "owned." It still is not large enough. Another 980 acres of "Private" tidelands are needed to forestall continuing attempts to exploit the bay. (If all the proposed marinas were built, the bay would be shore-to-shore stinkpots.) Further, a "research reserve" is not a sanctuary. Despite federal auspices and state management, the protection is less than perfect even within the present boundaries. The 1972 authorization under the Federal Coastal Zone Management Act is little more than a pious expression. Since 1979 the Washington State Department of Ecology has sought a formal "Reserve" status with teeth. So far, no luck. There would be little long-range hope of victory had not the Washington Supreme Court, in 1987, stated that the Public Trust Doctrine has clear priority over Orion's Private "rights."

The species of plants and wildlife will not be enumerated here; the visitor will want to make a first stop at the Breazeale Interpretive Center, just north of Bay View on the 64 donated acres of the Breazeale farm. In addition to permanent displays, the center offers a year-round program of lectures and walks. To be placed on the mailing list for the quarterly announcement calendar, write to Breazeale Center, 1043 Bay View–Edison Road, Mt. Vernon, WA 98273.

Upland Trail, 0.8 mile, and Padilla Bay Shore Trail, 2.25 miles

For *Footsore 3* the older surveyor walked and described 11 miles of dikes from Swinomish Point to Bay View State Park and 8 more miles north to Blanchard. He stated, "The dike-walking around the south end of Padilla Bay is the best...." Ah well, get to a library and read the rest. Much of that walking was on highly un-Public dikes (two shotgun blasts close by the surveyor's ear) where the surveyor put himself at risk for the sake of alerting the Public to its opportunities—though he realized that when the alerted Public arrived, it would have to be held on a tight leash for the sake of the wildlife. The time for the leash grows nigh.

The *Upland Trail* begins near the Breazeale Center barn and winds through meadow and forest. The trail guide supplied by the Center has explanations corresponding to numbered posts. Binoculars and field guides may be checked out as well. The first half of the trail is paved for wheelchairs, the rest is gravel.

The *Padilla Bay Shore Trail* starts from a county parking lot at 2 Street in Bay Shore, 1.1 mile south of the Breazeale Center. Interpretive signs on the diketop route explain estuary, open bay/mudflat, sloughs, and tidal marshes. The south end, at Indian Slough on the Bayview-Edison Road, is handicapped-accessible from a handicapped-only parking area; a key to unlock the gate can be checked out at the Breazeale Center.

The ¾ mile to the mouth of Indian Slough has views of Padilla Bay islands and points, 120,000-ton supertankers anchored off March Point, and the San Juans. In the ¼ mile along bay shore, by a long line of pilings, seameadow isles decorate the bay, hawks patrol the fields, views are tremendous. But this is *not* a foot-only trail: bicycles are permitted and their speed is such that it is not a true "trail" at all and certainly not a way to enjoy birding; the walker would be happiest on a February weekday. Neither is it a peaceway; gunners are permitted from October to January. Says the trail pamphlet, "PROCEED WITH CAUTION." Yeah. Tell it to the birds.

COLONY CREEK

Go off I-5 on Exit 231 and follow Highway 11, Chuckanut Drive, to the moldering hamlet of Blanchard (1885). Turn left on Legg Road and then right to parking at the mouth of Colony Creek.

Colony Creek was named for a Utopian community which briefly flourished early in the century. The creek hugs the absolute north edge of the Skagit delta; long long ago the Skagit itself flowed here. At the delta edge a hiker from the south who has spent days traversing Flatland is consternated. Who'd have thought the old world had so much verticality in it? The abrupt leap of Elephant Mountain (Blanchard Hill) and Chuckanut Mountain is a textbook of various geological matters.

The plunge of the Cascades to the Whulge necessitates a walking route that is not dikes, nor yet is beaches. What else? Railroad! Differing from the Seattle-to-Everett scene, where beach was pre-empted, here there wasn't much beach, short scoops only, separated by juts of hard rock. The Jim Hill Trail made a route for feet where previously there had been none.

South from Colony Creek to Edison Creek, 3 miles

The last of the delta is some of the best. Dikes round the shores of Samish Bay, bounded on the south by the long finger of Samish Island. Its companion San Juan Islands show unfamiliar faces. A look backward gives close views of the slot-narrow canyon of Oyster Creek, which separates Elephant Mountain from Chuckanut Mountain's dun slopes of sandstone, brushy outcrops burned nearly bare by the mid-1960s fire.

The easy-strolling dike rounds little peninsulas and little bays, cute geography. The bay side is lined by rotting pilings and planks, a stockade reminding of Boonesboro. Early in the century a great storm washed over

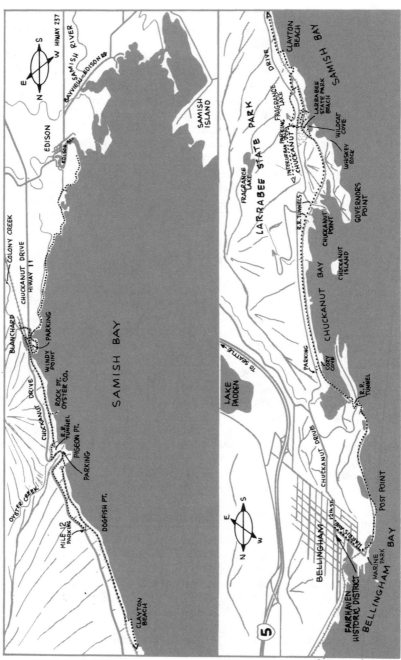

Secluded beach in Larrabee State Park

the then-new dikes, occasioning this defense system; the surveyor suspects a C/4. In season, gunners crouch in duck blinds, shivering and cramped, making noises they think sound like ducks. See mallards and buffleheads and goldeneyes, brant and snow geese, herons and gulls and hawks, plovers and peep.

Nearing Edison Creek and the hamlet of Edison, humanity crowds in; a start at Edison is uncomfortable if you don't live there.

North from Colony Creek to Larrabee State Park, 5½ miles*

A refreshing change from sand and silt: cliffs of sandstone, conglomerate, shale, coal, and fossils. Differential erosion by waves sculpts knobs, scoops, and filigrees which would, if done by humans, bring big prices in art galleries. Shifting views of bays and islands, barges, tugs, sailboats, oyster dredges, and supertankers.

The trail is plainly marked by two parallel steel rails—*watch your back*. The shore is always close below, just steps away, but there's not much beach. Close above is Chuckanut Drive; at several points paths provide safe accesses through cliffs for short walks.

---

*See the publisher's note on private property on page 11.

The railroad tracks cross the mouth of Colony Creek and thereafter are beside the water, passing Windy Point, views over Samish Bay to Samish and other San Juan Islands, the Olympics, and all. Ahead are the striking barrens of the Chuckanut Burn.

At 1¼ miles is the Rock Point Oyster Company, selling fresh oysters. The family-run operation is open to examination, from the dredge to the oyster-sorting room to the retail store. No parking except for customers.

Just north are the Samish rail siding, the mouth of Oyster Creek, and Pigeon Point, bored through by a ¼-mile tunnel too dangerous to walk. So, at the mouth turn off on a path to the Rock Point access road, climbing to Chuckanut Drive. A few yards north, past Milepost 11, is a parking area atop Pigeon Point, 2¼ miles from Blanchard and a good spot to start a hike south or north.

A little road-trail drops back to the tracks north of the tunnel. The way goes 1 mile by a huge heap of ivy-overgrown oyster shells to a pretty waterfall; here a trail climbs easily to the highway, attained just north of Milepost 12. At the parking area here, find the trail on the water side of two large firs whose leaning trunks form a v.

In ½ mile the rail trail rounds Dogfish Point, whose impressive sandstone cliffs are fenced by a wire mesh that catches small rocks and has a sensor wire to warn trains of big rocks and the bodies of idiots who try to clamber down here from the highway. A grass-topped sandstone point is a nice spot to sit and look south over Skagit to Cultus and north to the spectacular looming of Lummi Island.

Lovely madronas hang over the water. Blackened fir trunks tell that the Chuckanut Burn came down to the very shore. At 1 mile north of Dogfish Point the tracks are separated from the beach by a sand terrace; go onto it, or down onto Clayton Beach, marked by stubs of old pilings—relics of the Mount Vernon–Bellingham Interurban Railway.

In ¼ mile sand ends in sandstone and the best part of the whole Blanchard–Bellingham route. There is sand, sand, sand. Moth-eaten sandstone containing lenses of conglomerate forms buttresses enclosing tiny coves. Formerly the midnight rendezvous of wild and crazy guys, Clayton Beach has been purchased for the State Park and will be civilized.

For the shortest access to this ex-party spot, drive Chuckanut Drive to Milepost 14, enter Whatcom County, and pass the unsigned south entry to Fragrance Lake Road; just beyond is a sign, "Emergency Phone ¼ mile," and then on the left are three wood-concrete posts and a sizable parking turnout. From here a trail reverse-turns south, following the grade of the old interurban railway down through good woods, over a nice creek, to reach the railroad tracks in ½ mile, a short bit from Clayton Beach.

North from the beach the tracks go inland; paths lead out through the sandstone knolls to lovable coves. In ¾ mile is the main developed section of Larrabee State Park.

To Start from the North. The start from Larrabee State Park is the equal of the start from Colony Creek. But most walkers will find so much entertainment in the coves and sands of Clayton Beach they may not have time left for Dogfish Point, Pigeon Point, Rock Point, and Windy Point. Pity.

LARRABEE STATE PARK

Go off I-5 on Exit 231 and follow Highway 11, Chuckanut Drive, to just south of Milepost 15; take either entry down into the state park.

In the hundreds of miles from California through Oregon and Washington, the Cascade Mountains sit far back from saltwater. But here at the north edge of the Skagit delta the range juts to the very shore and dives to deep water. Spectacular. Maybe a geologist would say these aren't the Cascades at all, but an extension of the drowned range that forms the San Juan Islands. One of those pesky tectonic plates. Overthrusts. Hokey-pokey.

Put this splendid lump—Chuckanut Mountain—together with lakes fragrant of wildness, lakes lost behind the ranges, wave-swept shores of Whulge, and what have you got? Larrabee State Park, some 3000-odd (more coming) acres of glacier troughs in fault-line valleys, glacier-streamlined ridges, deep forests and sky-open, wide-view rock balds, and salt-water beaches. Add some 8000 adjoining acres of other state lands (Department of Natural Resources) and you've got something exceedingly good. The largest wildland with one foot in the Whulge.

The upland area of the park is too grand to be treated as a mere appendage of the beach. The 2-mile trail to Fragrance Lake and an airplane-wing view over Samish Bay to the San Juan archipelago, and the 2½-mile trail to Lost Lake, on the Other Side of The Mountain, are matter for a companion book.

The main section of the park's beach, squeezed between intense Privatizing, is only about ⅓ mile.

Larrabee State Park

But good. Wildcat Cove is cozy-cute, as are the sandstone cliffs of points south and north.

North from Larrabee State Park to Fairhaven, 7 miles*

The tracks north cross roads sternly signed "No Beach Access." Purely for the feet of Privates are Governors Point and Pleasant Bay and Chuckanut Point. At least the view of Chuckanut Bay is Public, tiny Chuckanut Island a foreground grace note to looming Lummi. The tracks go in and out of two short tunnels dated 1912, cross two wild ravines, and pass houses by the water below the tracks and houses atop the rock cliff. Then the cliff cancels housing rights, its huge tilted slabs, 200 feet high, suggesting ecstatic rollerskate runs, one to a customer.

The north arm of Chuckanut Bay is enclosed on the west by a long point, mansions at the tip. On the railroad shore of the bay, just past a driveway down to a beach house, is a rock point, a white all-shell beach on one side, a snuggly covelet scooped in the other. And wild, because the forest rises a steep 200 feet to Chuckanut Drive. Precious. (A good trail comes down. Look for it just south of Milepost 18. Ancient firs up to 4 feet in diameter.)

The rails shortcut across the head of Chuckanut Bay on a causeway of granite blocks. The west shore is a stone fantasy, ribs of sedimentary rock pushing out in the bay, walls pocked by cavelets eroded in the softer or more soluble components. The tracks enter a tunnel dated 1913. Daring youth go laughing and shouting through the long, curving, dreadful night. Not the surveyors, no sir.

No need. A fine trail has been built up the steep slopes of the tunnel ridge. At the parking area on top is a happy sign, "Designated trail areas are open space area with access limited to pedestrians only during daylight hours.... No fires, camping, firearms, being naughty. Bellingham Parks and Recreation."

To drive here, turn left from Chuckanut Drive on Viewcrest Road 0.7 mile. Turn left on Fieldston Road through a ritzy subdivision to the road-end atop the tunnel.

Behind the Open Space sign the north-side trail follows powerlines a short way. The main trail bends left. Spot a sidetrail on the right, descending to the tracks. But first walk out on the main trail to a rocky-mossy point and panoramas of Bellingham Bay.

The way north passes a series of lagoons impounded by the track causeway. Wildwoods on the bluff yield to houses. At 1 long mile north of the tunnel is Post Point. Ah, rapture. Slabs shelf into water, separating private sitting nooks of just a size for tête-à-tête. Two trees on the grassy point pose prettily for the camera. The view over the broad reaches of Bellingham Bay is dominated by the massive bulk of Lummi Island and

---

*See the publisher's note on private property on page 11.

Fairhaven Historic District

the long thrust of Lummi Peninsula, but not to be ignored are Orcas, Constitution close enough to see the summit tower, and Cypress, Guemes, Samish, and Fidalgo with its hump of Erie and steam plumes of refineries. There are more plumes north, beyond now-appearing Bellingham.

At ½ mile from Post Point is a sewage-treatment plant and then Marine Park, a superb viewpoint. To start walks here, follow Chuckanut Drive into Bellingham; past Fairhaven Park and Bridge it becomes 12 Street. At the second stoplight turn west and descend Harris Avenue to Marine Park.

Having devoted all this effort to getting to Bellingham, the walker ought to see a bit of the city. The *old* city, that is. From Marine Park ascend Harris Avenue a long ¼ mile to Fairhaven Historic District. The red-brick buildings dating from the 1880s have been restored to house such modern enterprises as the 1890 Marketplace, the Monahan Building (the saloon transformed into the Picture Show Theater), two bookstores, the Colophon Cafe, and other eateries. Good coffee. Good ice cream. Good soup and sandwiches.

ISLANDS IN THE SOUTH SOUND: FOX, McNEIL, ANDERSON, HARTSTENE

Psychologists have written about the "island personality," and poets the "island psyche," and publishers exploit a dependable market for the "island book." Sales around the world of Hazel Heckman's *Island in the Sound,* the Anderson story, reflect the nigh-universal longing to be an islander, safely circumscribed by guardian waters. More's the pity that addled vandals are permitted to build de-islanding bridges. But "de-islanding" is a matter of degree. The "island feel" endures, and there is comfort in the knowledge that Washington State's engineers are famous for temporary bridges. (One of two Hood Canal bridges, sunk. One of four Lake Washington bridges, sunk. One of two Narrows bridges, fallen.)

The mainland pedestrian questing his/her inner child on a water-ringed Avalon really ought to get a boat. (Rowboat, canoe, kayak, sailboat. *No* stinkpot.) Still, the boatless pilgrim is by no means shut out.

Fox Island

Fox Island is sinking under the weight of money but has one fine stretch of below-the-bluff peace. McNeil is the future, a vast wildlife refuge within the megalopolis, a Blake Island writ large. Anderson will not soon be crowded, not while the ferry service is right out of the 1920s. Hartstene no longer has a ferry but is protected still by remoteness.

In 1990 State Parks acquired 109-acre Hope Island. "Low-intensity" use is announced, hiking trails and 1.6 miles of wild beach. What's a "low-intensity" stinkpot? Squaxin Island State Park, on lands leased from the Squaxin Island Tribe, was among the state's most popular (stinkiest) marine parks. Upon expiration of the lease in 1990 the Squaxins closed the park. Too many stinkpots. Not enough holding tanks. Too much straight-pipe pooping. Boats at the park contaminate the shellfish.

What's so different about an island? Not much, really. Uplands and beaches are about the same as the mainland. The getting there is the most of it. Evil spirits, so wise men said of old, cannot cross water.

USGS maps: Duwamish Head, Bremerton East, Vashon, Olalla, Des Moines, Tacoma North, Gig Harbor, Fox Island, Steilacoom, McNeil Island, Nisqually, Longbranch, Squaxin Island, Vaughn, Mason Lake

FOX ISLAND

Drive Highway 16 from Tacoma Narrows Bridge to either of the two exits for Gig Harbor and follow "Fox Island" signs intricately but infallibly some 5 miles to the bridge which in 1954 replaced the ferry over Hale Passage.

Towhead Island Boat-Launch

On the southwest side of the bridge. Limited parking.

Access to the northwest shore, which is intensely Privatized but tolerable for a short stroll in winter midweek.

Old Ferry Dock

Drive from the bridge on Island Boulevard 2.2 miles to a T. Turn left on 9th 1.7 miles to the road-end at the old ferry dock.

The dock is dilapidated and fenced off. A path descends to the Hale Passage shore, too populated for Sunday pleasure but lonesome enough on a drizzly weekday.

Toy Point

Drive Island Boulevard 2.2 miles to a T. Turn right on 9th 0.3 mile, then left on Kamus a short bit to a Y. Go right on Mowitsh 1.5 miles. Here the road turns right and becomes 13th. Stay on it to a turn circle on the bluff above the water.

A posted notice (1993) announces the intent of the state Department of Fisheries to build a fishing pier and restrooms, parking for twenty-three cars, and paths to the beach.

As of 1993, a road blocked by a ditch and a gravel berm descends through the bluff to the beach in a trench dug through the till. It has the look of a former port for mosquito steamers.

On the beach to the left, houses start and don't quit to Fox Point, so why bother?

Instead turn right, in a few steps round Toy Point, and pass a small cluster of houses. Then the splendid bluff leaps up 100–200 feet, so formidably steep the unseen people atop have only a couple trails down. Wildness rules. Vertical jungle alternates with vertical gravel in foreset beds. In 1 mile is the glorious tip of light-marked Gibson Point. Views north to Narrows Bridge and Titlow Beach yield to views south to gravel mines, Chambers Bay, and Steilacoom. Tugs and fishing boats ripple the waters. Iron horses sound horns on the Whulge Trail. Army guns boom at Fort Lewis. Rainier rises high. From here the way rounds into Carr Inlet and the views extend over to the penal colony of McNeil Island and beyond to Anderson and Ketron Islands.

At 1 mile from Gibson Point is Painted Erratic, a monster hunk of granite brightened by children's spray-can art. For a short walk (4 miles round trip) this is the proper turnaround; the solitude, to here total, now becomes intermittent. Yet still considerable. A little valley with a handful of cottages is followed by a wild stretch. Beyond a bulge to which cling several (trail-access-only) cabins is Fancy Valley, a wide beach terrace crowded with houses small and enormous. Wildness resumes and views up Carr Inlet grow, reaching to the tip of Fox Island, the mouth of Hale Passage, and Green Point on the other side. Across Carr are Still Harbor,

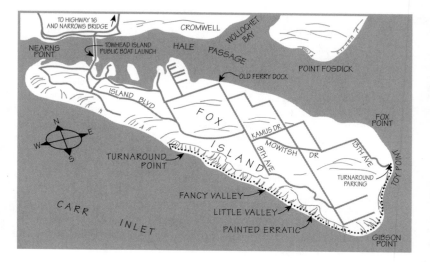

Great blue herons

on McNeil, and tiny Gertrude Island, site of the seal rookery. "Turnaround Point," the bulge of an old terrace at 2 miles from Painted Erratic, 4 miles from Toy Point, is far enough for a nice day.

MCNEIL ISLAND

Forget it for now. The island is forbidden to anyone not a criminal or keeper. In 1875 a federal penitentiary was established on McNeil, and in 1932 the entire 4413-acre island became federally owned, the last non-prison-connected resident expelled in 1936. The serendipitous effect of security precautions was to virtually freeze the island in the nineteenth century. The deer and the coyote and smaller mammals, the shorebirds and seabirds and waterfowl and raptors, go about their business as if glass-and-cedar ticky-tack never had been invented. Bald eagles nest. Great blue herons annually gather in a heronry to raise a new generation. The largest remaining harbor seal colony in Puget Sound sleeps easy, safe from subdividers and stinkpotters.

In 1981 the penitentiary closed and the U.S. Fish and Wildlife Service immediately moved to take over the whole island as a wildlife refuge. It withdrew, however, when the state of Washington obtained a lease on the prison, promising to continue the wildlife protection. Environmentalists have not been unhappy with this arrangement as an interim measure; great as is the recreation potential of McNeil's 16-mile beach, it ranks a distant second behind the immeasurable value as wildlife habitat. State plans to use the island partly for prison purposes, partly for wildlife protection under the Wildlife Department, partly for recreation under State

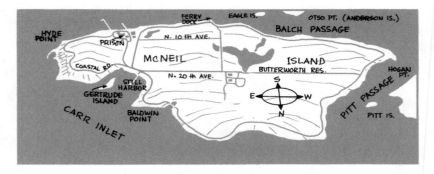

Parks, might be acceptably worked out—though the U.S. Fish and Wildlife Service surely is the preferred manager. The experiment on Squaxin Island has not established that the stinkpots beloved by State Parks are good neighbors.

ANDERSON ISLAND

Drive from Tacoma via 72 Street to Steilacoom and park as near the ferry dock as is easy. The ferry has four morning runs to the island and four in the afternoon. Arrive early to have plenty of time to park and buy a ticket at the restaurant on the dock. That's right—park your car on the mainland, ferry only your feet. Cheap!

The charm of Anderson is better savored in Hazel Heckman's books than from roadside views. And the beaches are good but not exceptional. Ah, but the ferry! There's the trip!

The thirty-car *Steilacoom,* built in 1936 at Bath, Maine, is the proper scale for the Whulge and takes the properly sedate pace, requiring 30 minutes for the 3½ miles over Main Street—more if barges or log rafts must be dodged. It's the happiest, old-timiest ferry ride left on the Sound. But to locals, it's the new ferry, only acquired from the U.S. Navy in 1976, put in service the summer of 1977. The former ferry, now the standby tied up at the Steilacoom dock, is the eighteen-car, wooden-hull *Islander,* even old-timier and better. Its backup was the nine-car *Tahoma,* and we're sorry we missed it.

An inch-by-inch survey of the island shore found no vertical Public access through Private uplands except at the ferry dock, from which a staircase leads to the beach.

South from the Ferry Dock*

A road runs beside the beach the first scant ½ mile to Yoman Point. A 200-foot wall of wildness ensues to Sandy Point, 2 miles from the dock.

---

*See the publisher's note on private property on page 11.

The bluff of gravel and varved clay and jungle is nice, and the trickle-creek waterfalls through masses of maidenhair fern. The view is the feature: the ferry shuttling to McNeil Island and past Ketron Island to Steilacoom, barges and boats on Main Street, iron horses galloping the Whulge Trail, north to Fox Island and Narrows Bridge, south to the wilderness of Fort Lewis (boom-boom-boom) and the Nisqually delta; over all, lofty white Rainier.

Just past the dock of Riviera Country Club are Sandy Point and stern signs. On a bleary November, quiet foreigners might not be yelled at in the 1½ further miles around the tip, into a lonesome cove with a tidal lagoon cut off by a baymouth bar, to Cole Point and its fine tall wall of sand and clay, and the next, nameless point at the mouth of East Oro Bay. From there one can view a bit of the "old island"—pastures edging the bay, farmhouses and barns from another century.

North from the Ferry Dock, 4 miles

The other direction's population is dense at the start, only gradually thinning. The beach is broken by a series of amusing estuary-gulches. Directly across Balch Passage is the McNeil ferry dock and the penitentiary. Aside from that, McNeil has the look of being totally abandoned by people except for seameadowlike pastures and onetime farmhouses now used for penal purposes. The wildlife sanctuary of tiny Eagle Island is passed, and then at 1¾ miles Otso Point is rounded and the intimacy of Balch Passage yields to the wide-openness of Drayton Passage, across which are Pitt Passage, Filucy Bay, and Devils Head, the tip of Longbranch Peninsula, beyond which lies Nisqually Reach. The way now becomes

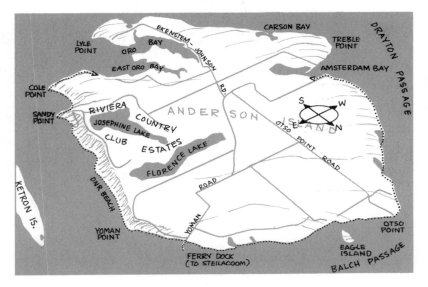

Ferryboat Islander *leaving Anderson Island*

excellently lonesome and is embellished by the two largest and best estuaries of the route (watch those tides, folks, or be prepared to wade channels on your return). After a brief interruption by houses, wildness resumes to Amsterdam Bay, 2⅓ miles from Otso Point, 4 miles from the dock.

More, 15 miles*

The island is of a size that a complete circuit might be done in an energetic day. However, Amsterdam and Oro Bays require detours via inland trails and roads. The trip would total about 15 miles, demanding steady pace and good tides.

The tempting morsel of Ketron Island was not surveyed except by eyeball. Still, the ferry stops there on some runs and the 3½-mile shore is virtually all pristine and obviously would fill several delicious hours. In the view from Solo Point on the Whulge Trail, the tip of the island is seen to be a formidable cliff of glacial debris, and the east shore a forest wall, no human presence visible.

HARTSTENE ISLAND

Drive Highway 3 to 8 miles northerly of Shelton, 10.5 miles southerly of Allyn, and turn east on the road signed "Hartstene Island" 4 miles to the bridge which at the end of the 1960s replaced the ferry.

Where the Whulge fritters away in reaches, passages, inlets, bays, and coves is one of its largest islands, 10 miles long. The location is remote and the population low. On winter weekdays the alien still may find a country chumminess, folks coming out to "howdy" and discuss the weather and the whales. (Of course, the times they are a-changing. Weyerhaeuser is on the island.) The canal-like waterways are intimate, the beaches vary from estuaries penetrating secret wildwoods to spits thrusting out in wild winds. South Sound and North Sound are married in the 30 miles of shore, nearly the whole walkable at the right tide.

*See the publisher's note on private property on page 11.

Latimer's Landing Park

On the mainland end of the villainous bridge is a Mason County park. This, and the former ferry landing 0.2 mile north, give access to the Pickering Passage beach. Graham Point Bay is ½ mile that way, Jones Creek estuary 1½ miles the other.

The footings of the island end of the bridge let feet on the beach. The shore is virtually houseless along Pickering Passage and then, where Squaxin Island divides the waters, Peale Passage. At 8 miles from the bridge is Brisco Point. Father and Mother Spring canoed these passages in 1914, from Olympia. They paddled through again in the 1930s from Shelton, accompanied by the twin photographers-to-be.

Brisco Point

Drive 0.2 mile from the bridge to a T and turn right on South Island Drive 3.3 miles to another T. Turn right 8.5 miles to near the south end of the island. Turn right at the water 0.5 mile, uphill to where the county road seems to end in three Private drives. The righthand drive actually is a county road, unsigned, dropping steeply to an abrupt end, at the beach— good reason to park up the hill.

The spit of Brisco Point juts out into the coming-together of Squaxin Passage, Peale Passage, and Dana Passage. Across the gulf are the mouths of Budd Inlet and Eld Inlet. Henderson Inlet is just around a corner. Traffic to Olympia funnels through Dana Narrows from Nisqually Reach. The horizon is the Black Hills and the Olympics. Here is the island's scenic climax.

The mainland bridge is 8 miles away on the west shore, Dougall Point 14 miles on the east shore—the wildest long walk of the South Sound, perhaps the entire Whulge. One must wonder, though, if the island has not been secretly bought up in toto by a mega-corporation based in Nevada or Japan or Federal Way; a legion of architects and engineers may now be drawing up the plat for 20,000 houses and the obligatory five golf courses and two airfields.

In 1993 the Department of Natural Resources and State Parks spoke of a "parcel 240 acres in size, at the south end of Hartstene Island," being considered for a new state park. Must be around here someplace. Watch the papers for the signal, "Gentlemen, start your stinkpots."

Jarrell Cove Marina

Drive 0.2 mile from the mainland bridge to a T, turn left on North Island Drive 2½ miles, and turn left on Haskell Hill Road 1 mile to the marina.

Department of Natural Resource lands adjoining the marina provide a start on 4-odd shore miles to the mainland bridge. Jarrell Cove blocks the footway east to the state park.

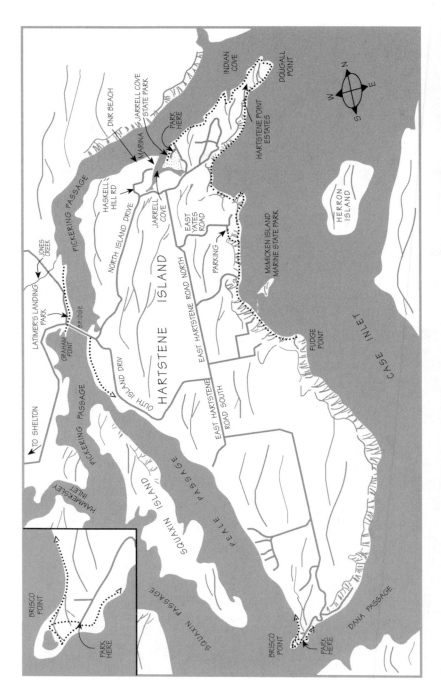

Jarrell Cove State Park

Continue past the marina turnoff to the parking lot 4 miles from the mainland bridge.

The estuary fingers on Jarrell Cove halt boots westerly but the other direction is open along the narrows of Pickering Passage. The bluff of iron-stained drift is high enough to guard the beach from scattered houses hidden in the trees. A mixed forest leans over the beach, which is thus a woodland walk even where the waves lap. Cool ravines break the bluff. In 1½ miles is Indian Cove, a boat basin. The estuary pokes deep in trees, where the green-shadowed creek can be crossed on a footbridge. After a scant ½ mile of cove-rounding the far tip is attained and in ¾ mile more is the north tip of the island, Dougall Point.

The shore rounds to Case Inlet, views north past Stretch Island to Vaughn and Rocky Bay and North Bay—the end of Puget Sound. For an introductory tour continue ½ mile more, by the dredged basin and picnic areas and whatnot and look south along Case Inlet to Herron Island. To the south 2½ miles is Fudge Point.

Note: The "house-growing company" (Quadrant) fronting for the "tree-growing company" (Weyerhaeuser) has erased "Dougall Point" from its map and replaced it with "Hartstene Point." A stinkpot basin dredged. Lots for sale. Operators standing by.

Fudge Point

From North Island Drive follow East Yates Road east 1 mile and turn right on an unsigned road ¼ mile to the beach trail.

The 2½ miles to Dougall Pont are lonesome and superb, though with Weyerhaeuser on the island only golly knows the future.

Southward is a long 1 mile of DNR beach, a good start toward Brisco Point.

Hartstene Island bridge

THE WESTERN ISLES: BAINBRIDGE, VASHON, MAURY, BLAKE

Any Puget Sounder who was around when the Model T yielded to the Model A, and that magnificent machine to the degenerate V-8, recalls how the water once set apart the Western Isles. Even then, however, the car ferries were transforming isolated villages to suburblets of Puget Sound City. After World War II, as engineers and land-developers were yoking up for a scorched-earth conquest of the republic, Bellevue clones grew feasible, more or less, on the islands. To the extent that they have not, there is room for the walker. Beachwalker, that is. What else is an island for?

Bainbridge Island has been de-islanded on one side by the Agate Pass Bridge. On the other, the jumbo ferries are so huge and swift they are not so different from mainland freeways. The older surveyor, who in his parents' memories if not his own vividly recalls the first Model A on the

Foot-bicycle trail at Fort Ward State Park

island, and how the entire population took turns flinging it about the washboard-and-rut roads, for auld lang syne circled the shore—again—in 1979, and again in 1988. The younger surveyor took her tour in 1993, accompanied (as in all the trips in this book) by the Youngest Surveyor in the family succession, who gave each beach the acid test of a 1½-year-old. Privatizers have been oh so relentlessly busy.

Vashon, sometime residence of the younger surveyor, is better. The sole water supply is the sky, barely sufficient for the present population; often there may be seen, fleeing from islander posses, the advance agents of developers. Further, the ferry services are neither jumbo nor truly super, and when you do manage to get to the mainland, where are you? West Seattle! Point Defiance! Southworth! You can't get anywhere from there. Nevertheless, the rule of Nature is no empty niches, for every meal a mouth, for every opportunity to make a buck a predator.

Sharing Vashon's permanent water problems, Maury has the added advantage of a longer drive to the ferry lines. Little of the shore is developed; that of the Gravel Coast is beneath bluffs so tall they scarcely have trails.

Then, Blake Island. Blake Island *State Park*. The *entire island* is a *park*. On the 4½-mile beach no Public ever will be chased by a Private brandishing hedgeclippers. Never will a clearcut let daylight into the green vaults of the forest. Additionally, visitors do not arrive here via car and car ferry. They voyage on the *Goodtime* fleet, modern mosquitoes.

USGS maps: Duwamish Head, Vashon, Tacoma North, Gig Harbor, Olalla, Bremerton East, Suquamish, Shilshole Bay

BAINBRIDGE ISLAND

From any spot in Seattle between Alki Point and Carkeek Park, look due west across the Whulge and what you see is Bainbridge Island, 10 miles north–south long and 4 miles east–west wide. The island is partly a suburb of Bremerton, mostly of Seattle, connected to the central city— and cut off from it—by the ferry. But as the century ends the central city itself is becoming an island, cut off by gridlock. Indeed, Seattle and Tacoma and Bellevue and Kent and the rest are an archipelago of islands separated and isolated by concrete. Bainbridge has, instead, water.

A walk on the island begins with a voyage over water—liberating, in absolute contrast to journeys imprisoned by concrete. But on a brilliant midsummer Sunday bring a book for the long wait while the ferries come— and go without you. The older surveyor's favorite scheme is to choose a February Tuesday of decent but not spectacular weather and circle the shore, piecing together short walks and their varied views in a good, long day. Enjoy the sunset from the ferry on the way home, arriving in Seattle after the evening commute. In these pages the entire shore is sampled, starting at Winslow.

For detailed information about bus service, call Kitsap Transit: (206) 373-BUSS.

Eagle Harbor

Park the car on the Seattle waterfront and walk on the ferry, paying only the foot-passenger fare (cheap).

Walk off the ferry, turn right, rounding the terminal building, and between the parking-lot fence and the ferry ramp find a rude path down boulders to the beach. On a medium-low tide the beach can be walked 1 mile, nearly to the battlements of Wing Point. In the beach gravel are rusted artifacts of a century of ironware. Views are excellent to the creosote plant, the shipyard, and the home port of Washington State Ferries. Ferry-watching doesn't get any better than this.

In the other direction from the ferry dock, walk the tidy main street of (New) Winslow and turn left, downhill, to Eagle Harbor Waterfront Park. A shore path gives close looks at the shipyard, where may be seen at close range the likes of *Amfish* and *Aleutian Bounty*. Return to the main street, proceed west, then sharply downhill, to (Old) Winslow. You wouldn't know that's where you are unless this book told you. On the survey for the first edition, the pilings and even some planks remained of the Winslow Dock, where the older surveyor and his parents used to catch the steamer *Winslow* to Seattle. A marina is there now. On that survey in 1978 the Galbraith warehouse was intact, complete with the holes accidentally shot in the wall by the surveyor's father and pals during midnight rat hunts. The sheet metal walls have been painted green and the birdshot holes plugged up. The structure, however, is intact—more so than its parent across the waters, the Galbraith Dock, the Seattle base of the *Winslow* and other steamers of the White Collar Line. Ivar's now sells steamers there—buckets of them.

Manitou Beach

Bus: 96

From the Winslow stoplight drive Highway 305 to a stoplight at 2 miles. Turn right and immediately park in the "Free Parking" lot. There is no parking at Manitou Beach.

Walk a few feet along the road to a Y and continue straight ahead ¼ mile to the beach. The way west is to the estuary head of Murden Cove, east to Skiff Point and views north along Rolling Bay, and past the ½ mile of beach houses to the nearly 2 bluff-wild miles of Rolling Bay. Views to Main Street ship traffic, West Point sewage plant, towers of downtown Seattle, Alki Point.

Fay Bainbridge State Park

Bus: 96

Drive Highway 305 for 4 miles, turn right at the sign for the state park, and follow signs 3.2 miles to the beach.

The 17-acre park has ⅓ mile of beach wedged between rows of houses. South is downtown Seattle, across the Sound are West Point and Shilshole Bay, and north over Port Madison and the Sound are Richmond Beach, Edmonds, and Glacier Peak.

Immediately south of the park are houses, a solid ½ mile. But beyond lie some 2 mostly wild, beneath-the-bluff miles on Rolling Bay.

Port Madison Park Nature Preserve

Drive Highway 305 for 5.8 miles and turn right on West Port Madison Road, which in 1.1 mile, after a sharp bend left then right, becomes County

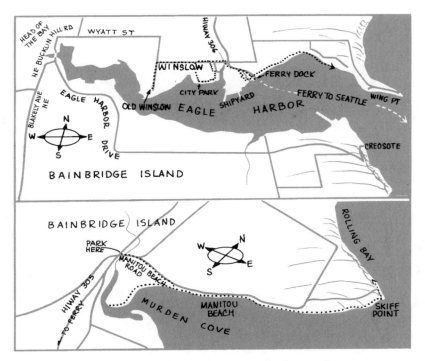

Park Road. Large signs mark a parking area for four to five cars.

Walk the road-become-trail ⅛ mile through a 13-acre (seems like hundreds) ancient forest, past picnic shelters. Near the parking area is a trailer housing the resident ranger and family, to the chagrin of wanna-be Saturday-night kegger-lads. The bluff is signed "Danger," which is true. So sit on the brink and gaze from the City of Bainbridge park across Port Madison to Suquamish and Indianola and Three Fingers. Old trees. Quiet views. Peace. A choice spot for reveries.

The short path down the near-vertical bluff is treacherous when wet, slippery as a greasy pig. Note the slabs of hard peat, lumps of blue clay, and clumps of living alders sloughed off the bluff. The beach easterly rounds to Hidden Cove, a cute estuary inundated by hundreds of stinkpots. The seals make sure to be elsewhere on Sunday. In the other direction, 1¼ miles, is Agate Point at the entry to Agate Pass.

Agate Pass*

Bus: 90

Drive Highway 305 nearly to Agate Pass Bridge and turn right on Reitan Road. In 0.3 mile, at a powerline tower, are a turnaround-type

---

*See the publisher's note on private property on page 11.

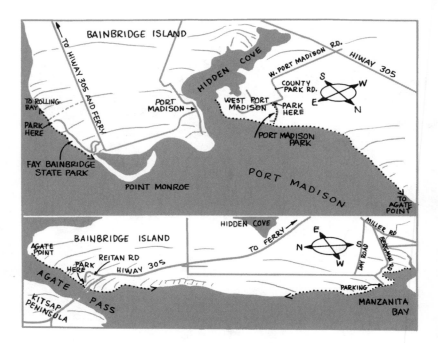

parking area and a short trail down to the beach.

Boat-watching is excellent on beaches of the narrow pass, where at the turn of the tide craft get either an assist or a tussle from the swift current.

The walk north 1 mile to Agate Point, views opening over the water to Suquamish and Port Madison and Indianola, is by a row of near-beach houses.

South beyond a couple of houses up on the bank, the tanglewood bluff rears up 100 feet and the beach is houseless and wild more than 1 mile and virtually empty the whole 2¾ miles to Manzanita. On the way, Agate Pass widens into Port Orchard. Views open around Point Bolin to the Navy installation at Keyport and south into Manzanita Bay and to Battle Point. On the Kitsap Peninsula rise the peaks of Green and Gold; beyond are Constance and Warrior.

Manzanita Bay*

Bus: 95

Drive Highway 305 for 4 miles, to where the road to Fay Bainbridge State Park goes off right, and go left at the sign for "Manzanita." Immediately go right (straight) at a Y, onto Day Road. In 1.1 miles turn left on

---

*See the publisher's note on private property on page 11.

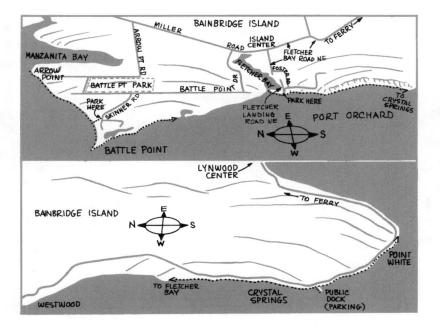

Manzanita Way. In 0.1 mile, on the right, are white concrete posts marking a street-end. Parking for a car or two.

The cozy bay beguiles. Views are over Port Orchard to Keyport. The Olympic skyline shines from Zion to Walker to Turner.

Signs imply evil awaits you. But north, beyond a handful of houses, is wild beach and, in 2¾ miles, Agate Pass Bridge. To the south it's ½ mile around the bay to the inlet estuary oozing muckily out of the forest.

Battle Point*

Drive Fletcher Bay Road to Island Center. Continue straight on Miller Road 0.5 mile and turn left on Battle Point Drive. In 1.7 miles turn left on Skinner Road 0.2 mile, down to beach level and a farm; at a left bend the road becomes Ollalie Lane. On the right is a field of grass and scotchbroom. Park on the shoulder and walk the path several hundred feet to the beach.

No "Private" signs as of 1993, but a realtor's sign, "For Sale." Some of the neighbors think the point is a park. Who knows? The lagoon-enclosing spit (should-be park) thrusts out in Port Orchard, a light at the tip. Views north to Agate Pass, south to Fletcher Bay and suburbs of Bremerton, and across to Keyport. Heavy water traffic, recreational and Navy.

Northwest 1 mile is Arrow Point at the mouth of Manzanita Bay. South-

---

*See the publisher's note on private property on page 11.

Agate Pass Bridge

west ½ mile is the tip of Battle Point sandspit; no houses near the water. The 1½ miles south to Fletcher Bay are thinly populated.

Who did the battling?

Fletcher Bay*

Bus: 95

Drive Highway 305 for 1 mile and turn left at the stoplight on High School Road. In 2 miles turn right on Fletcher Landing Road NE about 0.5 mile to Island Center. Turn left on Fletcher Bay Road 0.3 mile and turn left on Foster Road. In 0.3 mile is a T with Hansen Road. Go right a short bit, then left on Fletcher Landing Road. Parking for two cars at most.

Another of Bainbridge's South Sound–like fiordlike coves. The harbor is half-plugged with boats, dinghy to million-dollar yacht. Views along Port Orchard to Keyport and of the Olympics from Constance to Jupiter to The Brothers.

The street-end has been fenced. But the gate cannot legally be locked. Open it, walk through. The Privatizers cannot forbid you to walk to where the ferry used to cross Port Orchard to Brownsville, the route to Bremerton.

The beach leads north to the spit at the bay mouth, once the harbor for rowboats and naphtha launches bringing folks to trip the light fantastic at Ma and Pa Foster's dancehall. The older surveyor's father, when his battlewagon was in the Bremerton Navy Yard, had the loan of a cabin on

---

*See the publisher's note on private property on page 11.

the spit, courtesy of a retired veteran of the Great White Fleet. The beach leads south beneath a steep forest where all-year residences have replaced the cabins once served by steamers from Seattle. The surveyor's mother summered here with her mother and sister. At a beach fire the surveyor's parents met, so he danged well ain't going to be hollered off by modern Privatizers. Down the beach some 2 miles, wild then populated, is Crystal Springs.

Fort Ward State Park

Bus: 98

Drive from Winslow to Lynwood Center and continue straight on Pleasant Beach Road. At the Y in 0.6 mile keep right, and in another 0.6 mile come to the park gate and the parking area.

A beauty of a forest. A shore that can be walked on the dandy beach or paralleled atop the wave-cut bench which was elevated above the tides by that recent lurch of the Seattle Fault. Mountings of the gun batteries, strategically located to punish such Spaniards as got this far. Established in 1891, in 1958 the fort was surplused. In the 1950s Washington State Parks had little vision and less taxpayer support; of the 480 acres, only 137 were obtained for park.

A 2-mile loop samples the entertainments. From the parking area walk the ¾ mile of beach, featuring sandstone outcrops, ferries rocketing through Rich Passage so close you can watch the hamburgers being gulped, views of the Kitsap shore and The Brothers, Jupiter, Constance. (Also featured are masses of poison oak, so beware!) At high tide, walk the closed-to-vehicles road past toilets and picnic tables. A small gun emplacement is all that's warlike remaining, but here in War II were stretched the anti-sub nets that slowed each ferry trip by a quarter-hour as nets were opened. (After the war it was discovered a Japanese sub had gotten through to take periscope photos of the Navy yard. Very simple. Just follow the ferry in and out.) The park ends at the site of Timber Lodge, in previous incarnations an Army recreation center, then Sunset Lodge, then an amusement park.

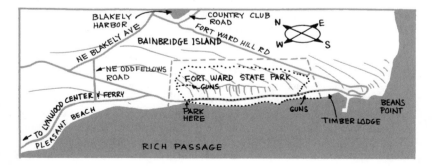

Now for the woods. Backtrack from the park boundary to the gun battery and spot a road-trail climbing a scant ¼ mile to the blufftop. (This upper park area can be driven to but why bother? No beach up *there*.) A road-path continues in the woods, ¾ green-shadow big-tree mile to the boundary fence, descends left, passing an ivy-overgrown gun battery, to the park entry road just north of the parking area.

Port Blakely

Bus: 98

Debarking from the ferry at Winslow, at the stoplight in town turn left at the sign "City Center," then right on Madison and left on Wyatt. Wyatt bends left and becomes NE Bucklin Hill Road, which then becomes Blakely Avenue NE. Continue on Blakely about 3 miles to the head of Port Blakely. Turn right on Country Club Road, which in 1 mile touches the beach. Park on the wide shoulder.

The first sawmill here, built in 1863 by Captain Renton, burned in 1888. Its replacement was bragged up as "the largest sawmill in the world" until it burned in 1907. The third mill was closed in 1914 and dismantled in 1923. At times more than 1000 workers were employed. Rafts of logs were towed in from all the nearer shores of the Whulge, literally filling the bay, barely leaving space for the ships docked there to load lumber for transport to San Francisco, Los Angeles, Peru, Chile, Australia, and South Africa. Lumber schooners remained moored in nearby Eagle Harbor long after; the older surveyor attended a birthday party on one. In 1937 the Black Ball Line moved its ferry landing from here to Winslow, previously a stop only for White Collar Line steamers, and Port Blakely was left to marinate in memories. Until now.

Unlike Eagle Harbor, Blakely lacks an underwater sill to block water circulation, thus permitting currents to flush the bay, steadily if gradually restoring the pristinity of waters and beaches. When the loggers went away in the 1920s, the forest ecosystem began to evolve toward ancience. But in 1992 the Port Blakely Mill Company, which since 1863 had made a series of fortunes from the land acquired by means that today would be prison offenses, decided to go for another. It proposed to build 843 houses on 1150 acres, far and away the largest development in the history of the island. A firm of sweet-talkers was imported from California to hypnotize the island community; to hear them, when good residents died they wouldn't have to go to Heaven because they'd already be there.

Drop off the low bank at a safe and easy place (there aren't many) and walk the beach ¼ mile west. Look out the harbor mouth to Seattle. Look around the harbor to a few old pilings, hulk of a wrecked ship, a couple remodeled houses recognizable as dating from the mill era, relict pilings of the ferry dock. In mind's eye reconstruct the mill and docks and stacks of lumber, the ships filling the harbor, the ferry shuttling in and out, the bustling town. Then, look into a future of 843 new houses, some 3000

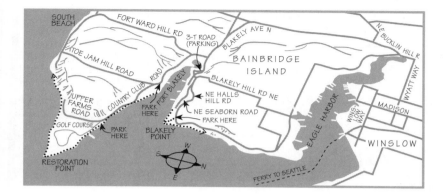

people, jogging paths, rowing club, Little League, and a "Japanese Village" to commemorate the folks who worked in the mill (300 of them) and then were prominent members of the farm community and then early in 1942 were hustled onto the Seattle ferry and shipped to concentration camps patterned after those run by the Nazis.

In 1994 the city of Bainbridge Island vehemently declared, "Not on *this* island, you don't!" Port Blakely Mill Company has called off its sweet-talking "Music Man" and is lying low.

Restoration Point

Bus: 98

Continue along Port Blakely on Country Club Road (see Port Blakely) to a Y where Upper Farms Road goes right. Park here—or if you've parked earlier, walk the beach to here.

Named by Vancouver, who sailed by the point's Indian village on the anniversary of the restoration of the English monarchy, this striking peninsula is the most spectacular natural feature of the island—indeed, of this entire sector of the Whulge—none other than a recent, geologically speaking, event on the Seattle Fault!

When there's beach, walk that, when and if you can get down to it. However, there's no beach at high tide, and the bank is mostly unclimbable because this is the center of the only extensive area on shores of Puget Sound where hard rock outcrops through glacial drift. From here to Fort Ward, and also across Rich Passage, sandstones, shales, and conglomerates often make buttresses and cliffs rather than beaches.

Sandstone-pavement beaches are ribbed and knobbed with protruding strata and nodules of harder rock. Here and there are pockets of dazzling-white shell beach. Above, on the former-island (tombolo) hill, are mansions built by some of the oldest money in the Northwest. Around the foot of the forested hill curves the onetime golf course, greensward rolling over the old (pre-earthquake) wave-cut bench to the edge of the sandstone scarp that drops a dozen feet to the new (post-earthquake) wave-cut bench, open to the feet at low tide.

The views! This way bustles the ferry to Winslow. That way hustles the ferry to Bremerton. And there's where they come from and go to, Elliott Bay, enclosed by West Seattle and Magnolia Bluff. Far south, beyond Blake Island, is still another ferry, from Fauntleroy to Vashon Island. Up the Sound is the shore from Alki to Tacoma. Rainier. Down the Sound, past Blakely Rock, is West Point.

Blakely Point: Beach Trail

Bus: 98

Drive Blakely Avenue NE (see Port Blakely) to the head of the bay and continue straight. At the junction of four roads go sharp right on 3-T Road. In a short distance the road turns right to a parking turnout and reader-board ("Recovery and Change"). A trail leads to the beach.

Blakely Point, across the mouth of Port Blakely from Restoration Point, is a companion jut of rock. From the history reader-board the shore rocks can be clambered from one pocket beach to another ½ mile to the point. At high tide the abandoned shore road can be walked beneath conglomerate walls, with madronas and firs leaning over the water. The tip is a fantasy of pillars and cliffs. The views extend from West Point to Alki Point, and beyond Seattle to the Issaquah Alps and Cascades. Ferries race every which way.

Blakely Point: Hill Trail

At the junction of four roads (see Blakely Point: Beach Trail) continue up NE Halls Hill Road to the top, 0.6 mile from the confusion. Park on the right shoulder.

Look for a road-trail concealed by a hellberry jungle. Past that obstacle the way down to the beach is steep but simple.

VASHON ISLAND

A 1983 study commissioned by King County established that rainfall was the sole source of the groundwater drunk by the 8300-odd residents of Vashon Island and that a relatively small population increase would quickly deplete and even more quickly pollute the water, and that therefore development should be strictly limited. Why isn't it? No guts in county government? Too much free enterprise? The scene strikes a visitor as rural, most settlements modest expansions of farming crossroads or summer colonies. But enterprisers come on and on, noses quivering, smart as weasels in the ways to sneak through loopholes in the law. Bumper stickers say, "Vashon is Sinking."

Vashon–Tacoma ferry

The attitude toward visitors is a genial (sort of) xenophobia. There is next to no tourist industry, next to no parks. Nevertheless, except in the summer season small groups of quiet, clean, polite foreigners are more smiled at than glowered. Be clean and quiet and civil and your encounters with residents are likely to be pleasant—they'll tell you about island history and give information on the Vashon Epic, the 35-mile around-the-island beach loop.

Precisely because it is so quick of access from Tacoma, Seattle, and Bremerton, Vashon "belongs" to a great many people. The existence of islandness is an opportunity potentially enriching us all. Therefore, we all should proudly say, to paraphrase President Kennedy on his visit to Berlin, "I am a Vashonite."

East Shore

Walk the whole east shore, miles of pure and semi-wildness, in ever-changing views across the traffic of Main Street to Seattle shores and to mountains. The beach is easy-open at all but the highest tides; rare are the beach-destroying "armorings" which bedevil the walker from Seattle to Tacoma; this beach is not starved, it's fat.

The bus enables an ingenuity: Take Metro bus 118 from 8 and Blanchard in Seattle. (Call Metro for times when bus 118 and the ferry connect to the bus on the Vashon side.) Get off the bus at Ellisport and walk the beach back to the ferry.

Be very sure to peruse the tide table. Choose a day with a morning high so the walk will begin on an outgoing tide. The first ¾ mile north can be walked on public road, climbing above the shore, then dropping to cross the lagoon onto the Point Heyer spit; aside from the KVI radio tower the spit is in a natural state of lagoon, dune, and driftwood. Waves and gulls, Rainier, rocket ships blasting in and out of Sea-Tac International Airport. When the water has lowered to 10 feet or so, continue north.

The 2½ miles to Dilworth Point (Point Beals) are virtually all wild beneath a tanglewood bluff as high as 300 feet. The trail-access cottages of Klahanie briefly interrupt, and a venerable mansion at historic Vashon Landing, and cabins in the valley-cove just north, but mainly the people are atop the bluff, not even trails down. Creeks flow from jungle over gravels—which by the unusual abundance of red-brick pebbles and cobbles tell of a past when the island had nine brickyards. Across Puget Sound is the thrust of Three Tree Point.

Dilworth Point (where in the 1930s, while swimming, the older surveyor watched an airplane fly over, carrying Wiley Post and Will Rogers to Alaska and eternity) is a logical turnaround; it's 3½ miles back to Ellisport, where any of five afternoon buses can be taken to the ferry dock. No time or energy is saved by turning back here, but more of the day is spent in wildness, because Dilworth itself is densely populated, as is the entire shore for a mile north.

The next 3½ miles to Dolphin Point have much interest. The architectural taste of beachdwellers entertains, especially in those constructions dependent not on tons of money but on beachcombing, scavenging, and do-it-yourself handicrafting. At 1¾ miles from Dilworth the wildness resumes for nearly 1 mile; then, at Cowley's Landing, is a vision of the past—a nearly intact dock and gangplank, artifacts of the mosquito fleet. Just beyond, on beach-invading riprap, is a short stretch that at above 7 feet of water cannot be passed without wading—the only such obstacle on the route.

Dolphin Point, thoroughly habitated, is yet a worthwhile viewpoint. Ferries shuttle to Fauntleroy, Southworth, Bremerton, and Winslow. Look south on the Sound to where you came from. And north to Blake and Bainbridge and Whidbey Islands. The Seattle shore is distinguished by the strikingly Green Mile of Lincoln Park.

At ½ mile south of the ferry dock a "Northeast Vashon County Park" reputedly exists and that's nice, except it is officially judged "not suitable for public use at this time." The final ½ mile is by cabins-cottages from Oz, home-made and homey. The escape from the beach is blocked by their bulkheads and requires less than 7 feet of water in order to reach the stairway up from the beach to a restaurant.

South End Loop*

Drive (or take the Point Defiance bus from downtown Tacoma) to Point Defiance Park (see Point Defiance Park). Walk on the nice little ferry for

---

*See the publisher's note on private property on page 11.

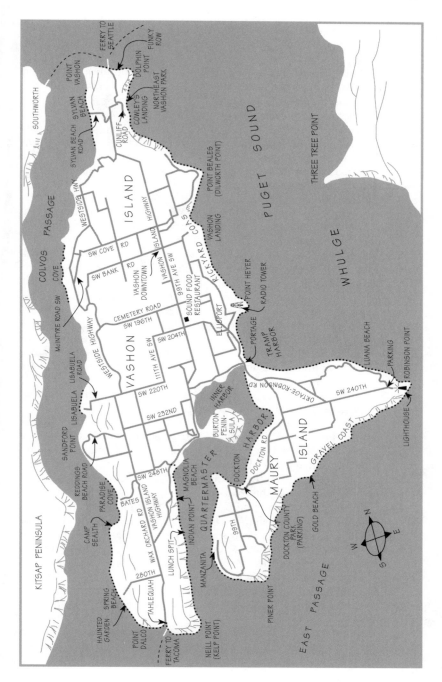

the 15-minute voyage over Dalco Passage to Tahlequah, an old village in and around the valley of Tahlequah Creek, the weathered houses grown comfortably into the landscape.

Wild beach beneath green-jungle glacial-drift bluff, views over busy waterways to the metropolis of Second City, and memories of the mosquito fleet. You can't beat it anywhere.

To loop is not compulsory. A person can stroll the west shore along Colvos Passage; Camp Sealth at 3 miles is a good turnaround. In the other direction, around Neill Point to Quartermaster Harbor, "Lunch Spit" at 3 miles is a satisfying goal.

The loop is the classic if time, tides, and energy permit. To do it clockwise, walk off the ferry dock, turn left to Tahlequah Grocery for nostalgia and some extra lunch supplies, and from it scramble down to the beach. In the first ½ mile are Tahlequah Creek, continuous bulkheads, and lived-in old homes. Views are east to Commencement Bay, downtown Tacoma, pulpmill steam plume, ships, and mountains.

Rounding Point Dalco shifts the mood to wildness, the jungle-drift wall rising a steep 260 feet. Views now of Point Defiance, The Narrows, and Gig Harbor. New vistas open north up Colvos Passage, tugs hauling log rafts, fishermen dragging lines. At 1 mile from the point is a wild valley where grow, mysteriously, tall poplars. Step in a bit from the beach and to a creek, a haunted cottage, flowers and beanstalks of a garden gone wild, overgrown by hellberries. A bit farther up the beach is a larger valley where part of a mosquito-fleet dock still stands, old houses line sides of the valley, and a large structure on the bulkhead by the beach bears faded lettering, "Miramar—Board and Room—And Lunches." This is Spring Beach; close your eyes and see the excursion steamer docking, hear the harmony around the bonfire.

Here is semi-secret Spring Beach (King County) Park. To drive to this point, take Vashon Island Highway SW, turn right on SW 280 0.8 mile to a y. Go left on an unsigned, narrow, gravel-dirt road 0.1 mile to a y where huge "bluff" signs tell great big lies. Stay right, dropping through magnificent old forest to the water, 0.6 mile from 280th. Best to park somewhere up on 280th, not at the road-end.

From Spring Beach 1 long mile leads to a wildland preserved by the Seattle–King County Council of Camp Fire Girls. Camp Sealth is fondly remembered by generations of girls and more than a few boys; it was in the spring of 1939 that Troop 324 voyaged here on the *Virginia V* to perform, as was the troop's wont, a Good Deed, brushing trails by day and at evening staging a little vaudeville.

Should you be confronted by functionaries and lectured on the shame of being a dirty old man (or woman), smile sweetly and offer to buy a box of mints.

"Sealth Point" is rounded to Paradise Cove. Houses start. At ¾ mile from the point, 4 miles from Tahlequah, a street-end at a tumbling-down boathouse provides a take-out for the loop.

Walk Bates Road up a forest ravine to the island top, 480 feet. Turn left on Wax Orchard Road SW a short bit, then right on SW 248 Street, which becomes Shawnee (Fisher) Road as it goes right and curves downhill to Vashon Island Highway. Cross to a lane that deadends on Magnolia Beach. This cross-island walk on country roads totals 2¼ miles.

Magnolia is a hotbed of Privates who stand 24-hour guard against Publics. However, a pedestrian who is a guest of residents—like, say, the Reizenheimers, who just moved in—can readily walk from the deadend.

Watch the tides. Ahead lie feeble-wave beaches overhung by alder and maple, cool retreats on hot days, but not so lovable when full of water, requiring a person to swim or fight hillside brush. The first 1½ miles south along Quartermaster Harbor, by Indian Point and Harbor Heights, views to Dockton on Maury Island, are mostly armored and populated, many boats moored.

In ½ mile more is "Lunch Spit," a tiny jut of sand enclosing a tiny lagoon. To the south 2 miles can be seen Neill (Kelp) Point and, in all that distance, no sign of humans. A second little spit is passed, several inviting ravines. Then houses do indeed exist, up in the trees, no interruption of the mood. (And providing emergency escapes to an overland return if, as happened on one survey, the beach is totally swallowed up.) Piner Point on Maury Island is passed and the water panorama widens, climaxing at Neill Point in a prospect across the Sound to Redondo, Tacoma again, and Rainier. A final 1 mile beside bulkheads and houses leads back to Tahlequah.

Note: For many years houses were built on this shore without permits, without King County enforcement. In the mid-1980s a millionaire Tacoma attorney/scofflaw built a pleasure dome, never so much as a by-your-leave. Others followed his example.

Northwest Shore

Bus: 117 on Westside Highway to Burton

In some opinion the northwest shore is the best of Vashon. Colvos Passage is so much narrower than East Passage that you can't miss the gray whales swimming by, and the view is not to Puget Sound City but such lesser megalopolises as Olalla and Fragaria. The beach seems lonesomer, the bluff taller and greener.

For *Sylvan Beach,* drive the highway from the ferry to the top of the hill, past the fire station, and go right on "Corbin Beach Drive–Sylvan Beach." In 0.1 mile is a junction. Park on a shoulder hereabouts; there is no room farther down, and certainly not at the beach. Go right and walk the ¼ mile from the junction down the narrow, winding, steep road, past the usual array of signs erected to frighten timid Publics. A boardwalk leads north and south from the road to a row of cabins.

For the next access, at *Cove,* drive the highway to just before beautiful downtown Vashon. Turn west on Cove Road 2 miles, then south on

McIntyre Road SW to a stop sign. Turn left (south) on Westside Highway 0.2 mile to SW 172 Street and an enormously hostile sign. Go west on SW 172 Street 0.1 mile and turn right on a one-lane road past three-storey Cove Motel to the water. Parking here is at a Public cable crossing; feel free. To the south are walk-in cabins. To the north the beach is beneath a steep and ever-sliding bluff overhung with alder; except at low tide expect to scramble over chunks of former bluff.

The next access south is *Lisabuela,* on a spit of driftwood and sandy beach poking out in the cove fed by lovely Judd Creek. In 1906 the community sought to secede from King County, next year tried to join Pierce County, and in 1912 almost got the legislature to establish Vashon County. It is not clear what was bugging them. What bugged islanders in the 1980s was a plague of realtors brazenly intending the Privatization of a Public treasure.

The Publics don't lose 'em all. As of June 1993 all Privatizers have been bought out and shipped out. Deconstruction of their shacks will ensue and then such construction of public facilities as is wanted for Lisabuela (King County) Park.

Check it out. At the Center stoplight south of downtown Vashon, turn west from the highway on SW 196 Street (Cemetery Road). Follow the twists (don't give up when it becomes Westside Highway) and turn right on SW 220 Street, which makes a sharp left, becomes SW Lisabuela Road, and drops to the water. On the way admire the waterfall of Judd Creek. Pretty!

Finally, drive the highway to Sound Foods Restaurant and turn right on SW 204th. In 0.8 mile it makes a sharp left and becomes 111 Avenue SW, which becomes SW 220 Street. Turn left on Wax Orchard Road SW 0.9 mile to SW Reddings Beach Road. Head west 1 mile to *SW Cross Landing Road.* Turn left 0.2 mile to the beach. Parking for one or two cars. In getting here you left just about everybody behind. Ah, wilderness! To the south are sandy beach, a navigation light on the spit tip, and a lagoon marsh. All the best stuff, and if you spot a surveyor hammering in stakes, report him/her to the Vashon militia.

MAURY ISLAND

Miles of beaches lightly populated or purely wild, a lighthouse built in 1915, some of the most stupendous gravel mines in the Western world, and views across ships and barges and sailboats in East Passage to the Whulge Trail from Three Tree Point to Point Defiance. Public accesses permit beach walks short or long—up to a complete circuit of the island. In 1993 the King County Council approved purchase of 300 acres, 7100 feet of shore, for a Maury Island Marina Park. Good news? The term "marina" implies stinkpots by the googol. Are we ready to accept the torpedo as a recreational device? (Recreational submarines are now on the market.)

Sweet Sampler

From Dockton drive 99 Avenue SW south to where it becomes gravel. Go right, signed "SW 280 Street–Manzanita Beach Road SW–SW Northilla," 1.5 miles to an end at Manzanita.

About five cars can park, so no mobs. Most days, nobody at all. The beach is sandy, driftwoody. Views are south to Dalco Passage and Tacoma.

The Complete Circuit

The 11-mile loop may be started (or ended) at Dockton. In 1993 Metro buses left the Vashon ferry terminal at 6:35, 8:05, and 9:27 A.M., arriving at Dockton at 7:01, 8:34, and 9:51 A.M. The last bus from Dockton to the ferry leaves at 7:13 P.M. Be sure to check a current schedule.

For an alternate start, requiring your own vehicle to be ferried, drive Vashon Island Highway from Vashon Heights or Tahlequah to 1.7 miles south of beautiful downtown Vashon and turn east on SW 204 Street, which in 1 long mile descends to the beach. Turn south on Ellisport-Portage Road 0.7 mile and park anywhere on the wide shoulders near Portage Grocery (1910).

Walk the shore of Tramp Harbor, leaving behind the isthmus that connects Maury to Vashon, looking over boat-busy waters to the Issaquah Alps. Though several gulches and benches permit houses near the beach, most of the way a 100-foot wildwood bluff keeps the peace. Stubs of pilings speak of the mosquito fleet. Bulkheaded dwellings of Luana Beach break the greenery for ¾ mile, then solitude resumes to the jutting spit and grassy fields of Robinson Point.

Dockton County Park

Here, 3½ miles from Portage, are a scenic climax and satisfying turn-around for a 7-mile round trip. The lagoon is filled but not otherwise intruded, the open fields grow wind-waving grass and wildflowers. Water views are unsurpassed. The lighthouse and keeper's house are pictur-esque; inquire at the office for possible touring of the light station, with a past dating to 1893.

To put in at Robinson Point for hikes south, drive from Portage 0.7 mile to a Y. The right leads in 3 miles to Dockton (King County) Park. Go left on SW 228 (Portage-Robinson Road), descending in 2.5 miles to a T. Go right on Wick Road 0.3 mile to a parking area on top of the hill above the lighthouse. A gated road drops to the keeper's house and the beach.

Around the corner, where lie the 1.3 miles of beach to be the new King County park, the pilgrim's vistas open southward past Des Moines Marina to Tacoma. Now begins the Gravel Coast from which a substantial portion of the mass of Maury has been removed. Two barge-loading docks have been active recently, two are in a condition of dilapidation, and others are reduced to piling stubs. The two newest pits are awesome desolations. Others have grown up in grass and madronas; in early summer, poppies, vetch, yarrow, and ocean spray in orange-blue-white-cream bloom are winsomely California-pretty. The oldest abandoned pits are so wooded one wouldn't know from a quick look they aren't enigmatic features of a natural landscape.

The first half of the 6 miles from Robinson Point to Piner Point is mostly uninhabited, partly due to mining and partly the imposing 300-foot bluff that plunges from the island plateau. The second half alternates between scattered houses and solid houses, notably at Gold Beach, where the removal of the primeval bluff by excavation has created a terrace ideal for subdivision. Piner Point is a wildwood bulge, views across to Dash Point and Commencement Bay, downtown Tacoma and Rainier. A nice spot for lunching and turning around.

If intent on doing the total Maury, proceed the 4 miles to Dockton Park. The bluff drops to naught, a hodgepodge of dwellings rich and poor push close to the beach, but the narrow waters of Quartermaster Harbor have charm. Dockton Point is rounded; the protected cove, now full of playboats and garbage, once was the site of a floating dry dock employing 400 workers, another 200 at other shipyards; many a vessel of the mosquito fleet was built here.

BLAKE ISLAND

In the middle of Main Street, ferries rushing this way and that, big ships and little boats and tugs and barges tooling around, jet airplanes thundering and propellor jobs clacketing and helicopters racketing, cities and suburbs humming on every side, are 475 acres of green peace. The beach and the big-tree forest are as wild now as when Chief Seattle (reputedly) was born here and tribes gathered to potlatch. Bought by William

Pitt Trimble in 1904 and kept by him as a summerhome until 1929, in 1957 the sanctuary became Blake Island State Marine Park.

For non-boaters, access is by craft of Seattle Harbor Tours serving Tillicum Village, an Indian-longhouse restaurant on 4½ leased acres. The *Goodtime* leaves from Pier 56 in Seattle, at the foot of Seneca Street just north of the ferry terminal and just south of Waterfront Park and Seattle Aquarium. Park in an Alaskan Way lot or on the street, or come by Metro bus. On a vessel of mosquito-fleet size, the trip from Blake to Seattle takes 45 minutes, a long view north to Whidbey Island, south to Rainier. The trip to Blake is 60 minutes, because a waterfront tour and a peek into the Duwamish Waterway are included.

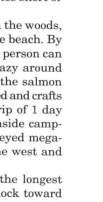

Replica of an Indian longhouse on Blake Island

The boat schedule dictates the hike itinerary. To learn the current schedule and make reservations, call Tillicum Village Tours: (206) 443-1244. The fare (1993) was—without the salmon feast at the longhouse—$19.96 for adults, less for children; with feast, $43 for adults, varied amounts for children, $40 for seniors. Having the schedule in hand, a hiker can plan any number of itineraries short or long, 1 day or overnight or longer.

A 2-hour layover suffices to circle the beach and sidetrip in the woods, or to circle the perimeter trail in the woods and sidetrip to the beach. By arriving on a morning boat and leaving on an evening boat, a person can do the whole trail system plus the entire beach, and then lazy around watching the sunset and eating a picnic supper—or buying the salmon dinner served at Tillicum Village, Indian-baked, dances performed and crafts displayed. Of course, the superior plan is to combine any trip of 1 day with any trip of the next, camping at one of the three beachside campgrounds, marveling at the all-around skyglow of the billion-eyed megalopolis. The east campground, by the dock, is $6 a night. The west and south camps are no-fee.

At any but high tides the first priority is the circuit of the longest purely wild beach so near downtown Seattle. Walk up the dock toward the longhouse, turn left, and go. (Left is advised in order to do the largely cobble east–southwest beach first, saving the mainly sand north beach for the end.) Village, picnic area, and campground are soon left behind,

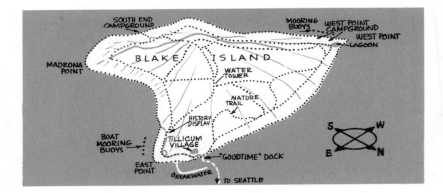

East Point rounded, and solitude attained—since the *Goodtime* throngs tend to stay near the longhouse. Grand fir, madrona, and maple overhang the beach. Views are to West Seattle and the Fauntleroy–Vashon ferry, Rainier and the Issaquah Alps, the Space Needle and grain terminal and Magnolia Bluff. At 1¼ miles Madrona Point is rounded and the view shifts to Colvos Passage between Vashon and Point Southworth, then across Yukon Harbor to Colby and Colchester. South End Campground, on a spur from the perimeter trail, is passed; the jungled bluff of glacial drift rears up 200 feet from the beach; fleeing herons "gark! gark!" The elevated terrace of a fossil beach (shoved up by the Seattle Fault?) begins, and on it is West Point Campground. Then the noble sandspit thrusts out in the waves, driftwood line and dune line enclosing a (usually) dry lagoon. At a scant 2 miles from Madrona Point is the tip of the spit, the climax delight; plan to sit a long while watching Seattle–Bremerton ferries dashing through Rich Passage between Orchard Point and Bainbridge Island. See the Olympics. A final 1¼ miles leads back under an alder canopy, in views to the Seattle–Winslow ferry and the metropolis, to the longhouse, completing the 4½-mile loop.

That's the half of it. Now, inland. Logged in the 1850s (except for some wolfish Douglas fir on the south side), the island has regrown a mixed forest that offers every variety of Puget Sound woodland experience—and meetings with some of the island's puny, half-starved, 120-odd deer, striving to survive in a habitat that can properly feed only 50 or so. (But if they swam to the mainland they'd get et themselves, by savage dogs or hunters.) To start the perimeter counterclockwise, walk by the right side of the longhouse to a bridge over a little gulch. To do it clockwise, meander through the campground any old way and near its end turn inland on the road to the foundations of the Trimble house. A few steps beyond is a Y; left is the island loop trail, right is the cross-island trail. The 4-mile loop is the basic trail but the cross-island trail offers additional green joy, as do the nature trail and lesser paths. Frequent spurs lead to the beach, permitting easy switches from one Blake mode to the other.

THE NORTHERN ISLES: INDIAN–MARROWSTONE, CAMANO, WHIDBEY, FIDALGO, GUEMES, SAMISH, LUMMI

Indian is hitched to the Kitsap Peninsula and Marrowstone is hitched to Indian, but don't let that bother you. A mainlander still most reasonably will voyage to the two hitched-up islands via ferry to the peninsula and thereby get the islandlike feel.

The 20-mile length of Camano is ringed by water, 50-odd miles of beach. Yes, there's a bridge, but blink your eyes and it's left in the lurch.

Whidbey, of course, is something else. In 1985 the U.S. Supreme Court ruled that New York's Long Island, 110 miles long, is not the longest island in the old forty-eight states because it's a peninsula. One wonders why the nine jurists felt compelled to meddle in the business of geographers. One further must ask if Isle Royale loyalists intend to seek *their* justice. In any event, Whidbey Island newly is officially the longest. How long *is* it? As the crow flies, about 35 miles. As the shoreline curves, 45, or

Joseph Whidbey State Park

60, or some other number. The miles of tideland total something like 135.

The hard-rock geology of Fidalgo is more hospitable to boating than footing. However, Bob Rose, who as Chief Thinker for the state Department of Natural Resources wreaked much good from the Issaquah Alps to the San Juan Islands, has retired to the Skagit delta to grow flowers and may as a hobby revive his 1970s vision of a Fidalgo Island Trail starting in Anacortes at the Guemes Island ferry dock (the former San Juan Islands ferry dock), following the shore to the new San Juan dock, passing en route the depot of the narrow-gauge Anacortes Railway, which began operating in 1887, and also the moorage of the sternwheeler *W. T. Preston,* retired in 1981 from active service with the U.S. Army. The way would proceed through Washington Park to the old city watershed at Little Cranberry Lake, to Heart Lake State Park (whose creation was an early triumph for The Rose), the old city watershed at Whistle Lake, Mt. Erie, Lakes Erie and Campbell, to Deception Pass State Park.

For an old-timey island, attainable only by old-timey ferry, go Guemes.

In an earlier edition we belittled Samish for having been attached to the mainland by mud-booted dikers. An island, is it? At the tip one feels far out to sea, sailing into the San Juans.

The looming of Lummi was omitted from our previous book for looking too spooky. Bravery has corrected the error.

USGS maps: Mukilteo, Maxwelton, Hansville, Freeland, Langley, Juniper Beach, Camano, Coupeville, Port Townsend North, Utsalady, Deception Pass, Anacortes

INDIAN–MARROWSTONE ISLANDS

Drive Highway 104 west 5 miles from Hood Canal Bridge and turn north at the sign "Fort Flagler State Park, Port Townsend." In 1.6 miles turn right on Oak Bay Road, signed "Port Ludlow." In 9.8 miles more turn right on Flagler Road. In 0.9 mile is the bridge to Indian Island.

An embarrassment of riches! Miles and miles of grand beaches in views of Main Street traffic and mountains from the Olympics to Baker to Glacier Peak to Rainier. And absolutely the bulliest of the three forts of the Death (or Devil's) Triangle that once protected cities of Puget Sound from the Spanish battle fleet.

Oak Bay Park

Before crossing the bridge to Indian Island, turn onto the road signed "Oak Bay Park" (Jefferson County). Descend to the beach and drive out on the spit to the road-end, 0.4 mile from the highway. Park.

Walk. To the spit tip, then along Portage Canal, which splits off Indian Island. Be surprised to see Port Townsend, pulpmill plume and all. Binoculars at the ready, return along the excellent ½-mile lagoon.

Cross the bridge onto Indian Island and immediately halt in Hadlock Lions Park, access to 2 miles of Public beach with nary a Privatizer, thanks to the close-by but non-invasive highway atop a short but sufficient bluff.

From Hadlock Lions Park, the South Indian Island Trail goes ½ mile along the channel between the mainland and the island in fir-cedar-madrona forest.

At 0.8 mile from the bridge turn right on a gravel road, signed "Jefferson County Park," to the beach and follow it 0.2 mile to the end at two picnic tables. Connoisseurs say this is one of the richest and most pristine saltmarshes we've got left, a saltwater museum, oozy-teeming saltgrass on the bluff side of the bars, wave-washed gravel on the bay side. A ⅓-mile lagoon empties into the bay (or, in flood, sucks in the bay) exactly at the picnic tables.

You may or may not wish to ponder as you walk the fact that Indian Island is Doomsday. Enough nuclear bombs are stored here on the U.S. Navy Reservation to wipe out everybody on the planet but the sludgeworms.

Kinney Point

At 1.7 miles from the bridge over Portage Canal onto Indian Island, a causeway hitches Indian and Marrowstone. Park here and walk 1 mile to the south tip of Marrowstone Island, Kinney Point. The state Department of Natural Resources has 80 acres here, ultimately to be a state park, developed only to an extent compatible with preserving the wildlife habitat, which includes eagle nests, one said by the Wildlife Department to be the most productive in the Northwest. Local folks see eagles every day of the year.

East Beach Park

Drive on north. Nordland is your next stop, to buy an ice cream bar at the Nordland Store, and mail a postcard at the Nordland post office. No

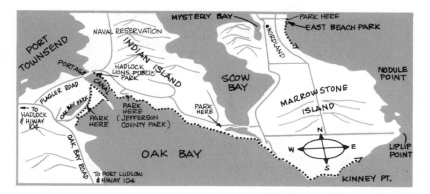

tourist boutiques here. This is the authentic 1930s. Pause for a look-in at Mystery Bay (State Park) Recreation Area, where the recreation consists of gunning marine motorcycles up and down Kilisut Harbor.

North of the Nordland Store go 0.4 mile, turn right at the sign "East Beach Park," and drive 0.3 mile to the driftwood, a picnic shelter, inviting beach (at low tide, broad sand) north and south, and views: Rainier, the shore of Whidbey Island, Baker and Shuksan, Main Street traffic up and down Admiralty Inlet.

Fort Flagler State Park

Though the island is not very distant in hours from Seattle, it's very far away in the past. The same water shortage (the sky is the only supply) that restrains development on Vashon Island has, in combination with the commuting distance, held Marrowstone, 6 miles north–south and up to 1 mile east–west, to a population of 500. "Pleasure driving" is still a reality. And—oh—the pleasure walking. A day trip from Puget Sound City can be olden-day relaxed. A better plan is to camp a night or two or several and be for that long an islander.

At 3 miles from Nordland, Fort Gate marks the entry. Three roads go to the beach. The road right leads in 0.4 mile, passing a battery of two 3-inch guns, to Fort Flagler Fishing Pier, a long reach of planks out into views. The beach access is the start for a ¾-mile walk to Marrowstone Point or some 7 miles to Kinney Point.

The road straight ahead passes through the main campus (handsome old officers' homes and utilitarian enlisted men's barracks converted to park headquarters, interpretive center, hostel, et cetera) and in 0.7 mile ends at Marrowstone Point Lighthouse. Look across to the loess bluff of Ebey's Landing and the green plain of Ebey's Prairie. Look south between Foulweather Bluff and Double Bluff to Puget Sound; the mainland shore

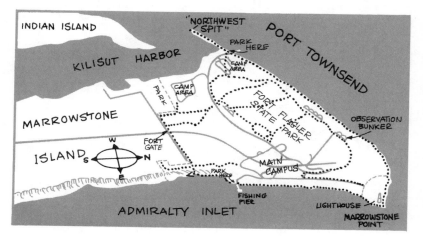

Fishing dock at Fort Flagler State Park

is a distant blue silhouette, seemingly at the foot of Mount Rainier.

For the suggested introductory walk, drive left from the main intersection 1.4 miles to the road-end at Northwest Spit. (On the way are a mortar battery, trails, and two campgrounds, one up on the bluff and the other down on the filled lagoon. Here is the sublime base for a Marrowstone vacation.)

First off, walk west ⅓ mile to the tip of the spit pushing across the mouth of Kilisut Harbor. Look over Port Townsend Bay to the pulpmill and town and Fort Worden, to the Olympics from Constance to Zion to Blue to Angeles.

Returned from this sidetrip, head east, leaving the spit flat for the base of the 120-foot vertical bluffs Vancouver called "marrow stone"—what we call glacial drift, here represented by concretelike till and some of the finest sand cliffs around. Ships, tugs and barges, sailboats, waves, birds, the Keystone–Townsend ferry. Across Admiralty Inlet, the Ebey's Landing section of Whidbey Island, Baker, Shuksan, Wickersham-Woolley-Lyman, Cultus, Chuckanut, San Juans. In a scant 2 miles are the flats of Marrowstone Point, the lighthouse on the tip, and views south to Whitehorse, Glacier, Rainier, and Foulweather Bluff at the mouth of Hood Canal.

Leave the beach (4 miles and never so much as a frown) and follow the road up the hill to the main campus and its well-kept 1900-era frame buildings. Keep right on an old, barricaded road-become-trail. The route from here the 2 miles back to the campground is partly on this or that old road, partly on trails; the rule is, stick with the easy going as near the bluff as feasible and safe. The way is in forest and sky-open, wide-horizon seameadow, passing (explore with care!) concrete emplacements of the 10- and 12-inch disappearing guns and 12-inch mortars and underground fire-control posts. Set aside as a military reservation in 1866, the fort was developed from 1897–1900 and declared surplus in 1954. Three wars in the memories here. Stand in the wind on the brink of the meadow-top precipice and look over the waters to the two other forts of the Death Triangle and visualize the climax, here, of a fourth war that never was; only in phantom history books is there, to rank with Trafalgar and Midway, a Battle of Admiralty Inlet.

Fort Flagler State Park is an enormous 783 acres, mostly a forest getting on to be a century old. The miles of woodland paths were not surveyed for this guide because a person wouldn't drive from Puget Sound City for their sake. Come for a stay of several days, though, a walker surely will want to intermingle the big sky of the sea with sorties into the little green rooms of the trees.

CAMANO ISLAND

From Stanwood drive Highway 532 over West Pass Bridge.

Camano Island has been so intensely loved, so Privatized, that the traveler from afar does best to be contented by the wealth of superb free-and-easy beaches in the Northern Isles and leave lesser strands to the locals.

Still, mention must be made in passing of a few of these lessers (driving directions left to highway maps except where needed).

Mount Baker from English Boom on Skagit Bay

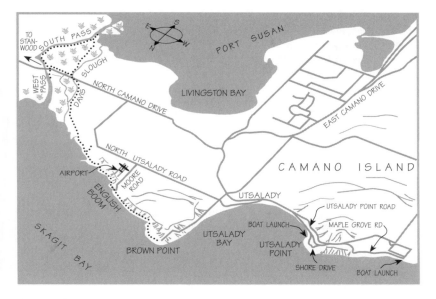

Lesser Interest

Davis Slough. A dike hike from Davis Slough Access, Skagit Habitat Management Area. Saltgrass meadows. Birds.

English Boom. A long stretch of Department of Natural Resources beach, but the upland is undergoing dense development. Best approach along the shore from Davis Slough. Smashing views over Skagit Bay to the delta and the Cascades.

Cavelero Beach County Park. Views and picnic tables on the east shore, which has a population density approaching that of Bombay; the C/4 will wash away billions of dollars of houses and toys.

Utsalady No. 1 County Park. Drive North Camano Drive to Utsalady Point Road. Keep right to the end of Shore Drive. A boat-launch hemmed in by Privates whose nerves when the weekend sun shines are hair-trigger.

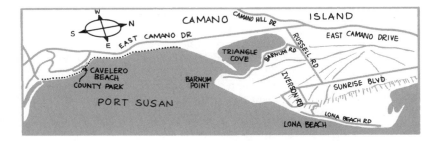

Maple Grove Boat-Launch.* Drive North Camano Drive to Maple Grove Road. Drop steeply to shore and houses and signs warning you to not even think about it.

Woodland Beach. Drive West Camano Drive to just north of Onamac Point. North of this noble thrust of spit are 1½ miles of bluff-guarded wildness. Superb erratics. An undisturbed kitchen midden. Forlorn ruins of a beach cabin. South from the point the beach and its monster erratics are bluff-safe the 1 mile to the old village of Camano. The next 3 miles, to Camano Island State Park, are sporadically habitated.

Camano. Public access at the little old village, where once the mosquito fleet brought summerers from Seattle.

Camano Island State Park

From the end of Highway 532 take a left, on East Camano Drive, 6 miles to a Y, both forks confusingly signed "East Camano Drive." Go right, signed "State Park," 2 miles to an intersection at Elger Bay Grocery. Turn west on West Camano Drive 1.7 miles and turn left on Park Drive. The park is entered and in 1 mile the headquarters passed. Just beyond is a Y, the left leading to parking on the beach at Lowell Point, the right to parking by North Beach.

Though Whidbey Island takes the brunt of the howlers from the ocean, the west side of Camano Island, the weather shore, gets its share of waves, enough for the pounded look walkers like. Saratoga Passage is busier than Port Susan, fishing boats going to and fro and log rafts south to Everett mills.

Near the entrance is the ½-mile Al Emerson Nature Trail. A 6-mile perimeter trail is planned through the 134-acre park. Presently there is a blufftop, wide-view path, the north end at the switchback on the road to North Beach, the south end in a ravine cutting the Lowell Point road at the foot of the bluff.

From North Beach to Lowell Point is 1 long mile of 100-foot cliffs of sand and gravel and varved blue clay, madronas hanging over the brink. Views extend across Saratoga Passage 2 miles to Whidbey Island, the Olympics beyond, and south to the island end at Camano Head and beyond to Gedney (Hat) Island. North of the park the beach is touched only by scattered communities the scant 4 miles to Onamac Point; southward the shore goes 2 miles into and around Elger Bay and another 3 miles to Mabana Shores.

The park of 134 acres and 1 mile of beach—that was the past. The park to be is 430 acres more (second-growth forest well along toward a century old) and 1 long mile more of beach. How on earth could the state acquire so much valuable land and precious waterfront in this Reaganite Age of cynical greed run amok? Because Karen Hamalainn and Sandra

---

*See the publisher's note on private property on page 11.

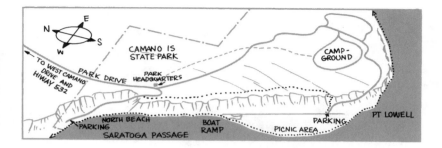

Worthington love their childhood home more than wealth. The possibility of seeing Cama Beach Resort, founded by their grandfather in 1934 and operated by their parents until 1989, developed into a row of yuppie condos horrified them. They rejected profit for principle and in 1993 arranged to sell out to State Parks at a ridiculously low price, on the easiest of instalment terms. The sisters hope that "our gift inspires others." It darn well ought to shame the swarm of weasels whose greedhead exploitations are described in this book.

Camano Head

Drive to Elger Bay Grocery (see Camano Island State Park) and continue on West Camano Drive a scant 4.5 miles to the Mabana fire station. Turn west 0.2 mile on Mabana Shore Drive, which becomes Seth Drive. Where it bends right, the second time, take the first gravel road (unsigned) down left to the parking area at the beach.

The southern tip of the island, Camano Head, is a 320-foot bluff of naked cliffs and sliding tanglewood. From the top look out over Possession Sound to Gedney (Hat) Island and Port Gardner and Everett's ships and pulpmills, and to Mukilteo's ferry and pastel oil tanks and, on the hill above, enormous buildings of Boeing's Paine Field complex, and to the Cascades and Olympics. That is, look if you can get to the brink. A plea to dedicate this vista point as a Public park was ignored in 1978 and 1988. As of 1993 the roads and powerlines and surveyors' stakes are in. The balcony thus is closed so go down to the orchestra pit. The beach walk around the base of Camano Head is a Whulge classic, 3 miles purely wild beneath that formidable cliff, the rest of the 7½ miles of beach south to and north around the Head only spottily inhabited.

Though not signed as such, the put-in is a Public boat-launch, the Port of Mabana dating from the mosquito fleet. Through this serendipitous intervention from the past, Publics of today can set foot on the beach. Once there, the mightily attractive 4 miles north to Elger Bay are so neatly tucked beneath the bluff a walker would scarcely see a house the whole way. But south is the way to Camano Head.

The beach goes south under a bully sand cliff footed by blue clay. Jungle

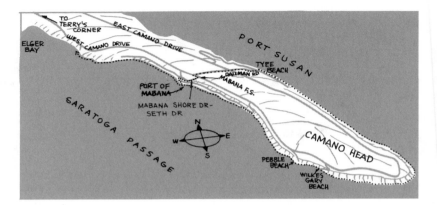

then alternates with bare walls; trails and perilous ladderways and aerial trams descend from unseen houses 100 feet up. At 1¼ miles a road comes down to a dozen houses on a beach-invading fill that must be passed via an inland detour on the community road. Solitude resumes to Pebble Beach at 2½ miles; the jutting spit encloses a driftwood-filled lagoon; several houses are here. Immediately south is Wilkes Gary Beach, ¾ mile of cottages, and then undiluted wildness. Across Saratoga Passage are Langley, on Whidbey Island, and Sandy Point and Columbia Beach, the ferry shuttling to Mukilteo. Now, around the bend, appear Hat Island and Everett. The bluff rears up to its full 320 feet, becomes naked white till and brown sand and blue clay, viciously vertical. At 4½ miles from the put-in the shore turns sharply.

What a spot! Camano Head. Sit for lunch. From the heart of wildness look to the harbor of Everett and buildings downtown. See the ferry and sailboats and mountains.

Now turn north into Port Susan. The bluff is less steep but an even more appalling (to property owners) 300 feet high. The view is over to the Whulge Trail and Index, Pilchuck, and Three Fingers. (On the first survey bald eagles were seen, and herons and ducks and fishing boats. A concrete chunk jutting into the beach suggested an old boat tie-up for a camp. Loot of clandestine cedar-mining had recently been hauled away by a small boat. Nearly rusted-away iron rails set in aged concrete on the beach, and an

Eagle in the wild forest on the bluffs of Camano Head

unnatural gully above, suggested a log skidway from the era of World War I.) The view opens to the head of the bay, Chuckanut, Baker. At 2½ miles from the Head start houses of Tyee Beach. In a scant ½ mile more a community boat-launch serves as take-out onto the road, which climbs the bluff ½ mile to East Camano Drive. Cross Dallman Road and in ¾ mile return to the fire station and thence to the Port of Mabana for a loop trip of about 9 miles.

WHIDBEY ISLAND

Bus: Island Transit 1A and 1B serve Clinton, Langley, the Keystone ferry, Coupeville, Oak Harbor, and waypoints; 4A and 4B serve Deception Pass and Oak Harbor

Take the Mukilteo ferry to Clinton and drive Highway 525, which becomes Highway 20. On summer weekends the ferries may be so jammed that the long way around via Deception Pass Bridge may be the shortest way home.

The beachwalker can get just about anything he/she might want at the Whidbey Island restaurant. Short walks on the lee side, where the storms are rarely furious and the history is always thick, and long rambles in horizons that extend to China and the dragons which in season come raging in from the Oceane Sea to roar their hatred of the continent and chew at its soft flank with big white teeth.

East Side

A lee shore, more comfortable for living and thus more heavily settled than the stormy west. Beaches that are generally less dramatic, appealing when the weather shore is too much so. Views over the water to the Cascades. More history. The entire shore is walkable. A number of Public put-ins permit sampling the scene on short strolls or long.

Lesser Interest

Not to bad-mouth this side of the island (there is no such thing as a bad beach), the eastern shore mainly interests folks who live there or close by. Visitors from Puget Sound City are more likely to head for the west shore, to see the dragons. Following are spots that demand mention (driving directions are given only when needed to supplement the highway map).

Langley. Settled in 1880 and for some years the major steamer port of the area. Walk down from the blufftop to the marina and south on the beach below the bluff 1¼ miles to the spit of Sandy Point or 4 miles north to the bar of Bells Beach.

Holmes Harbor. Wilkes named it in 1841. Soon the loggers were chopping and the farmers hoeing. In 1900 a splinter group from the Equality Colony on the Skagit delta moved here as the Free Land Association.

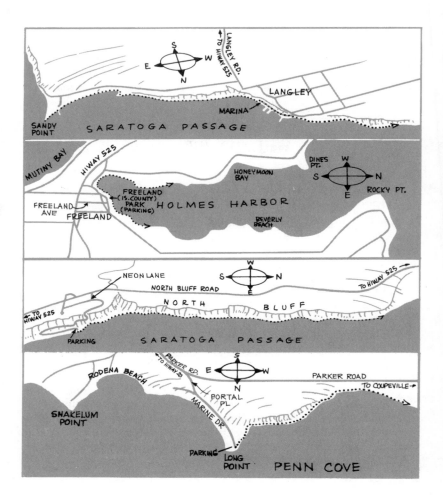

Freeland (Island County) Park is a start for walking under and around old docks and pilings, then 2 miles on under-the-bluff wild beach.

North Bluff. At Greenbank Country Store turn right on North Bluff Road 2.3 miles, then right on Neon Lane 0.4 mile down to the beach. Partly naked 200-foot bluff guards the walker's solitude 1½ miles.

Long Point. A lovely spit at the mouth of Penn Cove. Drive Highway 20 from Greenbank to Smith Prairie. Go off straight ahead north on Parker Road 1.2 miles. Turn right on Portal Place, which immediately T-junctions at Marine Drive. Turn left 0.4 mile to the road-end on the point. Gaze across Penn Cove to Blower's Bluff, beyond to Oak Harbor, and west to Coupeville. Beyond a few houses, a 200-foot bluff continues 1¼ miles to Lovejoy Point, ½ mile from the heart of Coupeville. To the east it's 1¼ miles to Snakelum Point, named by Wilkes for a Skagit chief.

Coupeville. The island's history hotbed. Blockhouse, museum, old houses, preserved wharf. Lots of good things to eat. The beach is less interesting but access is easy from the Coupeville Town Park and Captain Thomas Coupe Park (boat-launch).

Penn Cove Tidelands. Drive Highway 20 north past Libbey Road 0.5 mile to a gravel circle drive. Zylstra Road is just east of the turnout; if you pass it, you've gone too far. Access to lagoon and beach, courtesy of Department of Fisheries.

Monroe's Landing Park. Californialike golden fields slope gently down to the hamlet of San de Fuca on the north shore of Penn Cove. At the turn of the shore into Saratoga Passage is Blower's Bluff, the tallest and steepest piece of geography in these parts. Drive Highway 20 north from Coupeville. Turn right on Arnold Road. At the San de Fuca fire station turn south on Holbrook Street to Penn Cove Road. In 2 miles, where Monroe Landing Road goes left, turn right to a reader-board discussing the Original Residents. Beyond ½ mile of sandspit-lagoon the bluff grows to 150 feet. At 2½ miles is the Towering Erratic, quartz-veined gray metamorphic rock, 20 feet tall. The bluff soon drops off to the mouth of Oak Harbor.

Oak Harbor. When the time comes that the Top Guns are grounded, Maylor Point, Forbes Point, and Polnell Point (a tombolo) will comprise a topographically fascinating park. Until then, pause at a take-out for a hamburger and speed on. The statues on Flintstone Drive have been known to make the parents of small children fwow up.

Strawberry Point. Drive Highway 20 north from Oak Harbor. Turn southwest 1.8 miles on Auvil-Torpedo Road, then Crescent Harbor Road to Taylor Road. Turn north 0.4 mile to Silver Lake Road, which becomes

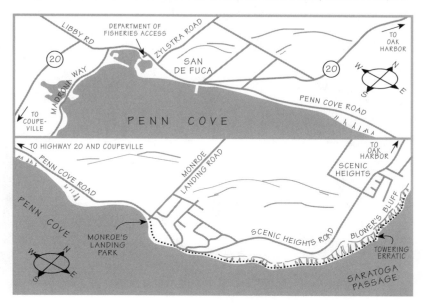

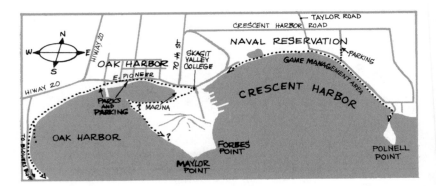

Strawberry Point Road as it turns south 2.3 miles to Mariners Beach Drive. In 0.4 mile spot a gap between houses, the Mariners Cove Public Boat-Launch.

A short walk to the south scoots under the shelter of an up-leaping bluff and remains lonesome-wild 2 miles to the sand neck of Polnell Point. A Navy road can be seen going the ½ mile out to the tip for unknown reasons. Picnics?

A long walk to the north begins past picture windows on the baymouth bar whose lagoon has been dredged for stinkpot basins. The bluff of glacial drift rises up and except for brief breaks remains at a height of 50–150 feet to Dugualla Bay, permitting only small and scattered structures on or near the lonesome beach.

In 1 mile from the boat-launch is Strawberry Point, bringing in sight the long, low horizon of the Skagit delta dikes. An ancient boathouse of

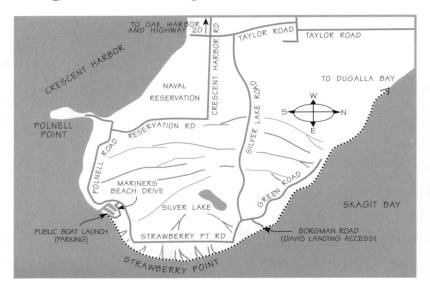

big timbers bears the faded advertisement, "Apples for Sale 50¢ Sack."

At 2 wild miles from the point are a wide valley, several houses, and a Public beach access at the deadend of Borgman Road. (Drive past Mariners Cove on Reservation Road; turn left on Polnell Road at the T and go 2.2 miles. Polnell Road becomes Strawberry Point Road; where it turns left, go right on Green Road, then right on Borgman Road—unsigned, just past "Davis Landing Mt. Baker Circle Private"—to the beach.)

Wildness resumes. Nice creeks are crossed. Alders lean a hundred feet over the beach. Enormous erratics are passed, one as big as a house, a forest of ferns atop. Each bulge in the shore yields new views north—to Ika and Bald and Craft and Goat Islands, the mouth of Swinomish Channel, and Hope and Deception Islands.

How far to go? There's nothing stopping feet or dulling interest in the 5 miles to Dugualla Bay.

Dugualla Bay. The mudflats do not invite boots, though the binoculars find much to focus on in the bay, and the dike leads to fine beaches south and north.

Drive Highway 20 to Frostad Road, which goes off east and becomes Dike Road. Two parking areas off Dike Road. The bay is the east end of Clover Valley, a swale that when sea level was 35 feet higher split off Whidbey's north tip in a separate island. Now the vale contains a large lake, formerly a tidal lagoon, a great flat farm, an infestation of great blue herons, and a jet airfield that harasses mountains and waters and countryside for hundreds of miles around.

The dike leads to wild beach 5 miles south to Strawberry Point and 3 miles north to Ala Spit.

Just south of Dugualla Bay, Sleeper Road goes off Highway 20 to a gate signed "State Park Boundary." No name for the park is given. From the gate the road becomes trail dropping through ancient forest by wetlands to 1 mile of pristine beach.

Ala Spit. Magicland! Particularly appealing for a short, slow, musing walk among the birds and toy islands, the spit also is a put-in for long

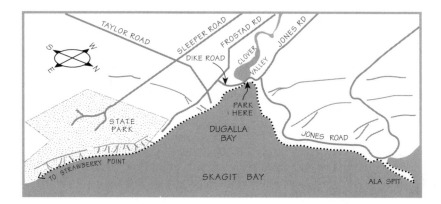

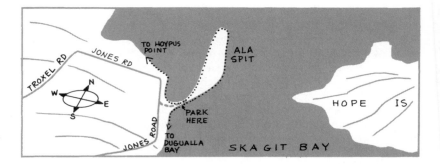

walks to Dugualla Bay and north the scant 2 miles, wild all the way, to Hoypus Point in Deception Pass State Park.

Turn east from Highway 20 on Troxel Road, which becomes Jones Road. Where Jones Road makes a sharp right to parallel the water, look left for an unmarked road down to Public parking on the spit.

On one side of the ½-mile-long driftwood-heaped spit is the bird-busy lagoon. On the other, across the narrow channel, are grass-tawny rock buttresses of Hope Island. South in the bay are Deadman Islands, Seal Rocks, Goat and Ika Islands, the opening to Swinomish Channel. North are Skagit and Kiket and Fidalgo Islands. Here the glacier-drift islands end, the rock-hearted San Juans begin.

Southwest Shore

The southwest is the weather shore, as exciting in a winter blow as a voyage around Cape Horn. From beaches of Seattle and from peaks high in the Cascades the tall naked bluffs are striking landmarks. A person canny in the ways of the Whulge cannot but hanker for a piece of the action on the prow of the "ship" which for thousands of years has been sailing southward, relative to the motion of the water, at a constant speed of many knots. Between broad, shallow, storm-open, useless bays, the jutting bluffs in a turmoil of rude erosion are on the sidelines of a big parade of Main Street traffic—ships to and from the ocean, tugs towing barges and log rafts, fishing boats, playboats, ducks.

Old Glendale retains the past in the present. Clinton once was the terminus of the only railroad ever built on Whidbey and in 1884 was a supply base for logging camps. Steamer service from Seattle began in 1907, the Mukilteo ferry in 1927. The history is thick but the beaches are too populated to be choice.

Possession Point–Possession Beach Park

Drive Highway 525 north 1.8 miles from the ferry and turn left on Campbell Road. In 1.6 miles turn left on Cultus Bay Road, signed "Possession Park." In 4 more miles, where this turns right, stay straight on

Possession Road. In 2 miles more turn right on Possession Park Road.

Sailing past on the day he took possession of New Georgia for his king, Captain Vancouver named the southern tip of the island for the event. Separating Puget Sound from Possession Sound, it is a magic spot to stand with steep bluff at your back and gaze across the broad waters.

The Island County park is a pretty little thing; especially nice are the bridges over the linear lagoon between bluff and dune line. The beach to Glendale, 4 miles, is attractive.

However, the big show is the other way. A 100-foot wall of vertical till announces the onset of wildness. Views north to the Mukilteo ferry, Three Fingers, and Baker yield to views south to the Edmonds–Kingston ferry, Seattle's West Point, and Rainier. The bluff leaps to its towering maximum of 380 feet. Boats cluster, fishing the legendary Possession Hole. Then the shore rounds to views of the Olympics and the 1 mile of wild beach ends at the flats of Cultus (Chinook jargon for "useless") Bay. Until the recent past the walk would have climaxed in a wondrous ½ mile along the spit of Sandy Hook, a superb lagoon on one side, the ¾-mile-wide bay (at low tide, mudflats) on the other. The Skagits had two longhouses here, the better to harvest the clams. Now the lagoon has been dredged to harbor a hundred or two stinkpots. Spit and upland slopes are a yuppie slum.

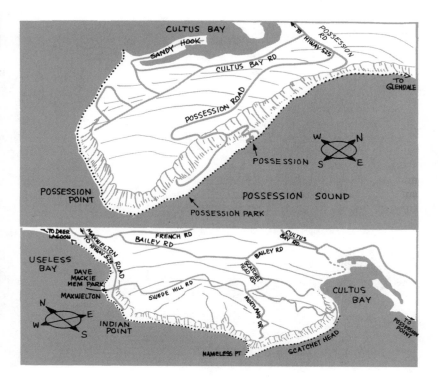

Indian Point–Scatchet Head

Drive Highway 525 from the ferry 3.7 miles and turn south on Maxwelton Road 4.7 miles to Maxwelton. Park at Dave Mackie Memorial (Island County) Park.

Though a bit lower than that of Possession Point, the bluff from Indian Point to Scatchet (a variant of Skagit) Head is longer—more than 2 continuous miles—and more vertical—a steep leap of 300 feet—and more naked. It thus is unmolested by subdividers, the longest stretch of wildness on the island's southwest shore.

Maxwelton dates to the 1890s as a resort community. A bit later, steamers from Seattle and Everett brought city folk to an amusement park and Chautauqua auditorium. The past remained alive in a venerable general store until its conversion to a home. Happily, in 1989 it was re-stored.

To the north, 1 long mile along the baymouth bar (the former lagoon is pasturized, though not occupied) brings the end of homes. A bluff as high as 200 feet rises, wild and free, 2 long miles to the double spit enclosing Deer Lagoon. The totally Private, built-out spit (Sunlight Beach) once was home for hundreds and hundreds of seals. It will be again after C/4.

The feature journey is the other direction. Walk the beach away from the village-on-the-sandflats (after 100 feet, on state Department of Natural Resources land) in views over Useless Bay to Double Bluff, out to ship

Maxwelton Beach

traffic of Main Street (here, still Puget Sound), the winking light of Point No Point, Foulweather Bluff and the mouth of Hood Canal, and the Olympics from Angeles to Zion to Constance and south. In ¾ mile is Indian Point and its 200-foot cliff, partly tanglewooded, then bare. The precipice steepens, rises to an awesome 260 feet in one lift from the beach, naked drift capped by vertical till. Among clay beds is a peat layer of leaves, twigs, cedar bark, and fir cones, not years or decades old but millennia. So steep the bluff becomes, a straight-up 300 feet, that chunks constantly fall; slides of huge clay boulders tumble far out in the water to be battered by waves.

At 1½ miles from Indian Point a nameless point thrusts out, the bluff lays back, and a trail descends from the rim, 340 feet up. Now the view is south up the Sound to Edmonds, the ferry, Appletree Point, West Point. The bluff loses its woods and is again steep and naked to Scatchet Head. A final ½ mile leads to a boulder bulkhead and a subdivision that is not thriving due to the heavy-heavy-hangs-over-thy-head bluff.

Double Bluff

Drive Highway 525 from the ferry 8.3 miles and turn left on Double Bluff Road, which in 1.9 miles ends on Useless Bay. The unsigned Public access has paved parking for some two dozen cars, but no boat-launch, and that's a mercy. (Kayaks don't need a ramp.)

The sand cliff is a noble eminence, the most awesome naked bluff on the Whulge, rising 367 feet from the water in a single vault. An Island County park's 1000 feet of beach connects the Public road to the Public tidelands and uplands of an undeveloped state park.

Birders should not ignore the wetlands east of the parking. Though the baymouth bar is built-up solid, the 1½ miles to the mouth of Deer

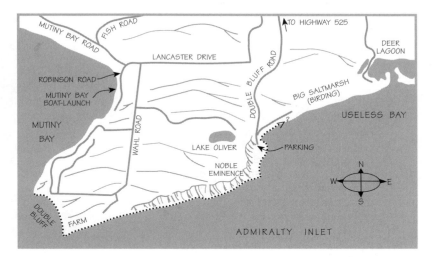

Lagoon, the saltmarsh behind the bar, a square mile of it, is partly pasture, partly wild grass and reeds, and a blending of fresh and salt wetness. Abandoned dikes and lines of fence posts testify to a victory of Mother Nature over the Pale Galilean. Approaches from Sunlight Beach and the adjoining upland are guarded by the Privates, though lone Publics are rumored to slip through the defenses to walk the old dikes.* Accesses via the baymouth bar and the Double Bluff Road appear feasible.

The other direction is the way to go for beach, bluff, and view. The sand beach quickly leaves domiciles behind and bumps against the foot of the noble eminence. A safe path weaves upward through sand cliffs to the top for a panorama of seas and shores. Hereabouts the name of Main Street changes from Puget Sound to Admiralty Inlet; the traffic is the same—heavy. Directly across the street is Foulweather Bluff at the mouth of Hood Canal, south is Edmonds, and north is Marrowstone Island. Beyond rise the Olympics, from foothills of Zion and Walker to snowy heights of Townsend and Constance. *Himmel.*

Descend to the beach and proceed by an exceptional variety of glacial drift from two ages, by eagle snags and maybe the eagles, and by a Grand Canyon–like gulch sliced in the sand.

The bluff dwindles and at 2 miles rounds a point, atop whose low bank is a navigation light and a spacious cow pasture, now as for a century. An idyllic scene. Will State Parks find the funds to buy the farm before it is cut up in lots? Probably not. In ½ mile more is the point named Double Bluff on maps. Here start Mutiny Bay and another mob of houses.

West Coast Trail

A visitor from Puget Sound City feels an exhilarating release from claustrophobic, mountain-walled confines of the inner Whulge. On a clear day you can see Asia, from whence roar the gales that stir oceanic surfs, sculpt the bonsai forests, wave the grass of the Mendocino-like sea-meadows. Despite subdividers braving the winds to trash the flats, the bluffs remain unconquerable and here is the longest stretch of unmolested beach this side of Olympic National Park. There are other attractions, too: the Olympic rainshadow, Main Street traffic of ships and boats, the Weird Pits of Point Partridge, old-lakebed Ebey's Prairie, spits and baymouth bars and lagoons, mementoes of ancient wars, and—climaxing all—Ebey's Landing National Historic Preserve.

The supreme walk of the island is ... the whole thing, of course. In 1962 four teenage lads circled the entire shore in a single backpacking go. Their report gives the shoreline distance as 201 miles and says the feat was accomplished in 5 days and nights.

In the 1970s a proposal was floated by the International Boundary Commission to establish an international park to knit together Cana-

---

*See the publisher's note on private property on page 11.

dian and American shores from Vancouver Island to Whidbey Island. It was like sticking a firebrand in a bee tree. Speculators and developers of two nations came out a-buzzing and a-stinging and brandishing their money. That was that.

The significance of the Whidbey West Coast already has merited a federal presence. Deception Pass State Park was shaped in the 1930s by Civilian Conservation Corps crews working under National Park Service direction. The Park Service is again on the island, supervising creation of Ebey's Landing National Historic Preserve.

There is the history, to an unusual extent preserved from the ravages of plat-happy exploiters. There are the plant and animal communities of sea and land, abiding side by side in a state of relatively undisturbed nature. And there is the beach.

Why is this the most-famed, most-acclaimed beach of the Whulge? Because of the vigorous weather and surf of the weather shore, where storms blow freely in from the ocean. Because of the wilderness that prevails due to the discouragement of dense habitation by the weather and the sea cliffs. Because of the storm-tortured forests, so much like those of the ocean coast, and the tawny seameadows, so much like those of green-and-gold California. Because of the busy Main Street waterway, always something going this way or that, and views from Baker to the San Juans to the Olympics to Rainier. Because of eagles and old forest. That's some of it. And unlike the wilderness oceans of Olympic National Park, it's all close enough to Puget Sound City for easy day hikes.

We describe beaches of the west coast as a linked "trail" because one leads inevitably to another and a hiker cannot but wish to connect them with his/her feet.

A note about Privatization here: Through some fortuity, long stretches of Whidbey shorelands which were granted by Congress to the state upon statehood never were put on the auction block. Upland Privates try here, as everywhere, to lay claim to the beaches abutting their properties. "Bluff" signs are ubiquitous, often quite menacing. For example, a "Please Respect Private Property Rights" is signed by "Washington State Department of Game" (which no longer exists) and "Island County Sheriff." The plea for "respect" is entirely proper, but the claim to "private property rights" is a sorry example of two law-enforcement agencies (one of them nonexistent) ignorant of the common law. But what the heck—yelling and screaming ruin a hike, so here we feature the beaches where nobody squawks louder than a gull.

Brief note must be made of two Public accesses of lesser interest to travelers from afar.

Mutiny Bay Boat-Launch. Drive Mutiny Bay Road south of Bush Point to Robinson Road, at whose end is a large parking area and Sanikan.

Bush Point. Drive Smugglers Cove Road to Scurlock Road (signed "Bush Point"), which becomes Main Street, which intersects Sandpiper Road. Turn right to the end. Parking for two cars (more along Main Street).

South Whidbey State Park

Drive Highway 525 north from Freeland and turn off west on Bush Point Road, which becomes Smugglers Cove Road and in 6 miles from the highway reaches South Whidbey State Park. Park at the entry lot if the park gate is closed, or at the main lot a short way north, or in the campground, farther north.

Walk on the beach, walk in the forest of ancient Douglas firs and cedars and hemlocks, an island of antiquity amid second-growth. Sky-open waters and green-twilight woods combine for an experience greater than the sum of the parts.

Several routes sample the 87 acres of park on the west side of the highway; these were acquired from trust lands of the University of Washington in the 1960s. From the parking lot picnic area at the entry, the Loop Trail goes ½ mile south on the bluff rim and returns inland for a 1-mile total. The Beach Trail and the Hobbit Trail take off from the network of paths in the vicinity of the main parking lot and campground and switchback down ½ mile in old conifers and younger deciduous trees; put the trails together with the beach between their outlets for a loop of 1 mile.

Inland of Smugglers Cove Road are the 250 acres of the "Classic U" tract, added to the park in 1985, again from University of Washington trust lands. The forest is partly second-growth getting on to be a century old and partly Douglas firs and western red cedars more than 250 years of age. Called "the true gem of South Whidbey," directly across the road from the park entry is the Wilbert Trail. Dedicated in 1982, it is named for Harry Wilbert, Colonel (retired) U.S. Army Corps of Engineers, the island resident who led the fight to save the trees. The 1½-mile path winds about to take in the choice groves, including a really big tree, and exits on Smugglers Cove Road at 0.3 mile from the park entry.

South from South Whidbey State Park to Bush Point, 2 miles

The next C/4 will permit the trail be extended south under a green riot of bluff to what will then be the cleansed site of the now-existing village on Bush Point, 2 more newly wild miles to Mutiny Bay, and excellent lonesome walking onward to Double Bluff.

North from South Whidbey State Park to Keystone Harbor, 12 miles

Were this the only Whidbey walk, it would be repeatedly featured in Sunday supplements and national magazines. But being on Whidbey, and the west coast at that, it is a largely overlooked overture to the grand opera. Several intermediate accesses split the route into day-digestible walks.

The 1 mile of park beach gets the boots going. The next 1½ miles to Lagoon Point, and the 1¼ miles around the point, are a high priority for C/4 cleansing. The primeval lagoon was among the finest on the island. However, the developer not only has put rows of picture windows along the dune line and the bluff foot but also in between has dredged two stinkpot harbors, used the spoils to build a peninsula between them, and

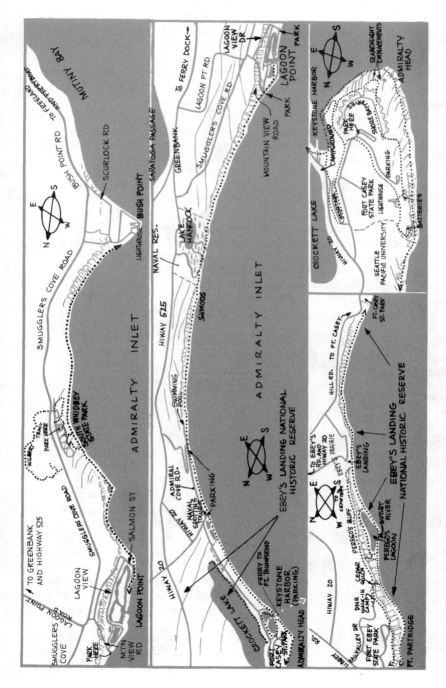

covered that up with houses as well. The spit has two Public beach accesses. For *Salmon Street,* drive Smugglers Cove Road to Lagoon Point Road and turn left to Salmon Street and the end. For *Mountain View Road,* drive Smugglers Cove Road to Mountain View Road to its end.

In the 1¾ miles north from Lagoon Point the bluff is exceptionally steep, too formidable to let Privatizers near the water. Where the cliff lowers to naught, a ¾-mile baymouth bar has completely cut off an ancient bay, enclosing a half-mile-square lagoon, mostly tidal marshes, partly Lake Hancock. The Navy owns the lake and the lagoon. A faded sign used to warn "Danger. Absolutely No Trespassing. Bomb and Rocket Target Area." However, the gate on the access road was in ruins and locals drove ¾ mile past the marsh to picnic at the beach. In 1988 the Navy repaired the gate to keep out vehicles, erected fences, and resorted to a new threat: "Warning. Keep out. Helicopter Practice Landing Area." A birdwatcher driving Highway 525 a scant 1 mile north of Smugglers Cove Road cannot but cast a fond eye on Lake Hancock, close by the highway. Just north is the gated road which certainly, in the very near future, will become the foot-only access to a state or federal wildlife sanctuary.

The 3 miles from the baymouth bar of Lake Hancock to the start of Keystone Spit (baymouth bar of Crockett Lake) are best accessed via *Driftwood Drive Public Boat-Launch.* From Highway 525 drive Ledgewood Beach Drive 0.4 mile to Fircrest Drive, turn left 0.4 mile to Seaweed Way, go left 0.3 mile to Driftwood, and 0.1 mile to the end. Between two houses is parking for five cars.

Great blue heron

These 3 miles are totally lonesome except for a handful of houses on a slump terrace at the halfway point. The bluff rises as high as 150 feet, in places vertical and stark naked. Particularly striking is a section of till just north of Lake Hancock where erosion has carved a badlands of cleavers and chimneys and pillars. The beach pebbles are outstanding, many agates. The most fun are the hard concretions formed in clay strata and now strewn about. The traditional name is "mud babies" but fans of Li'l Abner recognize his friends the Shmoos.

The swimming pool of Admirals Cove Estates preludes the 1 mile along the bar to Highway 20, the tidelands all Public, and that's good, but the upland, including the former dune line, all Privatizer glass eyes staring at the walker, and that's bad. The final 1¾ miles to Keystone Harbor also are on the bar, but thanks to environmental heroism of the 1960s and 1970s, almost entirely houseless; here is the longest beach walk on the island that (1) is essentially natural and (2) has no bluff; one is reminded of Dungeness Spit. Interestingly, those parts of the bar that were saved from the developer are now *Keystone Beach (Island County) Park*. Four plainly signed gravel lanes go between houses to the driftwood.

Many a hiker will leave the beach, cross Highway 20, and walk beside 600-acre Crockett Lake, feeding and resting ground for hundreds of waterfowl at a time, plus herons and their sort; one winter the older surveyor, driving by, exclaimed at the disgraceful roadside litter of white plastic bags, until he noted that some of them were snowy owls down from the Arctic. Developers once proposed to do a Lagoon Point job here, on a vastly larger scale, but were prevented by an outraged citizenry and a phalanx of good-guy attorneys.

Lake, spit (bar), and beach end at Keystone Harbor, where Fort Casey Picnic Area is located on an enormous fill. The earlier landing of the Keystone Ferry was so exposed the Army Engineers dredged the harbor for a new landing as well as a stinkpot shelter. The longshore currents that built the bar continue to dump loads, requiring the Army to return every half-dozen years to dredge.

One marvels that the ferry was so important to the nation. The voyage does make a dandy sidetrip for a passenger (no car) across Admiralty Inlet to Port Townsend and back again. Because the ferry must thread through ship traffic, barge traffic, and tug-and-log-raft traffic—all of which have the right-of-way—the crossing sometimes takes an hour. In a storm the experience is almost too thrilling.

Fort Casey State Park

For the complete tour, drive Highway 20 to Keystone Harbor and park at the Fort Casey Picnic Area. Other parking is across the harbor, at the campground entry, and on heights of Admiralty Head.

At the turn of the century, when the United States was conquering the Sandwich Islands, bullying rickety old Spain, annexing the Caribbean and the Pacific, it behooved the military to expect such truculence to make somebody angry. To guard Puget Sound from naval assault by any possible foe, Admiralty Inlet was fortified with the "Triangle of Fire," or "Death Triangle," or "Devil's Triangle," composed of Fort Casey, Fort Flagler, and Fort Worden. The guns of Fort Casey were mounted in 1900, test-fired in 1901, and melted down after 1922. In World War II the fort was reactivated as a training center, but in 1950 no further military use could be devised; in 1956 State Parks acquired 137 acres.

The recommended tour ascends a path from the campground entrance to the site of the mortar batteries hidden behind the hill from enemy

Old gun mount at Fort Casey

ships; proceeds along the park-entry road to the shore batteries, the concrete-and-steel emplacements so preserved and safeguarded that warlike children can easily spend an afternoon at games; and examines the spotting bunkers and searchlight emplacements. The walk culminates in the domain of Peace, the lighthouse. The original house, built in 1860, was torn down to make way for the batteries. The successor, erected in 1902, was retired in the 1920s and now serves as the park museum and interpretive center. So neat and tidy is the structure, metalwork painted black, walls white, and roof red, it's a pity the light is no longer there to keep company with those still winking through the night from the other old forts of the Triangle.

Admiralty Head is the climactic viewpoint of the West Coast Trail. North are the San Juan Islands, Vancouver Island, and, out beyond the water horizon, China. There are the Olympics from Angeles and Big Skidder Hill to Zion and Walker and Constance. In the distance is the plume of the mill at Port Angeles and directly across the waters is the pulpmill plume of Port Townsend; the lighthouse winking at the tip of Point Wilson marks Fort Worden State Park. Farther south is the third member of the Triangle, Fort Flagler State Park. The busiest Main Street marine-traffic view in the region has merchant ships and fishing boats and tugs and barges and playboats and Navy vessels and, dodging through it all, the Keystone–Townsend ferry.

North from Fort Casey State Park to Ebey's Landing, 2½ miles

At Fort Casey begins the longest stretch of undeveloped beach on the island, only minor intrusions for the north 9½ miles to Hastie Lake Road and the most of it Public. The rounding of Keystone Harbor and the jut of Admiralty Head cover 1½ miles of ferry landing, campground, and the beach below the guns. A portion of the old fort, some 87 acres, was acquired by Seattle Pacific University, whose hired hands occasionally put on Private airs.

The "Ebey-type" sand bluff (largely loess blown here by dry glacial winds) rises up, lowering on the north to Ebey's Landing. This stretch north to the Landing is exceeded in beauty and popularity only by the beach and bluff north from the Landing.

Ebey's Landing National Historic Preserve

Drive Highway 20 to a short bit north of the Coupeville pedestrian overpass, turn west on Terry Road, and when this bends left continue straight on Ebey Road, which in 2 miles from the highway dives off the brink of the table (ancient lakebed) to Ebey's Landing. (Just before the brink, look south to the Ferry House, built in 1860. Ebey's home was a few yards farther south.)

Many millennia ago the ancestors of the Salish arrived here, even before the saltwater flowed in to fill the savannah trough and form the Whulge. First hunters, then fishers, always gatherers, they became part-time farmers, annually burning the forests and undergrowth to provide more growing room for the camas, the blue-flowering plant whose bulb made so tasty a change from a heavily protein diet, and the bracken fern, whose root was ground into flour. In the early 1830s the Skagits, the island people, obtained potatoes from the Hudson's Bay Company; the tuber from the mountains of South America, via Europe, rewarded cultivation much more handsomely than native plants. So envious were neighbors across the water, the Klallams, that the Skagits looked to the fortification of their villages on Penn Cove.

European germs, and then European settlers, brought a new era. In 1850 Isaac N. Ebey filed his claim on lands from which the Skagits had evicted Thomas Glasgow 2 years earlier. By the next spring Samuel B. Crockett had filed on Crockett Lake. The Alexanders and the Hills soon arrived. Also in the 1850s came sea captains, first to trade, particularly for the oak that made stout hulls and the Douglas fir that made tall masts, and then to settle down as businessmen. Thomas Coupe gave his name to what became the dominant town.

On January 22, 1855, Governor Isaac Stevens snookered the Indians with the Treaty of Point Elliott. This and other swindles brought on the Indian Wars (White Wars). Many leaders of the Whidbey community of Europeans served in the Territorial Volunteers, an armed force (mostly colonels) whose savagery appalled professionals of the U.S. Army. Though the local Skagits didn't take up arms, the European squirearchy built eight blockhouses. It wasn't a bad idea. The Northern Raiders took advantage of the disquiet to intensify their regular visits. In the fall of 1856 a party got away with the Nisqually homesteaders' potato crop. A U.S.

Blockhouse near Ebey's Landing

Navy ship caught up with them and on October 20 fought the famous Battle of Port Gamble, killing and wounding half the 100-man force, capturing the survivors and dumping them at Victoria. Having lost a principal chief, reconnaissance parties of Northerners returned in January of 1857 to seek a suitably eminent enemy to provide them "a head for a head." They decided on Dr. John Coe Kellogg, the medicine man, but after waiting 3 days for him to return from a trip to Olympia, went for their second choice. The night of August 11 they removed Colonel Ebey's head and carried it away north. In 1859 a diplomatic mission by the Hudson's Bay Company recovered the head for burial with the rest of the colonel.

The prairies entered a shifting, tortuous, often hardscrabble, but continuous farming history—wheat, oats, potatoes, onions, garden truck, sheep, milk, whatever the market would accept. The farming continues to this day, the longest continuously farmed land in the state, the Europeans starting in the 1850s, the Skagits 20 years earlier with potatoes—and many centuries earlier with camas.

In the 1960s the farming, as inevitably for the European-Americans as it had for the Original Settlers, met its natural enemy—the subdivider. Keystone Spit and Crockett Lake were fated to become picture-window stinkpot communities of the wealthies. Ebey's Prairie was to be cut up in city-size lots of houses and carports and lawns. It was a consummation not to be endured by the Friends of Ebey. Their efforts culminated in November of 1978 with establishment by Congress of Ebey's Landing National Historic Preserve—the first such in the nation.

The reserve—officially created to commemorate the exploration of the Whulge by Vancouver in 1792, the settlement by Ebey and friends, the Donation Land Law of 1850–55, and the growth since 1883 of the town of Coupeville—cannot forget the Skagits, whose disease-decimated and demoralized remnant was deported in the 1850s, perhaps 13,000 years after their ancestors arrived. The boundaries of the reserve encompass Fort Casey State Park, Crockett Lake and Keystone Spit, part of Smith Prairie, Coupeville and the entire shore of Penn Cove, Fort Ebey State Park, and the shore of the adjoining Whulge. The National Park Service has purchased some lands where subdivision threatened and, elsewhere, development rights and scenic easements. Ultimately, when the preserve has been rounded out, management will be turned over to a non-federal agency.

In 1994, 15 years after establishment of the reserve (12 of these the park-starving reigns of Reagan and Bush), the Park Service lacks funds to supply interpretive materials and maintain a local staff. The best introduction to the reserve is the kiosk by the entry to the Coupeville Wharf (1900), where maps and text tell the history in some detail and point the way to the historic structures and sites. In Coupeville itself are a bit of the cross the Skagits made for Father Blanchett when he came in 1849 to instruct them; the 1853 house of Thomas Coupe; the Methodist church of 1853; the Alexander Blockhouse moved here from its original site; and the museum of the Island County Historical Association.

North from Ebey's Landing to Fort Ebey State Park, 6 miles

The Ebey Classic is from the Landing north to Perego's Lagoon, returning south atop Perego's Bluff, taking a sidetrip to the cemetery.

A few steps north of the beachside parking area is Landing Gully, dug through the 60-foot bank to the prairie to give wagons a way. Passengers and mail from the metropolis of Port Townsend destined for Coupeville ascended the gully. A canal was projected to Penn Cove. A city was laid out at the west end and named "Chicago." Its three-storey hotel collapsed and by the end of 1891 the bubble had burst. From the gully bottom a staircase climbs the bank to a brink trail at the edge of the cultivated fields; this is the way to Perego's Bluff. If the beach route is chosen, 1¾ miles of sublime shore lead to the north end of spit-enclosed Perego's Lagoon (Lake). (Note: Some years storms rip a hole in the spit and the usually brackish lagoon becomes subject to the tides. The outlet is then a wide and perhaps a roaring river, in and out. In such case it may be necessary to detour on a path along the lagoon at the bluff foot.)

From the north end of the driftwood-filled lagoon, a steep path climbs the tawny sand and green grass and (in season) brilliant flowers to the lip of Perego's Bluff, 240 feet above the brown-white driftwood line, the gray beach, the white breakers, and the gray-green sea. Views are over Main Street traffic to three mountain ranges—Vancouver Island, the Olympics, and the Cascades. Way out there is the water horizon, the edge of the world, source of the winds that so buffet the Douglas fir and Sitka spruce they have the appearance of being tortured for centuries by a Japanese bonsai artist.

The path passes the Cemetery Trail, a mandatory sidetrip. But the Classic can as well start and end in a loop from the cemetery. Drive Highway 20 for 1 mile north from the Coupeville pedestrian overpass, turn left on Sherman Road, then right on Cemetery Road, and 0.3 mile from the highway enter the cemetery parking lot.

Tour the headstones marking graves dating back to 1861. Find memorials to Ebey, Crockett, Alexander, and others of the pioneer community. George W. Samuel H. Perego was a latecomer, taking up a claim on a

Perego's Lagoon and the Strait of Juan de Fuca from the bluff trail north of Ebey's Landing

bluff he felt the Army would want. He chose the wrong spot for gunnery purposes and anyway died in 1897, just as the Death Triangle was being built. Until then he lived as a hermit with three dogs, watching for a hostile navy. Also at the cemetery is the Davis Blockhouse, one of the eight of 1855; it was a mercy for the settlers that they never had to stand a siege here.

A trail runs 1 mile from the cemetery to Perego's Bluff, and this walk is the quintessential experience of Ebey's Prairie, described in the Park Service brochure: "The square mile of primitive prairie that was Isaac Neff Ebey's by right of entry ... without question the prize acres of the whole of Whidbey Island, if not the whole of Washington Territory. No matter how you come upon it, you know when you are there.... The special ambience it radiates reaches to the visual horizons, and beyond, on all sides. It is not that this area has not changed; it is that the landscape has absorbed the impact of 13,000 years of human habitation and changed so little—and so gracefully." Contouring through cultivated fields on the slope, a hundred feet above the table-flat (old lakebed? old bay floor?) prairie, the dark soil exposed where newly plowed, the green carpet lush where crops are growing, the walker's eye mingles the land with the water; in early April the eye may spot blue flowers around the unplowed edge of the prairie—the camas—and gaze into that past where the entire prairie bloomed blue.

Nobody lives on the beach north of Ebey's Landing. Nobody lives atop the 200-foot bluff, largely composed of "Ebey sand," blown by winds from glacial-outwash plains. These 3¼ wild miles on the shore of the vasty

Whulge can be walked from either end or the intermediate DNR Point Partridge Beach Area.

At ¾ mile from the north end of Perego's Lagoon, the bluff is deeply notched by creekless Cedar Gulch, which stimulates an exercise in geo-morphological theorizing. A DNR staircase-trail ascends the north side of the gulch to the walk-in camps and picnic tables of the *Point Partridge Recreation Site*. The access, Hall Valley Drive (see Fort Ebey State Park), has been gated due to a slippage on the bluff but is planned for reopening in 1994.

Inland, this section of Whidbey Island is remarkable for the Weird Pits, the holes up to 100 feet or more deep that pock the ground east to Penn Cove, separated by ridges just as mysterious. The older surveyor, noticing them from the highway, supposed they were gravel mines. In time he began to wonder who on earth (or in outer space?) ever had such an insatiable appetite for gravel. It was on the bluff at Point Partridge the revelation came. This is hill-and-kettle topography. The glacier from Canada, in retreating, left chunks of ice buried in moraine; eventually melting, these produced the deep holes—the kettles.

From Cedar Gulch the way lies beneath the blufftop Fort Ebey State Park and Point Partridge Lighthouse 1½ miles to a little driftwood-filled lagoon the awakened eye recognizes as a kettle broken into by the waves. A major trail comes down the slope from a parking area near Lake Pondilla.

Fort Ebey State Park

From Highway 20 go off west on Libbey Point Road 1 mile and turn left on Hall Valley Drive 0.6 mile to the park entrance. For the north section of the park, turn right at the T just inside the gate 0.3 mile to parking for the Bluff Trail and Lake Pondilla. For the south section, turn left at the entry T. In 0.3 mile a sideroad goes right to the parking for the gun batteries and the Bluff Trail. A bit beyond is the campground.

Some people insist the fort was built before World War I to cover a blind spot not directly in line with the guns of the Death Triangle; never mind, they say, the "1942" set in the concrete of the ammunition lockers. Clearly, the fort dates from World War II, by which time the guns were long gone from the Triangle forts. The Army emplaced guns at several spots on the entry from the Pacific Ocean, including two 6-inchers at Fort Ebey. A major Japanese task force was not expected; it would, however, have been embarrassing for a squadron of destroyers to land a force of Imperial Marines on Whidbey and capture Coupeville.

The park was established on 227 acres donated to the state by the Army in 1968 and developed and opened to the public in 1981. In 1985 a 350-acre parcel of DNR land was transferred to the park. Most of the park is hill-and-kettle, second-growth Douglas fir, and thickets of salal and rhododendron, broken by small prairies (cleared by the military). The walking interest is close to the shore, on the beach and atop the bluff.

From the north parking area, a trail drops a short bit to Lake Pondilla, bilious green water beloved of ducks and binoculars; it is, of course, a kettle, the best of the lot. Another trail breaks through the thicket of wind-deviled trees to seameadows above "Broken Kettle Lagoon" and descends to the beach. The walker should not hurry down. Sit in the grass and train glasses on the enormous kelp bed, watching for diners, winged or flippered. (New Americans recently arrived from homelands where everything except rocks is considered edible if not a delicacy are wreaking havoc with kelp beds; they badly need education.)

The Bluff Trail runs 2 miles from Broken Kettle to Cedar Gulch, often on the brink of the bluff, in views over the Whulge to the Olympics and Vancouver Island, the rest of the time a few feet away behind the windscreen of tough trees and thickety undergrowth. The Point Partridge Light, a little automated box, is passed. The mounts of the 6-inch guns have some interest. The concrete ammunition lockers can be explored by flashlight. A broad terrace was bulldozed below the guns to permit them to bear straight down on the Imperial Marines as they waded ashore. Barb-wire barricades were supplemented by plantings of gorse, which blooms a pretty yellow the year round and viciously stabs anyone coming in touch.

The trail continues south to the campground at whose far end are other entries to the Bluff Trail through walk-in camps extending out to the brink of the bluff. On one visit the older surveyor encountered winds so strong on the open bluff he could scarcely stand—and a dozen yards inland, behind the screen of wolf trees and head-high salal, the air in the camps was virtually still—beneath a mighty river roaring in the treetops.

Beyond the campground the Bluff Trail continues ½ mile to Cedar

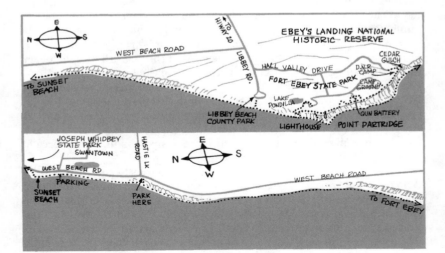

Gulch. Plans are eventually to extend it down into and up out of the gulch to Perego's Bluff.

North from Fort Ebey State Park to Joseph Whidbey State Park, 7 miles

If most of the best lies south, some of the darn good lies north. Intermediate accesses permit short walks.

At 1 mile from Broken Kettle Lagoon is *Libbey Beach County Park*. Drive Libbey Road west 1.3 miles from Highway 20 to its end.

Stand atop the beach meadows and gaze over the Whulge to the broad gap between America and Canada, to the water horizon of the Oceane Sea. For every dozen hikers who head south from Libbey Beach, only one heads north. The better for the solitude. Though rather different, the beach north is equally fine and, in its own specialties, more spectacular.

Public tidelands extend 6 miles north. The bluff rises to over 200 feet, stunningly precipitous much of the way, keeping houses from the beach the entire distance. Unlike the "Ebey-type" sand bluff south of Point Partridge, here the mix is a standard clay and sand and gravel and till, some rocklike, from older glacial times, forming noble tall cliffs.

The view rounds to northward vistas into Rosario Strait, past the lighthouse on Smith Island, to the San Juan Islands and the heights of Erie and Constitution.

Then the bluff drops to houses and the *Hastie Lake Road Boat-Launch,* 2½ miles from Libbey Beach. The kelp beds attract throngs of binoculars—and, disastrously, harvesters.

Beyond a short row of houses, the bluff leaps up once more. In 1 mile the beach rounds 100-foot-high "Vertical Till Point" and enters a shallow cove. Now the clay-sand precipice rises steadily higher, finally to 250 feet—as exciting as anything south of Point Partridge. In a most impressive stretch the alternating strata of sand and clay form Grand Canyon–like steps.

Then the bluff drops to nothing and man snuggles up to the water. A Public parking area here is reached by driving West Beach Road north 2½ miles from Hastie Lake Road. The ancient bay, now Swantown Valley, is shored by 1 mile of Sunset Beach houses. However, at the north end of the onetime baymouth bar is good news again.

Joseph Whidbey State Park

Drive Highway 20 to Swantown Road. Follow its sharp bend right to Crosby Road, which leads to parking, picnic tables, and a beach trail.

The Navy has leased 112 acres to State Parks. These end in a long ½ mile but feet proceed unmolested on 3 miles of beach that are lonesome-wild except for little-used Navy-only picnic sites. The shore from Swantown Valley to the north tip of the island is very different from that to the south. The bluff lowers, recedes inland, and virtually vanishes, replaced by a series of cutoff bays where the winds blow free, blowing up sand dunes, or trying—Navy bulldozers flatten them out.

At 1¾ miles the bluff briefly rears up. Here, at Rocky Point, is Whidbey's

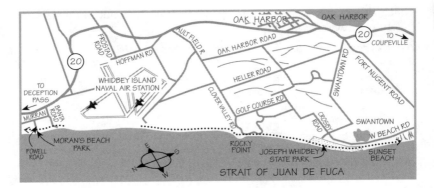

southernmost west-side exposure of non-glacial, San Juan–like bedrock, intricately eroded by the waves. In another 1¼ miles of solitude, a little bluff rises to a Navy park. Beyond its bulge are Clover Valley and Ault Field. It is technically conceivable for a walker to scamper across the 1 mile of jet strip to the West Beach of Deception Pass State Park. However, given the average of one takeoff/landing every 15 minutes the day around, the year around, the odds are the scamperer's brains would be scrambled by a Top Gun.

Moran's Beach Park. If you enjoy watching the Top Guns from the south side of Ault Field, you won't want to miss the north side. Turn west from Highway 20 on Banta Road, then right on Murran Road, and then left on Powell Road to its end at the beach. When Ault Field is closed, as the Navy will soon be forced to do by regional hatred and national poverty, this Island County park will be part of the connection between Joseph Whidbey and Deception Pass State Parks.

Deception Pass State Park

Drive Highway 20 to Fidalgo Island and at a Y turn south, signed "Deception Pass." Or ferry from Mukilteo to Clinton and drive the length of Whidbey Island. The park lies on both sides of the highway and both sides of Deception Pass, on both Whidbey and Fidalgo Islands.

If a person were compelled to select a single spot for all wanderings of saltwater shores and forests, there could be no better choice than Deception Pass State Park. One would think Mother Nature felt cramped for space in Creation, forced to stuff so many goodies in such small room: ancient Douglas fir up to 9 feet in diameter, virgin grand fir, Sitka spruce, shore pine, juniper, and madrona contorted and sculpted by storm winds blowing from the Pacific Ocean; grassy seameadows, flower-bright in season, and rock gardens of moss and lichen on headlands looking out to the San Juan Islands; myriad surprising little coves and secluded pocket beaches, and islands and off-shore rocks, and former islands (tombolos) connected to the mainland by sand necks; kelp beds and rafts of waterfowl, seals cavorting, eagles nesting and hawks soaring, and mobs of herons flapping to and from a heronry; pretty-pebble beaches, tidal marshes, and a sand-floored, tea-water, sea-level lake, enclosed by a baymouth bar topped by the best sand dunes on the Whulge; buttresses of heavily metamorphosed volcanic rock polished and rounded and scratched by the glacier. To this man adds small boats (and sometimes, amazingly, log rafts pulled and pushed by tugs) navigating cliff-walled Deception Pass, where at turns of the tide the water runs river-swift and turbulent; and history of Indians, explorers, and the Civilian Conservation Corps—and a penal colony. All in the rainshadow of the Olympics, where mossy citizens of Puget Sound City flock in winter for a chance to see the sun.

The bulk of the park was preserved in virginity (or near such) as a military reservation until turned over to the state in 1925. In 1933 the CCC, supervised by the National Park Service, began developing roads and trails and building shelters, the craftsmanship in stone and timber contributing a rustic charm. The 3500-acre park hosts 2,000,000-odd people a year for camping (254 sites), swimming, boating, and hiking the dozens of miles of trails and beach.

So many are the delightful nooks, so intricately interwoven the paths, and so many the convenient parking areas, a pedestrian can assemble the ingredients in a virtually infinite number of superb recipes. Short walks can be taken, a mile or less, fun enough to keep a child—or adult—entertained all day. Or these can be linked in longer rambles. Described here, to stimulate the imagination, are combinations that among them pretty well sample the park.

(Note: The park is distinguished by unclimbable cliffs plunging to unswimmably swift water. The rangers annually rescue scores of bold idiots. Please stay on safe paths and beaches.)

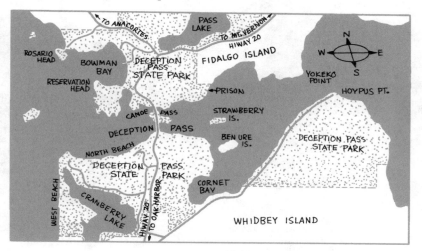

West Beach–North Beach

This tour will not be the first choice by the average walker but is the lead-off here because it is the denouement of Whidbey's West Coast Trail. We start by stirring together a melange of three strolls. The melange can be done from several parking areas. For one (no better than the others), drive the highway south of the bridge to the park headquarters entry. Following "West Beach" signs, drive to the large parking area at West Beach.

Stroll #1, a Partly Looping Round Trip of 4½ Miles. Head south on West Beach, walkable at all tides, in views to the San Juans and Olympics and the water horizon of the Strait of Juan de Fuca. At ¾ mile is the park boundary, beyond which houses have invaded the dunes, but set back far enough not to disturb enjoyment of waves and waterfowl, the parade of ships south to Puget Sound, and the Taiwan merchant marine carrying billions of quarts of oil to the refineries. At 1⅓ miles from the park the walk must halt, blocked at the outlet creek of Cranberry Lake by the U.S. Naval Reservation and Ault Field, the danger in proceeding lying not so much in being captured as a suspected spy but in being on the beach when a Top Gun passes inches overhead, the noise of his sky motorcycle turning you into a vegetable.

On the way here is *Moran's Beach Park,* already noted.

The beach is great, first cousin of the Dragon Whulge. An inland-looping return, however, leads to The Unique. Here where the rainshadow sun shines and the wild west winds blow there were, until the recent past, miles of sand dunes, far and away the most numerous and the biggest on the Whulge. The ½ mile preserved by the park from Navy and

Sand dunes trail

developers still is the grandest such display on the Whulge. In order to help the preservation, please view the dunes, and the sprawling mass of spruce, hemlock, and fir, from the blacktop paths; indiscriminate walking erodes. See the innermost and highest dunes, standing above the marsh-lake lagoon, representing a drier climate of the past and now mostly anchored by forest. See the outermost dunes, lightly vegetated, moderately active. From the dunes walk by Cranberry Lake, admiring the windblown sands invading water of "ocean tea."

Stroll #2, a Round Trip of 2 Miles. Returned to the parking area, walk north to the jutting rocks of West Point, and take the trail along North Beach, in views over boiling waters of Deception Pass to Fidalgo Island. North Beach consists of four shingle arcs separated by rock points; at moderate tides the route can combine beach and trees, at high it can stay on the forest trail. In 1 long mile North Beach is terminated by up-leaping cliffs.

Stroll #3, 2 Miles One Way. To complete the melange, from the picnic area short of the cliffs walk the trail in big trees up to the North Beach parking lot (alternative start) and proceed up its access road through an "Avenue of the Giants," huge Douglas firs and Sitka spruces and western hemlocks and western red cedars, and also-huge sword fern, to the park headquarters (alternative start).

A ¼-mile nature trail interprets the plant community. After walking that, descend by road or trail to the Cranberry Lake picnic area (alternative start), 1 mile from North Beach. Walk out on the dock to survey the lake, in mood and vegetation reminding of Ozette Lake in Olympic National Park. Follow the shore path, tunneling through 8-foot-high salal, to West Point Road. Soon leave it for trail again and walk by contorted shore pines out on a plank bridge to an islet's rock point, reminding of a lake at 10,000 feet in the High Sierra.

Cornet Bay–Goose Rock

More waterscapes and forestscapes and cliffscapes. Plus a miniature mountain, 475 feet high, giving broad views to far horizons. Goose Rock can be conquered from any number of starting points and by several routes. The surveyors' choice is a loop starting from the North Beach parking lot (closed in winter—park then at park headquarters).

Where one big wide trail drops from the road to the beach, find another boulevard contouring east into big firs, then climbing a rock-garden wall to cross under the highway bridge. The trail goes through woods, gradually dropping near the water, madronas leaning over the beach. Strawberry Island (park) is passed and then Ben Ure Island (private), as the shore rounds to Cornet Bay's marina and houses. At a Y take the right uphill (the left deadends on cliffs) to a moss-garden grass-meadow bald high above the boat-dotted bay. The trail then switchbacks down through wall-hangings of saxifrages and succulents to the beach and a junction 1¼ miles from North Beach.

The path straight ahead leads in ¼ mile to the mudflat head of Cornet

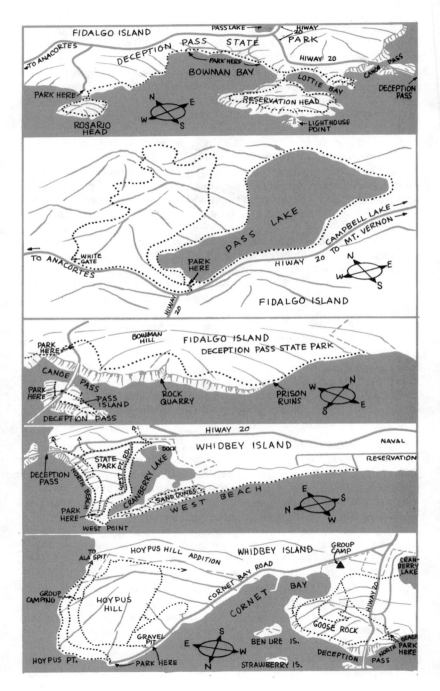

Bay and the park's Group Camp, site of one of the Civilian Conservation Corps work camps (others were at Bowman Bay and park headquarters). Two trails lead from the camp back across the highway, for variants on the suggested loop.

However, from the junction reverse-turn right, uphill, on the Goose Rock trail and switchback ¾ mile through rhododendrons and big, fire-blackened firs to mossy balds and onto the summit dome. Proceed over other ice-rounded rock domes to the west peak and the best views.

Zounds. See far down Camano and Whidbey Islands and Skagit Bay and Rosario Strait, out to the Olympics and Vancouver Island and Lopez and a mess of other San Juans. Especially interesting is the perspective on Cornet Bay, Cranberry Lake, and the dunes. And, on the Whulge, ships and boats, always something going somewhere.

For the looping descent, at the summit note another big obvious trail dropping into the woods. Descend it ½ mile to intersect the North Beach Discovery Trail (starting at the Group Camp). Following a former county road, the trail goes through stunningly huge fire-blackened firs, crosses under the highway, and in ½ mile from Goose Rock trail hits the North Beach road at ¼ mile uphill from the picnic area, completing a 3½-mile loop.

Hoypus Hill–Similk Bay*

Here is the forest primeval, the park's most pristine wilderness. Sheltered from ocean blasts, the trees grow notably tall and straight—it was here the CCC cut the timbers for park structures. The trails being largely overgrown, here too is adventure, and solitude. (For a mystic experience, walk these woods on a foggy morning.) Aside from all that, beachwalking. And entirely different views. Plus, probably, eagles.

Drive south past the park headquarters and turn east on Cornet Bay Road. Pass the Group Camp, a Private marina, and reenter park. Pass the boat-launch parking area and in 0.2 mile note a gated woods road climbing the hill to the right—this is the return leg of the Hoypus Hill loop. Drive on a scant 0.5 mile more to a gravel pit and park.

This is not a view walk, it's a tree walk through the Hoypus Point Natural Forest Area. Climb the woods road past the white gate. Soon the eyes bug, the Douglas firs are so incredibly big and tall. In a long ¼ mile a sideroad goes right; this is an alternative return of the loop (see below). The fire-road trail tops out and contours, passing trails down left to group pack-in camps (used by reservation) served by a hand-pumped well. At 1 mile from the start the trail hits Private property, steeply climbs the hill, and sets out on a compass course due east. To the left is the Hoypus Hill Addition obtained from the state Department of Natural Resources, containing groves comparable to those in the Natural Forest Area, and wetlands as well.

At 1 mile from the Private property line is a junction. The fire trail

*See the publisher's note on private property on page 11.

goes straight; instead, take the road-trail right. Pass two sideroads right which are alternative, shorter returns (see above). Switchback down to the shore road, reached at the white gate in 1 mile of walking from the park's south boundary. Walk the paved road—or beach—to the gravel pit to complete the 3½-mile loop.

A second Hoypus Hill hike combines monster trees with Similk Bay beach and views, plus a spice of history.

Drive past the gravel pit 0.3 mile to the road-end at Hoypus Point. What's this concrete bulkhead for? The ferry. What ferry? The one that until the bridge was built in 1935 crossed to Dewey Beach on Fidalgo Island.

At low tide the beach can be walked 2 miles south to Ala Spit. Across the waters are Kiket and Skagit Islands in Similk Bay. South are Goat and Ika Islands. Trees lean over the beach, including a grand fir that is horizontal 70 feet, its limbs rising straight up as a row of little trees. Look out for seals. (Or was that an otter swimming in the winter twilight?)

At any tide the forest can be enjoyed. From the road-end, scramble up the bank to what was in CCC days a big wide path but now, maintained only by thrusting bodies, is a slow go. But worth it for the jaw-dropping firs. In 1 mile are the pack-in campsites and then Private property.

At the right tide the correct route is forest one way, beach the other.

Canoe (Pass) Island

No short walk in the park is more scenic, more popular, and more dangerous. So take it easy—but take it.

Drive the highway over the bridge to the island-top parking area. Descend the alpine meadow–like rock-garden path, strawberry-blossom bright in spring, grass widows and mahonia blooming as early as February, to the east tip of the island and look to Strawberry Island and Hoypus Point and Yokeko Point. Stroll close by frightening eddies and whirlpools of loud waters, under the bridge, to the west tip and look to Deception Island.

You're really in the middle of things here, in the waterway called "Boca de Flon" by a Spaniard in 1791 and given the modern name the next year by Vancouver, who'd been deceived into thinking he'd found a peninsula until his man Whidbey explored the passage.

Rosario Head–Bowman Bay

Left for the last is what the mostest visitors take the firstest and consider the supremest and they never get to the rest. Only the aficionados explore two other Fidalgo Island treats, Pass Lake and the Prison Camp, where from 1909 to 1923 an average of twenty-five prisoners worked the quarry in the north wall of Canoe Pass.

Quintessential, that's what this melange is—most of the raptures promised by the introduction are delivered here. Three short strolls can be taken separately or combined. From Highway 20 at the south end of Pass Lake, turn right, signed "Rosario." Pass the sideroad down to Bowman

Canoe Pass and Deception Pass bridge

Bay (an alternative parking and starting point), continue 1 mile, and turn left down to the Rosario Beach parking and picnic area.

Stroll #1, a ½–1-Mile Loop. Walk out the grassy neck of the picnic area and up the forest-and-meadow heights of Rosario Head to broad views over Rosario Strait to Lopez Island, little lighthouse-blinking Smith Island, and the water horizon of the Strait of Juan de Fuca. Look across Northwest Pass to Lighthouse Point, next on the agenda.

Stroll #2, 1 Mile to Junction, Then a 1-Mile Loop. Returned to the picnic area, take the "Canoe Pass, Lighthouse Point, Bowman Bay" trail by the restrooms, into woods, along cliffs, ½ mile to Bowman (Reservation) Bay and another picnic area. On trail or beach proceed ½ mile more, by a boat-launch, onetime fish-rearing ponds, and old dock, along a marsh, to a wooded sidehill above the low neck connecting to Lighthouse Tombolo. Here is a Y; take the right, down onto the neck. On the far end the trail goes left around a corner and starts up the hill; spot a less-good path taking off from it straight up the hill—this is the return leg of the suggested (but not compulsory) loop.

Stroll #3, a 1-Mile Loop. Return to the Y, go left, round forest slopes, pass a sidetrail left (the loop return), switchback up a peaklet, and contour. Then take a sidetrail down to overviews of Canoe Pass, Deception Pass, Canoe (Pass) Island, the bridge, and boats; another path drops to the beach at the west entrance of Canoe Pass. Complete the loop back through a saddle and return as you came to Rosario Beach.

FIDALGO ISLAND

Not sands and gravels and clays but hard rock is the substance of Fidalgo. The geomorphology is such as to yield little beachwalking, most of it in Deception Pass State Park. But Fidalgo has one other shore spectacular.

Washington Park, 3 miles

From I-5 drive Highway 20 into Anacortes, turn left, following signs to "Victoria Ferry," and when the highway turns downhill right, to the ferry dock, continue straight on Sunset Avenue to the park entrance. At a Y the right fork, signed "Beach Area," drops to Sunset Beach; go left, signed "Camp Area, Loop Road, Boat Launch." At the next Y go right toward the boat-launch and park.

Better not schedule anything else the day you visit 220-acre Washington (City of Anacortes) Park. Don't be deceived by the shortness (3 miles) of the suggested walk. The long halts for views over waterways to islands near and far, to examine juniper and madrona groves and granite boulders dropped by the glacier, which also polished and scratched the buttresses, and sidetrips on seameadow bluffs and down balds to rocks jutting in the waves—well, better bring lunch, because you could be all day at it.

The park has innumerable trail signs pointing to Fidalgo Head Loop, Sunset Beach, Green Point, Rosario Strait, Juniper Point, Burrows Bay, Havekost Monument; the walker will want to take in all these delicacies in a big and simple 3-mile loop around Fidalgo Head on Loop Road, single-lane blacktop, speed bumps to encourage slow, quiet driving. Frequent sidepaths lure to wonders. Connector paths link many of these, eliminating returns to Loop Road. And so the whole day just melts away.

Find Loop Road above the boat-launch. Walk a roadside path in views over Rosario Strait to Cypress, Orcas, Blakely, Decatur, and Lopez Islands. See the ferry from Anacortes to Vancouver Island. In ½ mile round Green Point and from the green meadows look south to the Olympics. On or beside the road (at low tide, after a sidetrip down to West Beach), climb grassy opens.

After the road switchbacks left into forest, spot a good trail switchbacking right. Follow it away from the road and to the top of Juniper Point, 1 mile from the start. Now sidepaths proliferate, slowing progress, as do carpets of moss and grass and flowers, gnarled, wind-sculpted junipers reminding of the Sierra, views across the water to Burrows Island, Mt. Erie, fishing boats.

Burrows Bay and Mount Erie from Washington Park

Following this path or that, likely Loop Road will be touched here and there. And likely as not more trails will beguile, down ravines to secluded coves, out on high meadows. Chances are that after walking about 2 miles, exclusive of sidetrips, one will hit Loop Road at a view over the Flounder Bay Marina to Erie. If so, the Havekost Monument, commemorating the pioneer of 1871 who gave Anacortes this park, will be passed as well as concrete footings of the reservoir that served the Flounder Bay lumber mill until it was demolished in 1961 (all except the planing mill, now a boat shed). A final scant 1 mile on Loop Road, through fine cool woods, returns to the parking area.

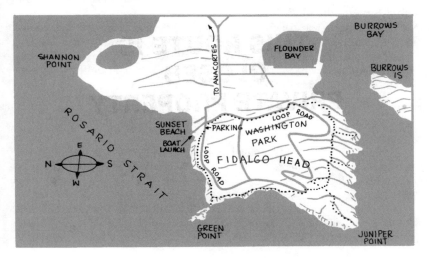

GUEMES ISLAND

Drive Highway 20 through downtown Anacortes. Turn left on 6 Street, signed "Guemes Island Ferry," to 1st, and right on 1st to the ferry dock. Ferries every half-hour (5-minute crossing) from 6:30–8:30 A.M., then every hour until 1:30 P.M., then every half-hour to 6 P.M.

The definitive day would be a 16-mile circuit of the entire island, and it might be done, because atypical of the San Juans, the beach is mostly continuous and mostly sand-pebble. However, the steep slopes of Mt. Guemes (720 feet) and other hard juts terminate in San Juan–typical rockeries, requiring inland getarounds. In contrast to such mountainous neighbors as Fidalgo and Cypress Islands, all of Guemes except that uppity southeast sector has the look of a great wave-cut bench lifted above the waves by isostasy or faulting. (Just guessing.)

From this point and that the views are splendid: over Guemes Channel to Fidalgo Island's March Point and Mt. Erie; over Padilla Bay to Hat and Samish Islands; over Samish Bay to Vendovi and Lummi Islands and Mt. Baker; over Bellingham Channel to Cypress and Blakely Islands and the Olympics; comings and goings of San Juan Island ferries and supertankers carrying millions of quarts of oil and never ever spilling a drop (well, hardly ever).

South Shore

West of the ferry landing the beach is bluffless and many-housed, except where a large saltmarsh holds off intruders. For the best access in that direction, drive South Shore Drive 1.1 miles to where it bends sharply north to become West Shore Road; go straight ahead on a dirt road to "Open Space" signs. A sandy-pebbly no-house beach rounds sandstone cliffs 1 scant mile to Kelly Point.

For access to the beach east of the ferry landing, drive South Shore Drive 1.3 miles. Where an overgrown road on the water side reverse-turns west, park in such fashion as not to block the way and find the path to the beach. Sand and pebbles, then rocks, gravel, and bouldery. Public. No houses in the ¾ mile to Deadman's Bay, where beachwalking is halted by San Juan–type rockeries in season a profusion of native wildflowers.

West Shore

From the junction of Guemes Island Road and West Shore Road, drive the latter south 2 miles to Lervick Drive. Just after turning onto Lervick see a road-blocking log straight ahead. Park there (one car) or on the shoulder (two more cars).

Houses line the (Public) beach 1 mile south to the uprising of bluff. Beyond the end of houses and past a small windmill the way is lonesome for 2¼ miles from the put-in, past Yellow Bluff to Kelly Point, neither of which can be rounded except at low tides.

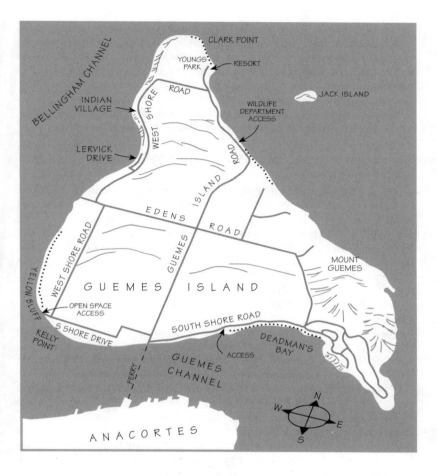

To the north are a few houses/shacks before the bluff rises up. Walking is peaceful beyond the point where the map shows "Indian Village." Not there no more, of course. The sandy-pebbly beach extends 2½ more miles to Clark Point.

Northeast Shore

Wildlife Department Access. Drive Guemes Island Road across the island to the northeast shore. At 0.2 mile from the turn northwesterly to parallel the shore, an unmarked road penetrates a thicket of roses between houses to a signed Public access; parking for three cars. The beach is open some ¾ mile southeasterly to the rocks of Mt. Guemes and 1¼ miles northwest to Youngs Park, though ¾ mile of that is bluffless and densely inhabited.

Youngs Park. From the Wildlife Department access, continue on Guemes Island Road 1.5 miles, passing West Shore Road and dropping to the water. The road bends in a horseshoe through Guemes Island Resort to Youngs Park. This is the chef's special, the surveyor's Guemes joy. Picnic tables, privies. Lovely sand-pebble beach, an agate-gatherer's heaven. Nearing Clark Point, a scant 1 mile from the park, huge glacial erratics on the beach. Great clambering for little kids after they tire of agates. The Youngest Surveyor recommends the park without reservation.

SAMISH ISLAND

Drive I-5 to Exit 231 and go off west on Highway 11, Chuckanut Drive. In 6.5 miles, at Bow Post Office, turn left 1 mile to Edison. South of that hamlet a scant 0.5 mile, turn west on Bay View–Edison Road. In a long 1.5 miles, where that road turns left to Bay View State Park, go straight, then turn and twist, to Samish Island. Beach-guarding uplands of the first island and the sand neck are elbow-to-elbow Private, the beaches a total loss. Just where the neck connects to the second island is a junction, identified by the fire station on the left.

Actually two islands joined by a sand neck, and now really a peninsula, Samish Island is a trip to sea. Miles and miles it thrusts out from the delta, dividing Padilla Bay from Samish Bay, seemingly striving to escape the mainland and join companions of the archipelago. Views are spectacular from the San Juan–typical grass-moss balds, flowers and Douglas firs and madronas atop, rock cliffs and deep water beneath.

To explore the outer island turn right and drive 0.3 mile along the north shore to Samish Island Public Beach and Picnic Site. Utilizing 1500 feet of Public tidelands and a bit of upland donated by local folk in 1960, the state Department of Natural Resources was first to save a portion of Samish for the Public. Descend the staircase to the beach (at high tide there is none), houses prevented by a bluff of glacial drift. In ¾ mile there is no beach at any tide, cliffs of metamorphic rock plunging to deep water. The cliffs may be scrambled and the thorny brush battled to the flattish island top, elevation 100–150 feet. Paths crisscross and fade but by trying this and that, trending inland from the bluff edge, a walker shortly emerges on an old woods road and is confronted by "Private" signs on the way to an old quarry.

Several paths lead northward to "North Point." From a clifftop seameadow the views are grand to Guemes, Cypress, Orcas, Vendovi, Sinclair, Eliza, and Lummi Islands—the latter displaying its amazing 1500-foot summit-to-beach western precipice. Only a scattering of distant houses is visible, the San Juan Islands seem a wilderness, and this point part of it.

After a certain amount of trial-and-error probing, the correct path can be found southward to William Point, site of a beacon light atop another seameadow bluff. Now the views are southerly. A short way from the point a path switchbacks down cliffs to beach that extends

William Point on Samish Island

onward to Camp Kirby, of the Samish Council of Camp Fire Girls.

At 1 wonderful mile from William Point is the tip of the long spit of Dean Point, where a person stands far out in the waters, swept by winds, the cross-chopping waves a foreground for views over Padilla Bay to Guemes and Jack and Hat and Fidalgo Islands, refineries on March Point, supertankers at anchor and supertankers underway north to Cherry Point refineries; south over the Skagit delta are Cultus and Devils.

Proceed ⅓ mile along the south side of the spit to the bluff and find a steep path up to the county road, attained near and outside the entrance to Camp Kirby. Walk the road a scant 1 mile back past the fire station to the start.

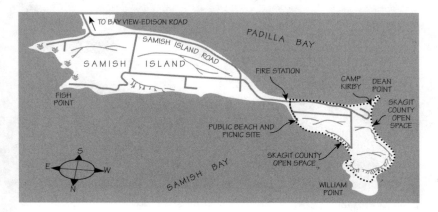

LUMMI ISLAND

Go off I-5 on Exit 260, signed "Lummi Island." Drive Slater Road 3.8 miles and turn left on Haxton Way, signed "Lummi Casino." In another 6.7 miles is Gooseberry Point. The Whatcom County ferry, *Whatcom Chief*, leaves 10 times in the morning and 10 in the afternoon. A 10-minute crossing.

As viewed from southward in the Whulge, Lummi is an awesome looming, the precipice of Lummi Mountain plummeting 1500 feet from summit to rockbound shore. No beachwalking *there*. But as with Guemes the island has a split personality. The northwestern half has the look of a wave-cut bench lifted above the water by crustal gymnastics. Stretches of beach along the Strait of Georgia and Hale Passage are hospitably Puget Sound–like, more sand-pebble than jutting rock. However, there are San Juan–like rock headlands, too.

Northeast Shore

Several hundred feet north of the ferry landing is a Whatcom County Parks stairway to the beach. The inner beach is glacial erratics and outcropping bedrock, the outer beach a wide strand of sand covered with eelgrass. Very little beach at high tide. Very little parking at any tide. Lummi Point, densely Privatized, is 1 long mile from the ferry. In another 1½ miles is the northern tip of the island, Migley Point, a rock headland, never to be rounded, though perhaps clambered over.

Lummi Island

Northwest Shore

Fern Point. Drive north 3.1 miles from the ferry on Nugent Road, which bends sharp left at Migley Point to become West Shore Drive. A row of condominiums is set back from the water and fronted by a broad lawn. Park where possible on a turnout.

Walk back north on West Shore Drive a short way to a sign, "Condo Beach Access," a stairway to the water, "Private." An obscure old path parallels the beach, a joyland of sand ½ mile south to Fern Point; houses quit as the bluff rises; beyond the point the surveyor did not survey.

Views are across the Strait of Georgia into the Gulf Islands (Canadian San Juans) and to Sucia and Orcas of the American San Juans. Ships to and from Vancouver.

Village Point. Continue 2.2 miles beyond the condo access on West Shore Drive, to where it takes a sharp left to become Legoe Bay Road, at Village Point. A turnout has space for several cars. Beach access to the Public shore by walking back west and north around Village Point.

Sand beach, gorgeous driftwood. A unique element of the view (in season) is the fleet of Lummi fishing boats in Legoe Bay. The long slender shells, resembling the dugouts of old, have wooden towers at both ends for putting out and taking in nets.

Congregational Church Access. Proceed from Village Point about 1 mile to a little white church topped by a steeple. Park in the vicinity and find a staircase to the sandy, pebbly, driftwoody beach. Few houses anywhere around. The lonesomest, wildest, least Privatized, loveliest Lummi beach. Walk some 2 miles south to where the rock heart of Lummi Mountain bulges out to halt the feet. A grand spot to sit and muse on the mountains of Orcas and Cypress Islands, ships traversing the Strait of Georgia.

Immediately north from the church access the shore rounds a rocky point, possible at low tide, into Legoe Bay and on to Village Point. Alternatively, scramble up an obvious trail to the windswept meadow atop the cliffs.

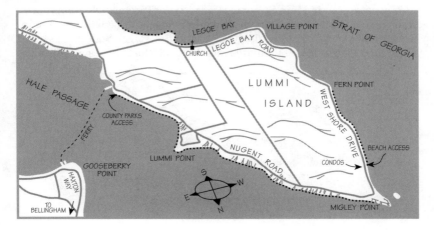

SOUTH AND CENTRAL KITSAP PENINSULA

Distance decreases the appeal of these beaches to folks in northern neighborhoods of Puget Sound City. So much the better for folks in southern neighborhoods—and for those northerners willing to endure extra hours on the highways.

The Longbranch (Key) Peninsula and the "Narrows Peninsula" (sub-peninsulas of the Kitsap) are within or adjoining the suburbs of Second City (Tacoma); good on *them*. In these pages are omitted many southerners' favorites but several regional treasures, some of them unique (or nearly) on the Whulge, demand attention.

As for Hood Canal, its Kitsap shores aren't next door to hardly anybody (well, Bremerton) and therefore have some of the longest purely pristine beaches east of Olympic National Park. A National Marine Wildland Park was proposed in the 1970s; the opportunity has not yet slipped away entirely; more beachwalkers must go there and return bearing witness.

USGS maps: Vaughn, Longbranch, Burley, McNeil Island, Fox Island, Gig Harbor, Olalla, Bremerton East, Bremerton West, Duwamish Head, Suquamish, Belfair, Lake Wooten, Holly, Seabeck, Brinnon, Poulsbo

LONGBRANCH PENINSULA–CASE INLET

Thrusting out in Main Street to close views of Tacoma–Olympia shores, and within a half-hour's drive of Narrows Bridge, the Longbranch Peninsula, enclosed by the twin fishhook termini of Puget Sound, Case and Carr Inlets, nevertheless remains mostly rural, the beaches largely wild.

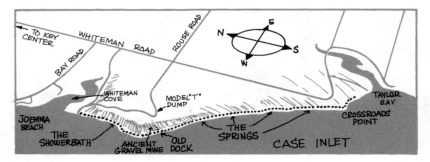

The hiker's pal, the bluff of glacial debris, helps. So does the lack of a mountain-fed river to keep the lawns of city-type subdivisions green. So do soils that are reluctant to "perk." However, Privatization is as persistent as glaciers in the Ice Age and suffices here to seriously hinder Public feet; developers are ever on the sniff for weaknesses in the natural and social defenses.

State Parks is planning development on the 178-acre "Haley Site" 5 miles southwest of Key Center, 1700 feet of Case Inlet waterfront plus marshes and a 6-acre lagoon. A community group wants the site kept undeveloped, designated a Natural Area.

Robert F. Kennedy Recreation Area

Robert F. Kennedy Recreation Area*

From Highway 3 or Highway 16, drive Highway 302 to Key Center and there go south on Key Center–Longbranch Road, signed "Penrose Point State Park." In 5 miles is Home, a utopian colony when it was founded in 1896. From the bridge at Home continue south 1.2 miles and turn right on Whiteman Road. In 2.2 miles turn right on Bay Road, which leads 1 mile to Joemma Beach in the Department of Natural Resources Recreation Area.

A host of South Sound–typical treats—estuaries, spits, islands combined with the North Sound–like excitement of a weather shore. Views are across to the wildness of great long Hartstene Island, then over Nisqually Reach to suburbia of Tacoma–Olympia, whose lights at night enhance the peninsula darkness. Wilderness! Barely a half-hour's drive from Narrows Bridge, some 11 miles along Case Inlet can be walked, only a few minutes of the journey in close sight of houses.

For how long? At the time of the first survey, in 1978, the area was just about empty and the scattered natives amiable. In 1993, however, aliens ("inlanders") are building on the beach and brandishing scraps of paper.

Joemma Beach to Taylor Bay, 3 miles

The DNR site is hemmed in by Privatizers who suffer the invasions of pirate stinkpots and thus are suspicious of any stranger, aboat or afoot. The beach north is long and lovely. South is Whiteman Cove, a lagoon converted to a lake by raising and widening the baymouth bar. Beyond

---

*See the publisher's note on private property on page 11.

the Privatization zone, jungled bluff commences and the beach turns fully wild for miles beneath the 200-foot guardian wall. The nearly 3 miles of unbroken solitude would be reward enough but there also is *The Showerbath!* Water cascades down a clay cliff and splashes in a green-lit forest cave hung with maidenhair fern. On hot days nymphs and satyrs disport.

At 1½ miles from Joemma Beach is an odd terrace above the beach; a person may search for the expected kitchen midden, be puzzled by heaps of cobbles, expanses of "moss meadows," and realize the terrace is not natural; this is a gravel mine dating from early in the century. Thus are explained the piling stumps on the beach and the midden of rusting automobiles from the 1920s.

A short way south are The Springs. Dozens of creeklets splash down walls of gravel or clay, a series continuous more than a mile. At a short bulge where an old road-trail descends to the beach is Best Waterfall; ascend the trail a bit to another showerbath, a 30-foot two-stepper down a clay cliff.

The bluff becomes vertical, a garden wall colorful in summer with yellow monkeyflower around the creeks and, in fall, on drier sites, pearly everlasting's white and goldenrod's yellow and the ominous maroon of poison oak.

Pause at "Crossroads Point," where the shore bends into the nook of Taylor Bay and Dana, Henderson, and Case Inlets and Nisqually Reach meet. Look down Nisqually Reach to the Nisqually delta and beyond to the Bald Hills. Look out Dana Passage past the end of Hartstene Island to the Black Hills. Look back up Case Inlet to the Olympics.

The first houses appear and at 3½ miles the trip ends at piling stubs of the dock of the old ferry over Nisqually Reach. This spot is reached by driving south on Whiteman Road, which becomes 76 Street, 3 miles from the Bay Road turnoff, and turning right on 182 Avenue to the dead-end. Note: Taylor Bay has one of the densest concentrations of "No Trespassing" signs in the Western Hemisphere—including signs claiming the county roads are Private! A person starting the trip at the piling stubs should not whistle while he walks. Perhaps check out the street-end of 182nd; a huge pile of gravel and dirt is no barrier to the beach, though the hellberry slope may require a set of bush-choppers.

LONGBRANCH PENINSULA– CARR INLET

The lee shore of Longbranch Peninsula is the most comfortable; winds and waves usually are quieter and the bluffs mostly shorter or absent and the cozy bays more numerous. Population thus is greater. Nevertheless, stretches of solitude are many and views are superb. On the south tip is one of the peninsula's two greatest walks.

Burley Lagoon, at the head of Henderson Bay, which is the head of Carr Inlet, has almost as much right as North Bay to be considered the Terminus of Puget Sound. Thus, as the barb tip on one of the twin fishhooks, it is Momentous. However, the lagoon is better for musing than walking, though the ¾-mile baymouth bar, augmented by riprap to be a causeway, is a pleasant highway-side stroll. Pilings of old booming grounds provide perches for a huge colony of gulls. Oyster-industry paraphernalia is strewn across the mudflat. The tidal rush through the lagoon mouth and the views down Henderson Bay to the Black Hills catch the eye.

South along the beach 3 miles is *Minter Bay,* very nearly closed off by a ½-mile baymouth bar. The cove is (or was?—pollution hereabouts puts the fear in oyster-gobblers) the home of Minter Brook Oyster Company. The baymouth bar, "Ship Bones Spit," summarizes the Götterdämmerung of the mosquito fleet. Skeletons of a dozen or more vessels expose rib cages in the waters and sands, naught left but timbers and rusted iron. (The hulks were beached here to provide oyster habitat.)

Maple Hollow

Drive Highway 302 to Key Center and go off on Longbranch Road, signed "Penrose Point State Park." In 3 miles turn left on Vanbeek Road. In 0.2 mile turn left at the "Maple Hollow" sign to the parking area.

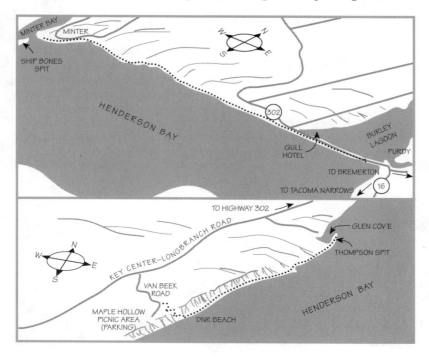

In 1987 the Department of Natural Resources sold the trees. The trail passes new houses to a narrow strip of surviving forest and drops to the water. The way south to Home on Von Geldern Cove is quite solidly populated. North, though, is mostly wild the 3 miles to Thompson Spit at the mouth of Glen Cove. Look south to Penrose Point and South Head, green pastures of McNeil Island, Fox Island, and the Steilacoom gravel mines. Look across to Raft Island and cupcakelike Cutts Island.

Penrose Point State Park

Drive from Key Center on Longbranch Road, following state park signs 8 miles through Home and Lakebay to the park entrance. In 0.2 mile, past headquarters and campgrounds, the entrance road T-junctions. For the recommended complete tour, turn right 0.2 mile to the picnic area.

Only 146 acres? Nonsense! What with inlet dips and peninsula juts, at low tide there are 2 miles of beach. And the paths that loop around in bigtree virgin forest total golly knows how many miles. A long day is scarcely enough to sample this compact treasure trove.

First, Mayo Cove. By the privies find a trail through the mixed forest to one of the campground parking areas and down to the dock. Admire the picturesque estuary and circle back via either beach or the banktop path, returning to the start to complete a 1¼-mile loop. (At low tide a bar miraculously emerges in the middle of the cove; the sidetrip out and back amid sands and gulls, ducks and crows, adds nearly 1 mile.)

Now, the point. Round the swimming beach cove, cross a trickle-creek at the mouth of a tiny lagoon ("Ark! Ark!" squawk the herons), walk the little spit to the start of low bank topped by madrona and fir—and poison oak, gaudy red in fall, a peril to harvesters of the black-fruited evergreen huckleberry. In ¾ mile is the tip of Penrose Point. Look up Carr Inlet, across to Fox Island, down to McNeil Island; between Fox and McNeil see Chambers Bay and gravel mines on the Whulge Trail. Continue a scant ½ mile from the point, past a grassy terrace and shells of a kitchen midden, and spot a trail obscurely signed "Underground Cable."

Now, the forest primeval. A network of paths has been tunneled

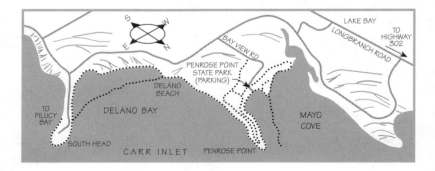

Maple Hollow, Longbranch Peninsula

through the peninsula's wildwoods to make it seem enormously larger than it is. Just inland from the beach, turn left on one trail—or a bit beyond, right on another. Either way, loop around and then take the other loop. Often the way is on a bank close above the beach, trenched in head-high salal and huckleberry. Often the way is in cool-shadowed alder-maple-sword fern, or madrona groves, or ancient Douglas fir. A straight shot from the beach to the picnic area is only ⅓ mile but wiping out the whole trail system adds 2 miles.

South Head*

A lovely gooky bay mudflat, a peninsula thrusting far out in the water, and then miles of mostly wild beaches along Pitt Passage, in close views of McNeil Island.

From the trail south of Penrose Point continue south on the beach. Wildness yields to mossy cottages and venerable mansions of Delano Beach. At medium tides the head of Delano Bay must be rounded, crossing a trickling creek (watch for wood ducks) to the resumption of tanglewood-

---

*See the publisher's note on private property on page 11.

*Devils Head on Longbranch
Peninsula*

guarded beach; at low tide an elegant shortcut over the mudflats squishes along far from land, out amid the clams and gulls and peep. Mainland is regained, and a 100-foot bluff. At 2 miles (or via shortcut, 1½ miles) is South Head, the views to Pitt Island in Pitt Passage, which separates the peninsula from McNeil Island. Watch for spouting whales.

The surveyor did not proceed farther, disconcerted as he was by learning from shore folk, at first quite surly, that he had the look of a convict who had just paddled a driftwood log over Pitt Passage and squished through a mudflat. To explore hereabouts, dress neat, keep clean, and comb your whiskers. The beach appeared virtually all wild, and fascinating, the 4 miles to Mahnckes Point at the mouth of Filucy Bay.

Filucy Bay Boat-Launch

From the bridge at Home (see Penrose Point State Park) continue on the highway south 4.5 miles to Longbranch on Filucy Bay. Continue 1.2 miles on Key Peninsula Highway and turn east on 72 Avenue, which in 0.7 mile dead-ends at a boat-launch.

North from the Boat-Launch to McDermott Point, 1 mile

Walk north under a rusty gravel wall from whose top leans a spreading madrona. In fall the evergreen huckleberry (sweet) and bitter cherry (bitter) tempt, and the wine-red leaves of poison oak warn to pick fruit carefully. The bluff lowers to a cluster of cottages, rises again, and drops to naught at McDermott Point. On the tip of the spit is the concrete foundation of the vanished lighthouse, amid scotchbroom and grass where the Coast Guard once kept a kempt lawn.

Around the corner is darling little Filucy Bay to whose green shores cling old houses of Longbranch, whose moored boats dot the bay. Up Pitt Passage, leading to Carr Inlet, is little Pitt Island. The beaches of McNeil Island make the feet itch. In Balch Passage, the slot between McNeil and Anderson Islands, is Eagle Island; out the slot are Main Street and the Whulge Trail.

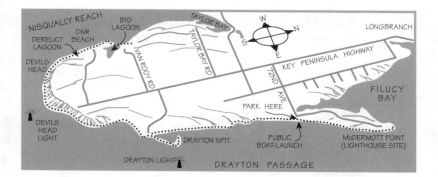

South from the Boat-Launch to Devils Head, 3 miles*

A perfect spit, two baymouth bars enclosing lagoons, a charmer of a bay, two navigation lights, close views of tidy little isles, and a headland thrusting boldly out in Main Street traffic. What more could one ask?

In the first 1 mile are trails and bulkheads and the genteel decay of the once-palatial Kraemer Estate. Wild bluff then rises, maples arching over the beach. Chunks of bluff that have slid down on the beach require a tide below 5 feet to get easily by. The first spectacular is Drayton Spit, hooking north to enclose a lagoon. Out in Drayton Passage is Drayton Light. Across is Anderson Island, whose entire west shore is paralleled on this trip. At Treble Point sidetrip ¼ mile out to the spit tip. At the spit base are a big lawn and picnic shelter; don't loiter.

In a scant ½ mile are a boat-launch and bulkhead and lawns. The bluff then leaps to over 200 feet in walls of vertical clay and jungle. In the next 1 mile Devils Head Light is passed and the shore rounds to its bluff apex, Devils Head, the tip of Longbranch Peninsula.

Don't rush away. It's a Momentous Spot. Drayton Passage has been left for seascapes of Nisqually Reach. Views extend past Anderson Island to the Nisqually delta and the green land whence come the booms of Fort Lewis war games, and to Johnson Point at the mouth of Henderson Inlet, and to Case Inlet and Hartstene Island. Here in "The Crossroads" see tugs and barges, fishing boats, sailboats, and, if lucky, that nostalgic anachronism, a rowboat.

Now for the baymouth bars. In ¼ mile is the first, enclosing a lagoon where two derelict houses sag into the forest beside the mud and driftwood. In ½ mile is the next, an increment of fill making it a lake. Beware of croaking herons, quacking ducks, squealing killdeer. Don't bother walking the populated final ¾ mile to Taylor Bay, whose ferry-dock piling evokes memories of the golden age of the Water Road.

---

*See the publisher's note on private property on page 11.

THE NARROWS–COLVOS PASSAGE–
RICH PASSAGE–PORT ORCHARD

North of Longbranch Peninsula is "The Narrows Peninsula," separating Carr Inlet from Gig Harbor. Shores of the (main) Kitsap Peninsula then follow Colvos Passage some 15 miles around bulges, in and out of coves. The valleys permit many a shore village, but much of the beach is bluff-wild for stretches as long as a mile. Playboats cruise the canal-like passage, and fishing boats and tugs and barges. And whales. Views are across a mile of water to Vashon Island, forest-green and mostly bluff-wild the entire length from Dalco Point to Point Vashon. The shore then turns west into Rich Passage, the waterway to Port Orchard, which completes a half-circuit of Bainbridge Island at Agate Pass, the waterway to Port Madison.

The beachwalker's friend, the high bluff, alternates with the beachwalker's nemesis, the low banks and estuaries which invite houses to cuddle up to the water—and, as often as not, invade it with beach-destroying, armoring bulkheads.

Kopachuck State Park

Drive Highway 16 from Tacoma Narrows Bridge to the Gig Harbor vicinity. Take either of the two exits signed "Kopachuck State Park" and follow those infallible signs some 6 miles to the entrance. Pass the campground to reach the parking area.

Old forest and fine views over Carr Inlet in the 109-acre park, a maze of paths up and down and across the slope, through big firs and spruces and cedars and maples. The ½ mile of beach gives views past cute Cutts Island to Raft Island and over to Penrose Point and Glen Cove. A person might venture south another mile into Horsehead Bay—but never on nice sunny weekends.

The Narrows

Drive Highway 16 to the west side of Narrows Bridge and turn off on the road signed "Airport–Wollochet–Point Fosdick." This road loops under the bridge, permitting easy egress from the highway and easy return, from whichever direction you come. Find parking space on shoulders under

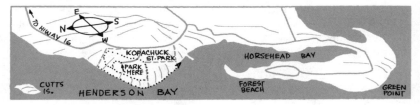

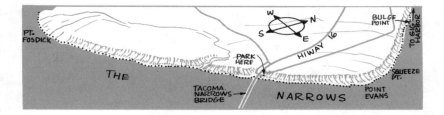

the bridge or someplace in the vicinity. From the shoulder on the north side of the loop road a trail descends a forest ravine to the beach.

Incredible! In the confines of Second City, 6 miles of almost perfectly wild beach, in close view over the skinniest section of Main Street to the jungle-bluff wildland from Point Defiance to Titlow Beach. No, it is not "*outer* wilderness." This is a prize specimen of "the wildness within." The beachwalker shares the scene with fishing boats, tugs and barges, playboats, and occasional ocean ships. And, of course, the herds of birds which hitchhike rides on the logs running on river-swift tides through The Narrows.

South from The Narrows to Point Fosdick, 2 miles

Barking dogs and occasional paths are the sole evidence of houses atop the bluff. The only habitation on the beach is in the ravine at ½ mile. Fir and madrona lean over the beach, decorated with red-in-autumn poison oak, maple and alder arch over, "Ark! Ark!" go the herons, "Splash! Splash!" go the leaping salmon, "Or-or-or!" go trains on the Whulge Trail, a mile across the water. In 2 miles the bluff drops to a mere bank at Point Fosdick and houses crowd the shore, including what the newspapers describe as the largest house ever built in Pierce County, the only one boasting a 50,000-pound theater pipe organ. Enjoy views over Hale Passage to Fox Island, up to the mouth of Wollochet Bay, and turn back. Especially on foggy days be sure to take a picture of the bridge overhead.

The Narrows from Kopachuck State Park

North from The Narrows to Gig Harbor, 3½ miles

Wild just about all the way—blufftop mansions out of sight, as is the city across the way. Just water and woods and fishing boats. True, one work of man is evident, indeed dominates—the bridge—but that is no less a landscape ornament than the Pyramids at Giza.

At 1 mile is the light on Point Evans. A woods road descends the precipice from a massive blufftop development that can't do much to the beach, the bluff is so unstable. For nearly 1 mile beyond the point the beach is dramatic; bare cliffs of sand and gravel form vertical cliffs and jutting ribs—at "Squeeze Point" narrowing the beach to a meager 5 feet at medium tides, nothing at high—beware! Tree clumps slid from above may force brushfights. The view over the waters is enhanced by Bennett Tunnel, swallowing up and disgorging trains, the ¾-mile strip of Salmon Beach's below-the-bluff cottages, and the great big green of Point Defiance Park.

The beach smooths, the bluff gentles, though still a steep jungle, gashed by several ravines (creeks and trails from above). At 2¼ miles "Bulge Point" is rounded, fully opening the view to Gig Harbor and Colvos Passage and Vashon Island. Wildness continues another 1¼ miles to houses near the mouth of Gig Harbor.

Colvos Passage

Sunrise Beach Park

From Highway 16 drive through Gig Harbor to Crescent Valley Drive. Turn left 0.5 mile, then right on Drummond 0.7 mile to a T; turn right on Moller 0.2 mile, then left on Sunrise Beach Road, and descend a valley 0.5 mile to just above the water. Spot a driveway on the left and proceed to the parking area. Formerly a private park on the Moller homestead, it now is a Kitsap County park, "Dedicated to memory of Rudolph Moller, 1868–1944, Mathilde Moller, 1880–1953, homesteaders of this property—1986."

The choice trip is south, in fine views to Point Defiance and Rainier. After ½ mile of Sunrise Beach homes is ½ mile of wild bluff. Then, past a shorter row of houses, is 1 wild mile under a formidable 280-foot bluff. At the end is the baymouth bar of Gig Harbor.

North the populated gulches and wild strips alternate the 2¼ miles to Point Richmond.

Olalla Bay

From Gig Harbor drive Crescent Valley Road to Olalla Bay. Parking just north of the bridge.

The drowned lower length of Olalla Valley, an estuary snaking back into muck and trees. Anciently inhabited: just south of the baymouth bar is a small building on sagging piles, ruins of the Olalla Trading Company, offering (it did) "General Merchandise"; on the hill above is a gracious mansion, cupolas and widow's walk and all.

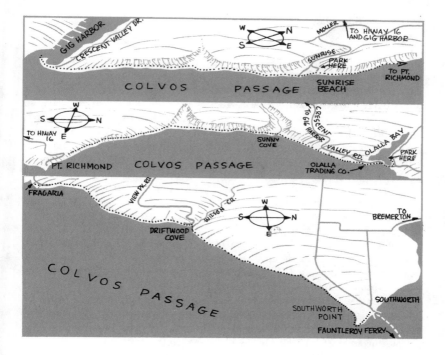

Walk south past the Trading Company and immediately onto below-the-bluff beach, 3½ lonesome miles to Point Richmond.

Southworth Point

Now for something completely different. Park at Fauntleroy in West Seattle and walk on the ferry to Vashon Island and Southworth Point. At Southworth, drop from ferry dock to beach and head south. Around the corner is a grassy spit. Views are north to Blake Island, across to Point Vashon, and beyond to the Green Mile of Lincoln Park, Alki Point, and Elliott Bay.

At 2¼ miles, mostly lonesome, is Driftwood Cove at the mouth of Wilson Creek. Houses. Several more settlements come to or near the water in the next 2 miles to Fragaria.

Rich Passage

Harper Park

Bus: 86 and 87

From the Southworth ferry dock, drive Highway 160 (SE Southworth Drive) west, then north to SE Olympia Drive.

A beach access on Colby Bay. Walk north to Manchester.

Manchester State Park

Bus: 86 and 87

One approach is via the Seattle–Bremerton ferry, Port Orchard, and Annapolis along extravagantly scenic Sinclair Inlet and Rich Passage. Another is via Fauntleroy–Southworth ferry, Harper, and Manchester along extravagantly scenic Yukon Harbor. Another is via Narrows Bridge and Highway 16 to either of these approaches, both of which become Beach Drive. From the north at a long 0.5 mile from Point Glover on Rich Passage and from the south about 2 miles from Manchester, turn east on Hilldale Road.

Anybody who has ferried through Rich Passage, close by rock-walled Middle Point, must wish to walk there. The 111-acre park, formerly part of Fort Ward (which occupied both shores of Rich Passage) has diverse habitats—beach, grassy meadow, dry (madrona) forest, cedar stands, and, to the right of the entry gatehouse, a swamp. Frank Beyer, the 87-year-old (as of 1993) volunteer park naturalist, says there are bear, red fox, over 105 species of birds, and over 300 species of flowers. At one time there were goats from Bikini Atoll, survivors of the first hydrogen "device," brought here to live out their irradiated lives.

The park's information boards have maps showing some 2 miles of trails, including an interpretive trail (poorly maintained) from the gatehouse. (Frank leads walks and on Saturday nights presents an interpretive program.) For the best walk, drive to the picnic parking on the knoll above Building 63, a handsome brick edifice that has been placed on the National Register of Historic Places (one of three in the park) and under the name of the Torpedo Warehouse serves as a picnic shelter.

Walk down to Little Bay. Watch the waterfowl, who find a degree of

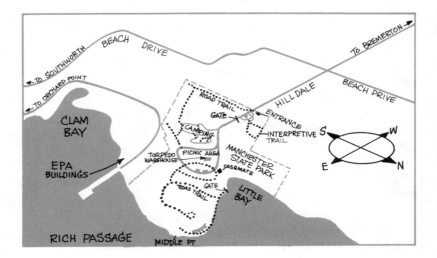

Bremerton–Seattle ferry in Rich Passage. Olympic Mountains in distance

refuge here, and the ferries. Then go east from the Warehouse on the gated shore road, passing a road up the hill (to be walked later). The way partly rounds Middle Point, a 90-foot hillock that was an island when sea level was a dozen feet higher, to fenced-off Battery Robert B. Mitchell, mostly underground. Its guns—with those of Fort Ward on Bainbridge Island—prevented foreign navies, the swine, from bombarding Bremerton. A concrete wall on the shore anchored the south side of the anti-submarine nets that impeded ferry traffic during World War II. The sedimentary outcrops (presumably lifted above the water by the Great Convulsion of the Seattle Fault) enclose nook beaches, jut out in picturesque buttresses. Madronas overhang the waters and poison oak is insidiously everywhere, beware, beware.

The views feature the big white-and-green jumbo ferry thrashing past just offshore and long looks to Blake Island and the Green Mile of Lincoln Park.

Return from the battery (the shore trail peters out beyond a rock point) to the road up the hill and climb to a large grass meadow (home of the hot goats, R.I.P.). The summit views are through madrona forest over Clam Bay to the green buildings of the Environmental Protection Agency. Beyond, on the larger, higher former island that now is Orchard Point, is the Navy's Manchester Fuel Depot—here, when time renders war obsolete, will be *the* park of this scene.

Return down the road to an unsigned trail on the left, entering alder-maple forest. In a short bit is a Y, both forks descending to the parking. The right is better because it passes Mining Casemate, an historic building that served as command post for mine patrol from 1900 to 1910.

Port Orchard

Ross Point

Bus: 4 and 7

Drive from Port Orchard on Bay Street to just short of Retsil Street Veterans Home, and a blue-gray sewage plant.

A Wildlife Department Public access, lots of parking. The beach is yucky, slimy, mucky cobbles, too mean to walk far. But this sort of habitat is exactly what turns on yuck-loving biologists. Turn over a rock and be nauseated by creepy-crawlies. Watch the gulls sweep in, squealing "Yummy." Bald eagles also appreciate the cuisine.

Waterman

Bus: 4 and 7

Continue from Rose Point on Bay Street, which becomes Beach Drive E, to the Port of Waterman Public Pier and Beach Access.

Access to Waterman Point and Point Glover.

Illahee State Park

From Bremerton drive north on Warren Avenue (Highway 303) to the entrance. Descend the loop road, passing a parking area with trailhead and a sideroad to the beach parking. For the best walk continue on the loop to another parking area and trailhead.

A splendid old forest and a dandy little beach, just enough room to dip toes in the water, in the north suburbs of Bremerton. Masses throng the 75-acre park on weekends; try a bright spring morning or a moody winter afternoon, weekdays. Descend a great gulch in gorgeous maples and firs a scant ½ mile to the beach. Lollygag south along the sands. Sidetrip on the dock for maximum views up and down Port Orchard, across to Bainbridge Island and to ferries rocketing through Rich Passage. In ⅓

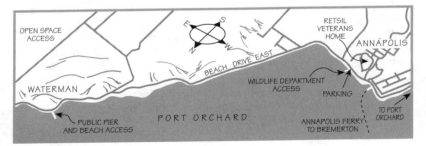

mile, when a fence bars the beach to feet, climb the trail high on the precipitous bluff. What appears to be the gully of an ancient logging skidway is passed. Douglas fir up to 5 feet in diameter, and cedars and maples and ferns—the climax is a fir snag, bark still on, 9 feet in diameter, wow. Return to beachside parking and climb back up the great gulch.

Brownsville

From the turnoff to Illahee State Park continue north on Illahee-Brownsville-Keyport Road 5.5 miles to the bridge over the estuary of Burke Bay. Just across, turn right to spacious parking areas of the large marina.

Brownsville was the terminal of the long-ago ferry from Fletcher Bay on Bainbridge which permitted sailors on leave and Navy Yard workers to commute from the island. Most of the vicinity lacks the standard shore-defense (against houses) system and the beaches are insufferably populated. Here, though, a bluff leaps up a dandy 200 feet, giving the longest lonesome walk hereabouts.

A fishing dock and float ("Use At Your Own Peril"), reached by a bluff-edge path behind an old boathouse, permit close looks at costly stinkpots and long looks north to Liberty Bay, Battle Point, and Agate Pass. Access is easy to the beach, alder-overhung, little molested by humans at the start and less so as the bluff rises to full height. Views of Fletcher Bay yield to views of Manzanita Bay. Liberty Bay grows, and the Navy torpedo installation at Keyport. In 3 miles the fences of that reservation halt progress at the mouth of Liberty Bay.

Suquamish

Bus: 91 or 92

Drive Highway 305 from Winslow to the west end of Agate Pass Bridge and turn off right to the parking area of Access No. l. Or shortly after crossing the bridge, turn right on Suquamish Highway 1.2 miles and just beyond a shopping center go right on Division Street, then left on

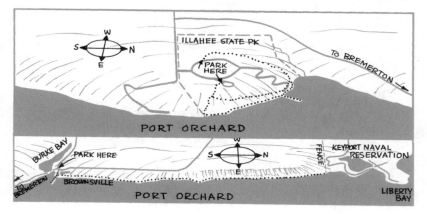

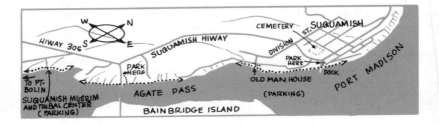

McKinstry, in 0.4 mile from the highway arriving at Old Man House State Historic Site, Access No. 2. Or continue on Suquamish Highway into Suquamish to the Suquamish Dock, Access No. 3. Or drive Highway 305 beyond Suquamish Highway 0.4 mile, turn left at the sign "Suquamish Museum and Tribal Center," and in another 0.4 mile turn left again, down to the parking area, Access No. 4.

Cars whiz through the air over Agate Pass dividing Bainbridge Island from the Kitsap Peninsula and noiseboats through the waterway from Port Orchard to Port Madison. Just beyond the memory of people now alive, the waters were plied by dugout cedar canoes of the Suquamish people headquartered here under their leader, Sealth.

From Access No. 1, a path drops through woods to the beach, lonesome-wild under the protective bluff for ¼ mile in either direction. To the north, front-yard beach continues 1 mile to Old Man House. To the south the clusters of houses are widely scattered and mostly up on a high bank the 2 miles past Sandy Hook to Point Bolin, at the mouth of Liberty Bay.

From Access No. 2 a path leads to an interpretive shelter which tells the tale of times just barely beyond the memory of people who live here now. On a fossil-beach terrace elevated barely above high tide was the largest known longhouse, 500 feet long, 60 feet wide. Construction began about 1800, at the instance of Sealth's father, and was completed under Sealth. In 1870, after his death, the U.S. Army burnt the ruins.

The beach south goes under Agate Pass Bridge. The beach north comes in ½ mile to Suquamish Dock.

At Access No. 3 walk out on the dock for views down Agate Pass, across Port Madison to Agate Point and Point Monroe, across the Whulge to Shilshole Bay. North 1 mile on the beach are the entry to Miller Bay and a close look at the spit that was supposed to become a state park but was snatched by Privatizers. In Suquamish visit the Memorial Cemetery, where rests Sealth (1786–1866), who signed the 1855 "Treaty" of Point Elliott which "gave" his Suquamish and Duwamish peoples the 1375-acre (reduced from an initial 8000 acres) Port Madison Reservation. (In 1979 Judge Boldt, then already suffering from the Alzheimer's disease that in 1984 killed him, ruled these two peoples didn't exist and never had. He signed virtually unchanged a proposed order written by a government lawyer. It was his last official action before retiring, and startled objective observers, who said it was uncharacteristic.)

At Access No. 4 the museum and tribal headquarters, built in the early 1980s, have supplied the Original Residents an organizational focus of sorts in their attempts to prove they exist. Spend half a day in the museum. Then descend to the beach and walk this way to Suquamish, that way to Agate Pass Bridge.

HOOD CANAL

Old country. "Head of Canal" (Belfair, now) was settled in 1859, though not reached by overland road until 1918, despite an 1895 "gold strike" on Mission Creek. The water road was about the only way to go in those days and steamers from Seattle called at the major fishermen-sheltering ports of Holly and Dewatto (where, in the mid-1880s, a boat-building enterprise began) and especially Union, the metropolis. When settlers arrived in the early 1850s the Indians had more than thirty villages from "Head of Canal" to Dewatto Bay; they were moved to reservations, such as Squaxin Island, to make room for loggers—by 1876 there were fifty logging camps on the Canal, bullteam operations, logs flumed down the scarp from the plateau to the water and rafted to mills. The walker still finds traces of Indians, loggers, mosquito fleet.

Rhododendrons above Hood Canal near Dewatto and Mount Washington

Beautiful country. The fiordlike waterway voyaged by fishing boats. Playboats. Olympics rising abruptly and high.

Even now, mostly lonesome country. Solid houses extend from "Head of Canal" to the Great Bend and have crept around Bald (Ayres) Point. And US 101 on the west side is continuous cars, trucks, resorts, and homes. But on long stretches of the east shore deer nibble seaweed oblivious to the hiker, and crows harass nesting bald eagles, and creeks ripple from forest ravines. It won't last—the end is nigh. But it's a creeping doom. Walk now and weep later.

Or maybe not. Friends of the Earth has proposed that Congress protect the treasure by creating a Hood Canal National Scenic Shore administered by the National Park Service. There may yet be time.

North from Dry Creek to Dewatto Bay, 7 miles

Drive west from Belfair on Highway 300, which becomes North Shore Road. At 17.5 miles round Bald Point and in 1 long mile more come to suburbia's end in the wide swale of Dry (Rendsland) Creek. Park on the south side of the creek's splendid delta in what some signs call "Port of Tahuya–Menard's Landing–DNR Access" and some books call "Harvey Rendsland State Park."

The shore north from here was a roaring wilderness until the late 1960s, the only overland access by a disconnected net of rude and crude

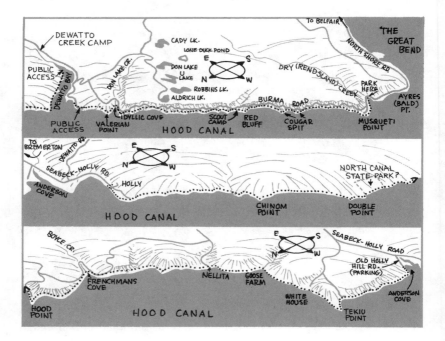

roads. According to local oral history, a county official who owned a vast tract of the empty land he had purchased for nickels and dimes diverted taxpayer funds to construction of an unauthorized road from Dry Creek to Dewatto. Though a twisty, tortuous, narrow lane winding in and out of ravines slicing forests of the 600-foot cliff, the "Burma Road" has opened up the country.

From the creek, the far south of Vancouver's 1792 voyage of discovery, walk the ½ mile to Musqueti Point, whose scattering of beachside homes is being joined as of 1993 by a huge development ("Utilities In—Lots for Sale"). Past Musqueti Point much of the beach is guarded by drift bluff that will keep the way wild. But there are pleasant deltas and terraces where Indians once camped and the heirs of their terminators soon will crowd in.

Across the 1½-mile canal, plied by sailboats and noiseboats and oyster dredges, is US 101. Hoodsport and its valley of Finch Creek stand out and, south of that, Potlatch and the Tacoma City Light Powerhouse. Dennie Ahl Hill and Dow Mountain rise above; above them, Ellinor and Washington.

A long 1 mile from Musqueti Point is happy little Cougar Spit, a pretty creek running through it and a half-dozen cabins continuing their mellowing. In ½ mile more is another nice point with a shack bearing a sign protesting that the map is wrong and *this* is Cougar Spit. In a scant 1 mile more is Red Bluff, a 120-foot naked wall of iron-stained gravel, an old Scout headquarters building, pilings of the dock where Scouts used to debark onto their Hahobas Reservation; here are the delta point of a gorgeous creek sparkling from the forest, the rhododendron, madrona, dogwood, and evergreen huckleberry vividly blooming in May.

Burma Road is high in the forest, unseen from the water, though always ready to rescue the walker whose beach retreat is cut off by a rising tide. However, getting *down* to the beach from the road is not so simple. The one sideroad not signed "No Trespassing" (1993) is about 3 driving miles north of Dry Creek and reaches the beach (one old cabin only) at the (veritable?) Cougar Spit. This hospitable (?) road is readily identifiable, being the only one lacking (1993) a hostile sign. After ½ mile of wild shore the shore becomes crowded (by local standards)—in the next 2¼ miles a couple dozen cabins cling to the bluff. The shore bulges out, swings in, the forest and waves go on, creeks waterfall to the beach or rush from ferny-green gullies or sprawl across gravels of delta points. Throughout here, and all the south Canal, the beach shingle is strikingly tawny, unlike the gray shingle typical of the Whulge elsewhere, including the north Canal; the main constituents are sandstone and basalt, iron-stained, from the Skokomish Gravels washed out from the front of an Olympic glacier. This stretch culminates in the gasper of the trip, the bay and estuary delta of "Don Lake Creek," a creekside, mudflat-side meadow, an orchard, and a comfortable old house and two old cabins. Look from a distance. No touching.

In a scant ½ mile from the bay's south point is "Valerian Point," where in May the grassy wall is bright with Scouler's valerian, paintbrush, vetch, and lupine. In the final scant 1 mile are another lovable creek, a couple more cabins, and the rounding into Dewatto Bay, deepest indentation for miles—and presumably connected by a fault to Lilliwaup Bay on the opposite shore.

Admire Lilliwaup town and Washington, The Brothers, other Olympics, and turn around to begin the 7 miles back, by beach and/or the Burma Road. You'll have had a nice day.

As described below, as of 1993 the hike now can be done from the north, starting at Dewatto.

South from Holly to Turnaround Camp, 6 miles, and Dewatto Bay, 9½ miles

From Bremerton drive west past Wildcat Lake and Symington Lake. Just west of Camp Union, at a T, go left on Seabeck-Holly Road. Drop off the plateau to water level at Anderson Cove, pass Dewatto Road, and enter Holly, originally "Happy Valley" and home port of many fishermen, now inhabited by about three dozen families. The problem is ditching the car. There's no provision for invaders—not so much as a road shoulder to park on. This must be done wherever opportunity affords, maybe 1 mile away at Anderson Cove. Do not park on roadway or in driveways—not only would you mess up the good life for residents but you would mess up the hospitality.

To start the hike from the south, drive Holly–Dewatto Road south about 11 miles to Dewatto. Gone from the bay is the boat-building industry of 1884. Gone too is the fleet of fishing boats. Moldering ruins remain—and few of them. Until recently it was not a hiker's put-in (unless, like the Photographer, he/she had a canoe). However, in the 1980s the DNR opened a Public access just beyond the bay's south point, letting feet on the beach for the route south toward Dry Creek. The DNR also installed a delightful campground in the green woods of Dewatto Creek and a beach access on the north shore of the bay, letting feet on the beach for the route north toward Holly.

The bay therefore is not, as on the first survey in 1978, a route-stopper. However, the walk is best done from Holly because the 6-odd miles to "Turnaround Camp" (where the older surveyor lunched and turned around in 1978) have most of the best. A return in 1980 found the wildland forests south from there to Dewatto gridded and flagged.

Walk down Allan King Road, past Holly Beach Community Club, to the beach, and turn left. In a scant ½ mile a point is rounded and the last houses passed. The way now is securely wild, guarded by the steep jungle that rises to the plateau at 400 to 600 feet. At the start the drift bluff has much blue clay and is slidey—in the first stretch the beach may be blocked by pants-ripping tangles of seaweed-hung, barnacle-encrusted tree clumps.

Small inlet leading to Hood Canal near Holly

After that the erratic-strewn "brown beach" is easy open at tides of 8 to 9 feet or less, often canopied by alder and maple.

The quiet of this shore is underscored by the hum-roar of US 101 across the waters. A deer steps out of the evergreen-huckleberry thickets and calmly inspects you. Great blue herons protest your intrusion—the surveyor saw twenty-odd, four in a single surly gang.

Across the Canal the mountain backdrop shifts as the walk progresses, from Jupiter between the Dosewallips and Duckabush valleys, to The Brothers and Bretherton and the Hamma Hamma valley, to Pershing, Washington, and Ellinor, and, at last, past the Lilliwaup valley, up the Skokomish valley.

The beach curves in to coves, out to points, requiring many foot miles to make any heron miles. The way is enlivened by gulches, ravines, and minivalleys, most with creeks, some with deltas. Now and then terraces of old beaches are elevated above the tides. At 2¼ miles is the first civilization since Holly, a valley where several trailers are parked. In another 1½ miles is Chinom Point, most prominent feature of the route, its valley and delta spit and filled-in lagoon sporting a dozen flossy summerhomes. Several ancient homes/modern camps are passed in gulches the next 2 miles to "Double Point." The bluff now is mainly gravel, drier, grass slopes breaking a forest of fir and madrona.

Poignance. The past lives. A pictograph on an enormous erratic. A lone apple tree bearing a lush crop of some antique species. Ironware of ancient logging rusted nearly to nothing. A huge stump grooved for a cable, at the mouth of the gully, route of a skid road down which bull teams dragged the logs to booming grounds. Remnants of a waterwheel, a primitive hydroelectric plant. Stubs of old pilings, dwellings collapsed to litters of rotten lumber. More people lived on the Canal in the 1930s—the 1910s—the 1880s—than now. Met on the 1978 survey was an old settler, 77, who told how on his place, a fossil beach just several feet above high tide and no more than 30 feet wide from beach to bluff, there was in the 1930s a chicken coop 60 feet long—the supplier of eggs and drumsticks to the entire south Canal. Until nearly War II a freight boat ran once a week, down the west side of the Canal in morning, returning up the east side in afternoon, nosing to the beach to load and unload. In earlier decades the Canal was busy with mosquito-fleet traffic and among the settlers on fossil-beach terraces and deltas were many who made their living cutting cordwood for sale to passing wood-propelled steamers.

Just past "Double Point" begin some 2 miles of DNR tidelands. The survey proceeded only ½ mile past "Double Point" to a camp in a valley, a grand spot to lunch and turn around. And so the surveyor did. On his next survey he didn't and wished he had. The DNR lands south of Double Point have been proposed for a North Canal State Park. The wildwood then would be concrete-padded for Winnebuggers and Silver Slugs, a marina installed where stinkpotters could play their boomboxes and jettison their empties and flush their toilets in the water. If a park must be built here, it *must* be inland, a ½-mile strip of wildwood buffering the shore from high-impact, toy-based recreation. Access to beach, *foot trail only*. (If this be treason, State Parks, make the most of it.)

North from Anderson Cove to Hood Point, 6 miles

Drive toward Holly and 1 mile before getting there, just before crossing Anderson Creek, turn right on Old Holly Hill Road along Anderson Cove. In several hundred feet park in a turnout.

South of Holly wilderness is the rule, civilization the exception. Now, north, the balance swings the other way—the bluff relents, lessening in steepness for long stretches, more frequently breached by gully-ramps to the water. However, the mood still is dominantly lonesome, though interrupted by summerhomes and a scattering of year-round residences.

The way curves out of the cove around a head. In the first scant 1½ miles to Tekiu Point (including ¾ mile of Public tidelands) are several cabins at the start, then wildwood bluff broken by tanglewood creeks, and one substantial old home. Tekiu Point is a splendid unmolested spit poking out in wind and waves, the views across to Triton Head and The Brothers.

The shore turns from a northerly to easterly trend and the route ahead can be seen all the way to the next spit, Hood Point. In a vale is a gracious two-storey, two-chimney white house, and in another wide valley are a sizable creek and a picture-pretty little farm where watchgeese waddle out to the driftwood to hiss at beachwalkers. But that's the most of civilization in the 1½ miles to Nellita, a cluster of well-worn summer cottages by the beach.

Herons "grawk!" and kingfishers "ti-ti-ti" and cormorants pose on old pilings and bald eagles soar on high. Cedars and firs and madronas overhang the beach. Another cluster of cottages on the hillside, and another farm/greenhouse in the orchard, big delta of a babbling creek. Wild bluff leaps up again. At 1¾ miles from Nellita is the major valley of the route, Frenchman's Cove, accommodating several houses and, inland, a fine big pasture and barn. Boyce Creek must be leapt or waded—or crossed inland on a plank bridge.

In 1993–94 Kitsap County Parks acquired (by State Wildlife and Recreation bond-issue funds and donations by Ariel Reynolds Parkinson and children) the Guillemot Cove property on Frenchman's Cove, some 190 acres, ¼ mile of beach, ½ mile of Boyce Creek. An interpretive center is planned. Low-impact recreation, including *nonmotorized* boating, praise be. Road access (in 1995–96?) will be from the Seabeck-Holly Road; watch for signs when they are installed.

The final 1 mile is mostly inhabited. Several cottages are on a bulkhead, a couple more on a bulge, and at the base of the spit of Hood Point are a dozen fancy houses. Ignore them. Put them behind you by going out on the tip. Look far south to Holly, across to Black Point and the Duckabush valley, to Olympics from The Brothers to Jupiter, and north to Scenic Beach and Dabob Bay and the Dosewallips valley.

Although not surveyed, the next 2½ miles to Stavis Bay appear mostly wild.

Scenic Beach State Park

Exit from the Bremerton ferry dock and go right on Washington, then left on Burwell, the new name for 6th (Highway 304), and continue on this thoroughfare as it changes name to Kitsap Way. Or, if driving from Tacoma Narrows, exit from Highway 3 onto Kitsap Way. From the High-

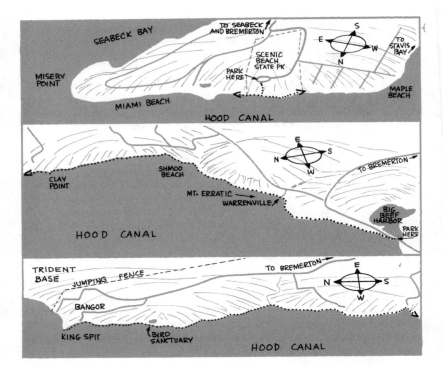

way 3 underpass drive Kitsap Way 1.5 miles to a Y; go left, signed "Kitsap Lake, Seabeck, Holly." In 1 mile go left, signed "Wildcat Lake, Holly." Stick with this highway some 7.5 miles to Big Beef Harbor and continue 2.5 more miles to Seabeck Landing, whence once the *Lake Constance* ferried Model As and Trapper Nelsons over the Canal to Brinnon. About 0.2 mile south of town turn right, following "Scenic Beach" and "State Park" signs here and at the Y (go left) in 1 more mile, in a final 0.7 mile entering the park and descending to parking areas near the beach.

Scenic it surely is. More scenery than beach, though some strolling is to be done. And oh the looking!

An old farmhouse and orchard, a log cabin roofed by moss and ferns, fine fir forest, and ¼ mile of beach are the standpoints for the views: across Hood Canal to Oak Head at the tip of enormous Toandos Peninsula, and into enormous Dabob Bay, within which is smaller Jackson Cove, site of Camp Parsons. Rising above are Walker, Turner, and Buck. Higher are The Brothers, Jupiter, and Constance, the mountain masses cleft by trenches of Duckabush and Dosewallips Rivers. That's scenic.

The 71-acre park is mostly devoted to picnic spots and campsites. Beach population is high in summer but in winter lonesomeness the walk might be extended south 2 miles to Stavis Bay and north 1 mile to Misery Point at the mouth of Seabeck Bay.

North from Big Beef Harbor to Bangor, 6 miles*

To start the walk from Bangor, drive Highway 3 north from Silverdale Exit on NW Trigger Avenue, heading west 0.5 mile to Old Frontier Road NW. Turn left (south) 0.5 mile to NW Westgate Road. Turn right (west) 1 mile to Olympic View Road NW. (Just before Olympic View Road, cross tracks traveled by the dreaded White Train.) Head north on Olympic View Road beside the "Jumping Fence" of the Bangor base about 4.5 miles to the end at King Spit.

For the surveyor's preferred start, from the south, drive to Big Beef Harbor (see above) and park on the shoulder of the causeway which has augmented the baymouth bar.

Head what seems north but actually is closer to east. The wild Canal has been left well behind. Now the bluffs are lower, breaching gullies and valleys are numerous, highways from population centers short and fast, and people cuddling the waves many. Nevertheless, short below-the-bluff stretches are primeval. And the valleys themselves, most containing coves-lagoons-marshes cut off by baymouth bars, intrigue, and littoral architecture interests. And Olympic views are continuous and stupendous. Beach population is dense at the start, then thins.

The view is from Seabeck Bay across to Brinnon at the mouth of the Dosewallips and to Dabob Bay, enclosed by the Toandos Peninsula. The mountain front extends from The Brothers over the Duckabush valley to Jupiter, over the Dose valley to Constance, Turner, Buck, and Walker, and over the Quilcene valley to Townsend and Zion.

Continuous bulkhead quickly ends and a bulge is rounded to the creek, valley, baymouth bar, lagoon-marsh of Warrenville. The offshore tor of "Mount Erratic" is passed, then the concretions of "Shmoo Beach" and slidey "Clay Point" leading to the cove and valley of Anderson Creek. Fancy houses of Sunset Farm are left behind at 2 miles and henceforth solitude outweighs population. Here the shore, passing the across-the-Canal tip of Toandos Peninsula, bends sharply due north.

In the next 4 miles a half-dozen gulches-valleys break the bluff, most sheltering a few houses, though one has a wild lagoon signed "Private Bird Sanctuary." To be a Private isn't necessarily to be a bad person. Down the 100-foot bluff come paths and electric trams to camps or boathouses.

At 6 miles is the trip end, on the tip of King Spit amid driftwood and gulls. Look north to the past and future. Past: Old pilings of the mosquito fleet's Bangor Landing, where Bangor Boats on a pier and the mercantile mart of H. W. Goodwin on the shore have been restored. Future: The fence and the Trident and fence-patrolling sentries who glower at whiskered old surveyors carrying rucksacks and umbrellas who look as if they might any moment jump the fence or lie down on the railroad tracks to obstruct the White Train. (Does it still run, now that the Evil Empire has been dismantled?)

*See the publisher's note on private property on page 11.

NORTH KITSAP AND OLYMPIC PENINSULAS

Whan that Aprille with his shoures soote
The droghte of March hath perced to the roote ...
Thanne longen folk to go on ferry rides ...
The holy blissful Whulge for to seke ...

Granted, the ferrying from Seattle or Edmonds cannot be done in less than an hour, what with the loading–unloading and waiting in line. But the water road is nothing like the concrete road. Ferries aren't part of the agony, the disease—they're part of the fun, the cure.

Two walks on the Kitsap Peninsula can be done by parking the car in Edmonds and paying only foot-passenger fare (cheap) to Kingston. Even when the car must be ferried (expensively), the Kitsap beaches are so different from those facing across Puget Sound they're worth it. Wilderness! On Main Street! Also, history back to the earliest days of mowing

Edmonds–Kingston ferry docking at Kingston

down ancient forests to load on square-rigged ships, of the U.S. Navy firing broadsides at the canoes of Northern Raiders.

The next step, by bridge over Hood Canal to the Olympic Peninsula, entails a moderately to very long day, though a comfortable overnighter. When a walker yearns for a change from the intimate beauties of Home Whulge, yet hasn't the 2 to 3 days required by the Dragon Whulge, there is the Middle Whulge, the beaches long and lonesome, the surf often ocean-crashing, seascapes and mountainscapes enormous, Main Street traffic busy. Here, too, is where mossy citizens of Puget Sound go on pilgrimage to the rainshadow of the Olympics, to seek the Great Blue Hole which will help their spirits when they are sick of winter's semi-eternal grays.

USGS maps: Duwamish Head, Bremerton East, Shilshole Bay, Suquamish, Edmonds West, Brinnon, Port Gamble, Lofall, Hansville, Port Ludlow, Port Townsend South, Port Townsend North, Dungeness

MAIN STREET

The subtleties of South Sound persist well north on the Kitsap Peninsula. But at Port Madison, where the beaches come out from behind sheltering peninsulas and islands to the wide-open reaches of Main Street, goodbye to all that, hello to the naked power of North Sound, the Whulge Primeval.

North from Indianola to Kingston, 6 miles*

Drive from the Winslow ferry via Highway 305 to Agate Pass, turn north on Suquamish Highway to the head of Miller Bay, then south on Indianola Road. From the Kingston ferry the route is south around Appletree Cove on Indianola Road. Parking is scanty in the old summer-cottage settlement. Don't come on summer Sundays.

A mere 5 miles across the waters is the throbbing (and roaring, banging, rumbling, generally racketing) heart of Puget Sound City, and along Main Street the traffic hurries between points on the Whulge and the Seven Seas. But here one walks in wild quiet for miles, waves and gulls for company.

The Indianola dock is signed "Private Beach. No Trespassing. For Use by Indianola Residents Only." But the dock is the (Public) Port of Indianola, from the mosquito fleet. In the 1920s the older surveyor's mother debarked on this dock for family summering. He bases his rights on family history and the Public Trust Doctrine.

From the staircase to the beach the 1 mile of shore west is inviting, to the house-desecrated spit reaching nearly across the mouth of Miller Bay, but the memorable walk is 4 miles east and north, along Port Madison and Main Street.

---

*See the publisher's note on private property on page 11.

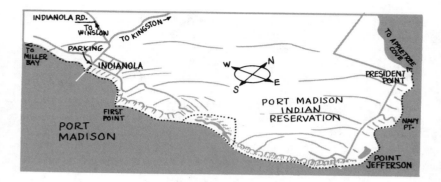

Houses on bulkheads are quickly passed and humans retreat to their proper place atop the bank. In a long ½ mile "First Point" is rounded and the bluff rears up a steep, partly naked 200 feet of till and sand and clay. The view back down Port Madison to Agate Pass is lost, that of Bainbridge Island continues, and across Main Street is Seattle.

At ½ mile from First Point is the most unusual geography of the trip. The bluff swings far inland around an ancient bay, long since closed off by the baymouth bar, inland of which are a lagoon/mudflat, a mass of bleached driftwood, and a broad marsh and great swampy forest. Birds! A crowd! What secrets lurk in the heart of the Port Madison Indian Reservation? Marred by a single edifice only, the entirety of closed-off bay half-ringed by hillside forest appears primeval. At medium-to-high tides the lagoon-mouth channel must be waded to the knees or detoured around on the driftwood; at low tides the channel can be hippety-hopped, the baymouth bar walked, ½ mile to a resumption of bluff.

After ¾ mile more of bluff wildness, a dock and road briefly intrude. In ¼ mile more is Point Jefferson, a dune line, a lagoon, and a half-dozen modest cottages. Now the far-shore view opens north past Carkeek Park to Richmond Beach, oil tanks of Point Wells and Edwards Point, and Edmonds. This may be far enough for many walkers, 3 miles from Indianola.

But onward ½ wild mile is "Navy Point"; atop the bluff is an aged warlike structure, below it another lagoon. And in ¾ bluff-wild (though the blufftop is inhabited) mile more, complicated by a beach-invading stretch of armoring riprap requiring scrambling at medium tides, are the wide flat and lagoon of President Point, sparsely dotted with houses. Now the view is north to Whidbey Island and Mukilteo. Here, 4¼ miles from Indianola, is a good turnaround, though in only 1¾ more (civilized, now) miles, past a beached hulk, is the point at the mouth of Appletree Cove, in close view of the Edmonds ferry arriving at and departing from Kingston—the alternate (carfree) start for the 6-mile (or any fraction) route.

North from Kingston to Eglon Beach, 5¾ miles

Leave your car in the Port of Edmonds lot. Voyage cheaply to Kingston. Walk up from the dock, take the first road right, and find the broad trail dropping to the beach.

The beach is a North Sound classic beneath a formidable guardian bluff and the route along Main Street is a walk through time. In the 1½ miles to Appletree Point, beneath a two-step bluff 60 to 100 feet high, houses are distant from the beach except at the halfway mark, where a boulder bulkhead invades, requiring a short wade at medium tides. The couple dozen modest cottages on the point are readily passed, but at the north end is a massively wicked bulkhead that is non-detourable via bluff, non-clamberable due to a house, and at middle tides and above requires a knee-deep to nose-deep wade. Face it—to do the whole trip to Eglon you're going to have to get feet and knees wet here, going or coming. (Of course you *can* walk *from* Eglon.) The beach then widens. North of the point begins an amusing ½ mile, a half-dozen quirky little cottages-castles, trail-access only, scattered along a slump terrace.

Now, 2½ miles from the ferry, begin 2½ utterly wild miles, the bluff a steep 300 feet. Chunks of it slide onto and across the beach. Gullies slice the clay. Waterfalls cascade from greenery. It's as solitudinous a beach as the Whulge has to offer.

Trails and staircases foreshadow the start of civilization, on the flat of a coastal bulge at the mouth of a creek. Oddly, the only development is a couple of small farms, several beach houses, and several bleached ruins. Very nice. Wildness resumes, though of a lower order, the bluff a mere 60 feet, the final ¾ mile to Eglon Beach Park.

Sit for lunch. Enjoy views of Main Street traffic, Whidbey Island's

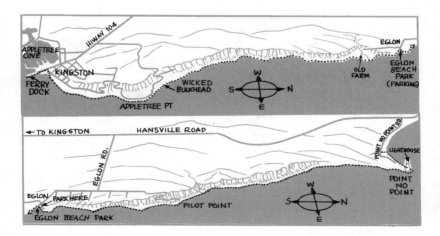

imposing bluffs. The Edmonds Ferry Dock whence you came. Pilchuck, Glacier Peak, Rainier. Far across the water, hear the rumble of trains on the Whulge Trail.

Eglon Beach Park

Bus: 66M

Drive from the Kingston ferry 2.5 miles to the Hansville Road, turn north 4.5 miles, and go right 1.7 miles on NE Eglon Road.

Another bounty of the mosquito fleet, a Public Port District which no longer has a dock but does have a dainty little Kitsap County park. You'll love the walk south 4½ miles to the Wicked Bulkhead. The 4 miles north to Point No Point are another epiphany.

South from Point No Point to Eglon Beach, 3¾ miles

Drive to Hansville. From the Winslow ferry the route is Highway 305 to just west of Agate Pass, then north on Suquamish Highway to the Hansville Road. From the Kingston ferry the route is west 2.5 miles to the Hansville Road. Upon descending to the shore plain, turn right on Point No Point Road 0.7 mile to the resort entrance. Park on a road shoulder back toward Hansville.

Point No Point Lighthouse

Walk through the resort to the beach, thence to the point; or, where the resort road turns left, walk the road straight ahead to the lighthouse, where very limited parking is available during visiting hours (Wednesday–Sunday, 8:00 A.M. to 4:00 P.M.). Dating from 1879, the light is worth a tour.

The view west is past Hansville over Skunk Bay to Foulweather Bluff, and north is across Puget Sound to the gray-white cliffs of Double Bluff and Indian Point and Scatchet Head on Whidbey Island.

South from the spit, jungled cliffs of glacial drift enwilden the beach. Bald eagles may be seen; a pair or two perhaps nest here. The view now is past Possession Point to densely inhabited slopes of Edmonds, oil tanks of Edwards Point and Point Wells, Richmond Beach, and towers of downtown Seattle. Beyond are the Cascades from Rainier to Glacier to Baker. And always ships passing, birds flying and swimming.

Paths indicate unseen residences above. Then, at Pilot Point, 2½ miles from Point No Point, a half-dozen cabins occupy a beachside flat. Wildness resumes the final 1¼ miles to Eglon Beach Park.

Foulweather Bluff

Drive to Hansville (see South from Point No Point to Eglon Beach) and keep going. Upon reaching the beach, Hansville Road turns west as Twin Spits Road. At 2.8 miles from the bend watch for a wide marsh to the left; summer vegetation can make it hard to spot. A bit beyond is an obvious path into the woods, signed only by demure "Nature Conservancy" tags and a little plaque identifying this as a Nature Sanctuary. If you come to Skunk Bay Road, you've gone 800 feet too far. Alternatively, drive on 0.7 mile to the road-end and a Public beach access beside Twin Spits Resort.

Talk about weather shores! Foulweather Bluff juts out where Hood Canal, Admiralty Inlet, and Puget Sound meet, and the weather comes at it every which way. The skinny beach at the base of the vertical jungle is a terrific viewpoint, resounding finale to a walk past two great spits and a marvelous nature sanctuary.

The Sanctuary is the unique treat. The footpath through the woods passes the marsh, then the broad lagoon, ⅓ mile to the beach. To appreciate how glorious a spot this is, and how fortunate we are that the Conser-

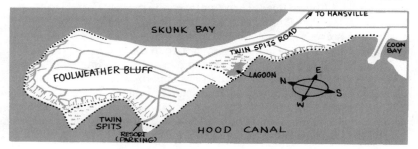

vancy saved it, walk 1¼ miles southeast, first along the baymouth bar that encloses lagoon and marsh, then under an 80-foot-high naked bluff, to the gross development on the spits of Coon Bay which forces any religious person to consider praying for the C/4.

But the main show (other than the Sanctuary, which a birdwatcher just may not want to leave) is the other way, on what was, when sea level was 20 feet higher, Foulweather Island. Houses are safely atop the 60-foot till wall the 1 wild mile to the southern of the Twin Spits, where are located Last Resort, Twin Spits Resort, and the Public beach access. Proceed by several beach-near houses ¼ mile to the northern spit and a resumption of wildness. At low tide walk across the lagoon outlet onto the spit and stick with the beach; otherwise, follow the foot of the bluff until saltgrass and driftwood can be walked around the lagoon to the beach. Views are superb south along Hood Canal to Hood Head, the floating bridge, Port Gamble, the mouth of Port Ludlow directly across the Canal, and Zion, Townsend, Walker, and Constance.

The spit beach is ¾ mile long, a lonesome splendor of grass-anchored sand dunes, driftwood and waves on the Canal side and birds on the lagoon side. Two modest summer cottages at the spit base briefly break the solitude, which resumes under the bluff as it leaps to 100 feet, then 220 feet, too steep and clay-slidey to permit trails from the top. The shore rounds from northerly to east, the view extending to Marrowstone Island and Fort Flagler State Park, to the distant San Juans. Directly across Main Street is Double Bluff, between Mutiny Bay and Useless Bay on Whidbey Island. Ocean freighters race by, stirring up wonderful crashing waves, ocean-size. Fishing boats work and sailboats play. Ah, but what's missing from the scene? The Edmonds–Ludlow ferry, scuttled soon after War II. Foulweather Bluff was a famous landmark to voyagers en route to the high Olympics, Trapper Nelsons lashed to fenders of the Model A. At 1 mile from the northern Twin Spit the bluff shore turns sharply south into Skunk Bay. About ½ wild mile more and the bluff dwindles to naught and houses begin.

Hood Canal Drive Creek

Drive Hansville Road north to Little Boston Road NE. Turn left (west) 1 mile to NE Cliffside Road. Turn right 0.6 mile to Hood Canal Drive NE. Turn north (right) 0.9 mile, winding down toward the water. Just before the almost-horseshoe bend which crosses the creek, spot a narrow dirt road and path to the beach. Parking for two to three cars.

Though the major creek of the north Kitsap Peninsula, no name can be found on our maps. Never mind. It is a superb creek for children-play, as attested by the Youngest Surveyor. Sandy beach beneath an 80-foot bluff stretches north 1 mile to the Coon Bay obscenity. South 1 mile is the boundary of the Port Gamble Indian Reservation, whose 2 more miles of beach reach beyond Point Julia halfway to the head of Port Gamble.

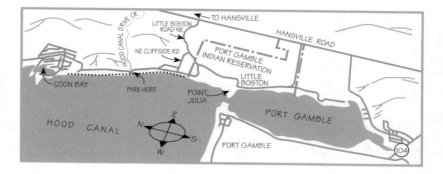

Views are directly across Hood Canal to Hood Head; north to Twin Spits; south to Port Gamble and Hood Canal Bridge.

Port Gamble

Parking areas in town permit walking tours from a number of starts. A nice way to grasp the geographical setting is to approach via beach from Salsbury Point Park. Drive Highway 104 from Kingston or, from Winslow, Highways 305, 3, and 104 to 0.5 mile east of Hood Canal Bridge and turn off on Wheeler Street to the park.

No museum specimen under glass is this, no artist colony or row of shoppes, but a lived-in working mill town and the oldest operating sawmill in North America. The hamlet seems too old for this raw young corner of the nation, looks like it belongs in New England. Indeed, when A. J. Pope, Captain William Talbot, and Cyrus Walker founded the town in 1853, they built it to resemble their native East Machias, Maine. Take away the cars and TV antennae, fill the bay with square-rigged ships, and you're in the nineteenth century.

Salsbury Point (Kitsap County) Park is walled in by houses. Still, when Private eyes are trained on the Nintendo a solitary Public can (on a low tide) speed quietly by to the shelter of Teekalet Bluff, in views south on Hood Canal to the Olympics, north to Port Ludlow and Foulweather Bluff. In 1 mile is the millyard, from which a road-path climbs to the town and the parking area across from the post office (Land Office) and the Port

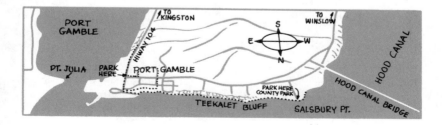

Port Gamble Centennial celebration

Gamble General Store (1853). Here too is the Pope and Talbot Office; the company restored and maintains the town and runs the mill on timber from lowland forests it has been logging all this while, one crop after another, and will continue to do so until the soil is exhausted or more money is to be made by replacing forests with retirement communities, which is to say shortly.

In the basement of the General Store is the Historical Museum, the basic introduction when open and providing a walking-tour pamphlet-guide. But there's plenty of history out in the open. Stroll the sidewalks along tree-shaded streets, by modest homes of the proletariat and mansions of the capitalists, in views down to the mill, rafted logs, and across Port Gamble to where the Indians lived, wondering at all this.

Ascend the bluff-rim lawn westward to the hilltop cemetery, where headstones bear such legends as "died at Teekalet W.T. 1860." Ponder the memorial to "Gustav Englebrecht–Germany–Cox US Navy–Indian War–November 21, 1856." When the Northern Raiders attacked, the millworkers called for help from the *Massachusetts*. During the desultory skirmish known to history as the Battle of Port Gamble, the coxswain poked his head over a bulwark for a better view of the action and became the first U.S. Navy man to be killed in a Pacific Ocean war.

Admire the view to Hood Canal Floating (?) Bridge, the Olympics, Marrowstone Island, the plume of the Port Townsend pulpmill, and Foulweather Bluff. In mind's eye see the tall ships spreading sail to carry Washington lumber the world around.

Hood Head (Wolfe) State Park

From the west end of the Hood Canal Bridge, turn right on Paradise Bay Road, and immediately right again on Termination Point Road, signed "Shine Tidelands State Park." Drive past the Puget Power transformer to the parking area by the beach. This is the south access. For the north

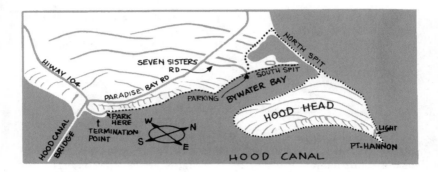

access, drive Paradise Bay Road 0.5 mile and go right on Seven Sisters Road (gravel) 0.5 mile to parking at a Public boat-launch.

Wolfe State Park is 131 acres of forest and marsh, 4 miles of tidelands. Stroll shores of a secluded little bay, poke around ducks and herons thronging a lagoon half-ringed by saltmarsh and forest, explore spits, venture onto a former island, now a tombolo, and from its tip gaze up and down Hood Canal.

Termination Point to South Spit, 1½ miles

Walk 1 mile on the shore of Bywater Bay and ½ mile more (passing the north access and then a log-filled lagoon) on South Spit to its tip. The spit thrusts out so far it nearly cuts off the head of the bay, forming a large inner bay/lagoon, mudflat at low tide, duck pond at high.

Boat-Launch to Hood Head Loop, 3½ miles

The tip of South Spit is just a spit away, but at unwadeably high water walk inland around the little lagoon/marsh to the west end of North Spit. In ½ mile go off the east end onto Hood Head. Walk the north shore beneath a high bluff of tree-tangled glacial drift the 1 mile to Point Hannon, a superlative viewpoint thrust out in Hood Canal. Look north to the entrance portals, Tala Point and Foulweather Bluff, and beyond to Marrowstone Island. Look across to the mill and town of Port Gamble, Rainier rising above.

The first edition of *Footsore 3*, delivered to the stores in February of 1979, said,

> *Look south to the bridge floating in the Canal (floating, that is, until the next approximately twice-in-a-century event, the last coming in the 1930s, a northerly gale on a bull tide, a combination for which the bridge was not engineered, and thus the fittingness of the location near Port Gamble).*

On February 13, 1979, the bridge sank. A new one was built. How will it do in a C/4?

The uplands of Hood Head, rising a mountainous 220 feet, are a wild-wood 1 mile long and ½ mile wide. The shore, too, is perfectly wild except for a dozen-odd cottages on the west side. The logical completion of the trip is to round the island, in a scant 2 miles from Point Hannon returning to North Spit.

FORT WORDEN STATE PARK

Drive west from Hood Canal Bridge and turn north on the highway signed "Port Townsend." Enter Port Townsend on Highway 20 and before downtown turn left at the sign "Fort Worden State Park," then turn right and left and right and left (always signed) and, voila, the park entrance. The car can be parked and the walk begun at any number of places.

How impoverished our park systems would be without wars—and foolish fears of implausible wars. Forest wildlands are preserved, and miles of lonesome beaches, all haunted by the past. Even if a person lacks a taste for ancient bloodshed, the Quimper Peninsula has plenty to enchant—history that is not military, oceanlike beaches, and unsurpassed water-and-mountain views. Three sample tours are suggested.

Old Fort Townsend State Park

First off, on the way to Port Townsend turn in to clearly signed Old Fort Townsend State Park. Unlike its neighbors, this was an Indian War fort, established in 1856, abandoned in 1895, the 377 acres deeded to the state in 1953. The beach is a dandy, extending north under guardian bluffs 1 mile to Glen Cove, nearly to the steam-spewing pulpmill, and south 1¾ miles to Kuhn Spit and Kala Point, all in broad views. The park is a lonesome woodland full of paths; a loop of some 3 miles is especially attractive in May when the rhododendrons are in bloom.

History Tour (War), 2½-mile loop

Had an Enemy tried to storm on through from the ocean into Puget Sound, the batteries of this vertex of the Death Triangle would've fired the first shells, perhaps leaving Flagler and Casey little to do but finish off cripples. Work on gun emplacements began in 1897 and in 1904 Fort Worden became headquarters of the Harbor Defense of Puget Sound. In 1911 the 12-inchers of Battery Kinzie were in place. In 1920 aerial warfare arrived with the construction of balloon hangars. On December 8, 1941 the fort briefly awoke. In 1953 it was closed, to become a 339-acre park.

To absorb all this, first drive around the parade ground, past the flagpole, to the park office, to obtain a copy of the park map and chronology. A methodical way to do the history is by a periphery tour on foot. From the chapel at the entrance, walk by the guardhouse, turn left to the balloon

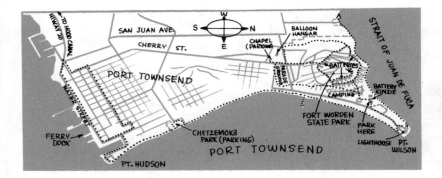

hangar and cemetery, turn right to bluff-edge views over the Whulge, turn right and prowl gun batteries, return right to the old barracks, now the Conference Center, and stroll the parade ground to the mansions of Officer's Row, now rented out as vacation homes.

On the Beach to the Old City, 3 miles

Drive by the parade ground, down to the beach, and north to the parking area at Battery Kinzie, just short of the Point Wilson Lighthouse.

First, of course, tour the lighthouse (visiting hours, 1:00–3:00 P.M. weekdays, 1:00–4:00 P.M. weekends) on the tip of the superb spit poking into Main Street, the Strait of Juan de Fuca on one side, Admiralty Inlet on the other, great ships often cutting the corner close to make the turn, sloshing exciting waves on the beach. Views are overwhelming to Victoria on Vancouver Island, the full east–west width of the San Juans, the loess bluffs of Whidbey Island, the shuttling Keystone–Townsend ferry, the Cascades from Baker to Shuksan to Glacier to Whitehorse and Three Fingers.

Walk south along the spit beach (wide, sandy, all-tides-walkable) by the driftwood line, the grass-grown dunes, the (filled) lagoon. South ¾ mile from Point Wilson is a pier providing out-in-the-water perspectives. Leave the spit for the foot of a wild bluff, pass under Chetzemoka Park, and at 2¼ miles from Point Wilson come to the end of beach, start of port facilities, at Point Hudson (parking, alternative start).

Port Townsend is worth walking. Turn onto Water Street, main drag of the lower, below-bluff town, visit the ferry dock, and tour the scene. A thriving seaport when Seattle was a real-estate speculation, Port Townsend lost the race to hugeness. That's our good luck, because the long languishing in a backwater preserved much of the nineteenth-century flavor of the would-be-but-never-was metropolis. The 1891 City Hall at Water and Madison houses a historical museum; the basement, when a jail, offered hospitality to Jack London. The Bartlett Building, when a

Old German Consulate and the City Hall at Port Townsend

tavern, specialized in shanghaiing seamen who didn't want to go to sea. The 1874 Leader Building is claimed to be the oldest remaining all-stone structure in the state. The upper, above-bluff town has many well-kept Victorian homes. Keep an eye out for poets.

Long Wild Beach, 7 miles

If it's a good leg-stretching you seek, a good lung-filling with salt winds, a good eye-filling with oceanlike marine vistas, the north shore of Quimper Peninsula is for you.

Park at Battery Kinzie and hit the north beach, walkable at all but the highest tides. Views are east past the Point Wilson Lighthouse to Whidbey Island bluffs and the white tower of Baker, north by ships to Vancouver Island. When a tall freighter rushes past, the surf turns ocean-size, scary for a walker with his/her back pressed against the unclimbable wall of glacial drift. Cormorants perch atop erratics. Grebes dive, oyster-catchers squeal, gulls soar, crows caw, plovers scurry, peeps run. After 1 mile of splendid isolation, the bluff drops away to a flat. Here are fields and homes and North Beach (Jefferson County) Park, alternative start

(from Fort Worden entrance drive west, then north).

After ½ mile the bluff rises, homes atop. But at 2¾ miles from Point Wilson the houses end, the bluff rears up to a frightful precipice, sand strata topped by vertical till, the brink 280 feet from the water, the tallest naked vertical wall of the Whulge. In a long 1 mile the cliff diminishes somewhat to McCurdy (Middle) Point, 4 miles from Point Wilson and a logical turnaround.

The wildness and isolation continue under a more-than-ordinarily-vertical bluff, a daunting 200 feet of clays and gravel and tills. Watch those tides, folks! Escape routes are few and cruel and mostly dangerous, not a single deep-slicing ravine to breach the wall. Spice is added by the fact that at high tides there is no beach much of the way, just clay walls battered by breakers and clawed by fingernails. Yes, a wilderness to sing in, and no fear that any developer will invade the combat zone where waves buffet the clay cliffs, great chunks of which slide down in counterattack.

At 3¼ miles from McCurdy Point (atop which is an abandoned military reservation) is Cape George at the mouth of Port Discovery, views to Olympic foothills, Miller Peninsula, and Protection Island. Time to turn around, because soon start houses of Cape George Colony, and who needs that?

MILLER PENINSULA STATE PARK

Middle Access. Drive US 101 west from Gardiner 1.5 miles and turn north on Diamond Point Road. In 2.2 miles the road curves left to a sign, "Northwest Technical Industries." A gravel road, gated, enters a 1989 clearcut at 0.9 mile from the gate. At 0.25 mile into the clearcut a sideroad curves left, uphill; stay right. Shortly the road is blocked by logs and heaps of gravel (to keep four-wheel cowboys from the beach). Proceed past the barricade, down the ravine to the beach, 2 miles from the gate.

West Access. Drive US 101 to the head of Sequim Bay and turn toward the water on Blaine Crossing (a street). Immediately turn right on East Sequim Bay Road. Ignoring sideroads, at 4.3 miles from US 101 go right on Panorama Vista Road to its end. Turn right on Buck Loop Road 0.2 mile to limited parking at the gate barring wheels from the county park beach trail, a grass-covered road descending a ravine to a short stairway to the beach.

Views across the great embayment to Canada and the beyond-Cascade mountains of the north. Ships of many nations passing to and from Vancouver and Seattle. Wakes of those ships washing up to the foot of the bluff, reinforcing the surf briefly to oceanic dimensions. Seals poking heads out of the water to watch seal-watchers on the beach. Bald eagles circling above, guarding their nests. Peregrine falcons, too. A riot of rhododendron bloom in mid-May. It is good, very very good. But the best, perhaps, is that in 5-odd miles of Miller Peninsula shore there is no intrusion by human machines or homes. Not very much by human bodies. The powerful longshore currents slim the beach so drastically that quite a low tide is required to do much walking, and so vigorously wash away sands and shingle, leaving ankle-twisting cobbles, that walking is tortuous. Few ravines breach the 200-foot bluff; watch those tides!

The parcel managed for years by the Department of Natural Resources has 1444 acres, more than 3 miles of tidelands. A deal to exchange lands to permit Mitsubishi Corporation to build a luxury golf resort was done in by the alert and determined citizenry of Save Our State Parks. Olympia officials retreated and the current intent is to acquire lands to enlarge the tract to 1700 acres, to become the third-largest Washington State Park. Planning is in progress for a park amply providing for wildlife, the handicapped, and other non-golfers.

Start by admiring Protection Island. Then walk east (from the middle access) 2 miles to Diamond Point. Well, maybe not the whole way; the magnificent spit has been littered with cabins and trailers set up in a row for the C/4 to bash to splinters and deposit in the lagoon. The best of the trip comes in ½ mile, Thompson Spit—actually almost a baymouth bar. Behind the driftwood line the dune line is greenly grassed. At the tip of

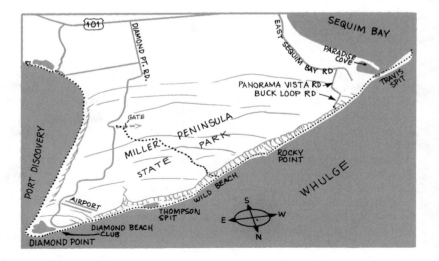

Miller Peninsula

the spit is a lone shore pine, tortured by storms to a stunted bonsai. Back of the murky orange-brown lagoon is an old hovel. The map shows a cross here and says "Grave." The younger surveyor saw six seals and four bald eagles.

Walk west ¾ mile to Rocky Point, distinguished by two enormous glacial erratics. The point cannot be rounded except at low tide. Not surveyed for this guide were the 2⅓ miles onward to the base of Travis Spit (on the way the bluff dwindles to naught) nor the ¾ mile of that spit, which very nearly closes off Sequim Bay to make it a lagoon.

GIBSON SPIT

Drive US 101 west toward Sequim. Turn right on Brown Road 1 mile to Port Williams Road. Turn right 2 miles to the end at Marlyn Nelson (Clallam County) Park.

Travis Spit, westernmost thrust of the Miller Peninsula, nearly meets Gibson Spit thrusting southward from the Dungeness flats, almost completing a baymouth bar closing off Sequim Bay as a huge lagoon. The views of all this business and The (little) Lagoon, Washington Harbor,

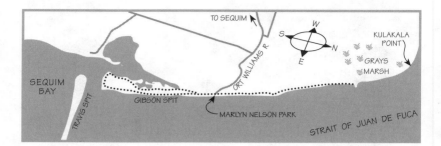

and The Middle Ground, are a textbook of shoreline morphology.

The feature show is the 1 mile along Gibson Spit to where the tides race through the narrow channel between the two spits. By no means to be scorned is the walk north beneath a low clay bluff (nesting area of the pigeon guillemot) 1½ miles to Grays Marsh and beyond to Kulakala Point. The near-tidal marsh is Grays Marsh Farm, a privately maintained wildlife refuge; Public walkers are welcomed subject to good behavior and temporary closures (posted) for the business and pleasure of wildlife.

DUNGENESS SPIT

Drive US 101 west from Sequim's town center 4.5 miles and turn north on Kitchen-Dick Road, signed "Dungeness Recreation Area." In 3.2 miles the road makes a right-angle turn east and just beyond is the entrance road to the recreation area, a 240-acre Clallam County park. Drive 1 long mile, passing the head of the horse trail, going by the picnic area and

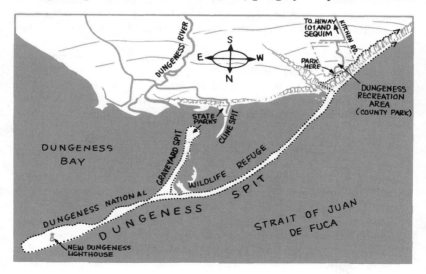

Driftwood on Dungeness Spit; Olympic Mountains in distance

through the campground, to the road-end parking area and restrooms and trailhead, elevation 120 feet. Entrance fee for trail-walking, $2 per family.

The longest natural sandspit in the United States thrusts 5 miles out from Olympic Peninsula bluffs into the Strait of Juan de Fuca, so far that on a stormy day a walker feels wave-tossed and seasick, and on a foggy day wonders if he/she has passed over to another and totally watery planet. Birds run the sands and swim the waters and fly the air. Seals pop heads out of breakers to wonder what you're at.

As a prefatory note, there's more walking here than the spit. Southwest are at least 4 miles of open-to-boots big-surf beach, totally wild below naked, vertical, 100-foot bluffs of glacial drift. In the same direction, an unsurveyed distance, runs a blufftop path through grass and wind-tortured scrub trees and broad views.

However, the spit calls.

Note: The Dungeness National Wildlife Refuge is *not a playground*. Kinetic sports are banned. Indeed, even foot traffic is growing so heavy as to endanger the wildlife. Added restrictions on human visitation are being considered. The trail ("no camping, no fires, no guns, no pets, no bicycles") enters forest, emerges to a viewpoint of spit and the Whulge, joins the horse trail coming from the right, and drops to the mouth of a nice little creek valley, in a scant ½ mile reaching the beach and the base of the spit.

So, there you are. Go. Via the outside route or the inside, separated by the driftwood jumble along the spit spine. The outside is the surf side, views to tankersful of oil and Vancouver Island, the San Juan Islands, Whidbey Island, and the Baker-dominated Cascades. The inside is the bay side, the first half a lagoon, often glassy calm and often floating thousands of waterfowl; the view is to mainland bluffs, delta of the Dungeness River, and the Olympics. But the inside is also the wildlife side and may have to be absolutely closed to feet and boats during certain seasons of the year.

Both end in the pretty government-issue lighthouse, the foghorn, and ⅓ mile beyond, the tip of the spit. A light has been on this site since 1857, earliest in the state. The precise name is New Dungeness Lighthouse; Captain Vancouver was struck by the resemblance to Dungeness "in the British channel."

There's a sidetrip. Graveyard Spit—commemorating the day in 1868 when seventeen Tsimshians were massacred by the Klallams—branches off, extending 1½ miles south, nearly touching Cline Spit thrusting from the mainland, the two enclosing the inner lagoon. This spit probably should be entirely closed to humans, in boats and on foot.

INDEX

About the Author

Harvey Manning is one of the Pacific Northwest's most influential and outspoken conservationists. His preservation efforts have ranged from protection of the "Issaquah Alps" wilderness near his home in the Puget Sound region to helping attain national park status for the North Cascades. Manning is the author of *Backpacking One Step at a Time*, and he and co-author Ira Spring have introduced legions of future environmentalists to the Northwest wilderness with their *100 Hikes in*™ guidebooks, *Hiking the Great Northwest,* and *Hiking the Mountains to Sound Greenway*.

THE MOUNTAINEERS, founded in 1906, is a nonprofit outdoor activity and conservation club whose mission is "to explore, study, preserve, and enjoy the natural beauty of the outdoors...." Based in Seattle, Washington, the club is now the third-largest such organization in the United States, with 14,000 members and four branches throughout Washington State.

The Mountaineers sponsors both classes and year-round outdoor activities in the Pacific Northwest, which include hiking, mountain climbing, ski-touring, snowshoeing, bicycling, camping, kayaking and canoeing, nature study, sailing, and adventure travel. The club's conservation division supports environmental causes through educational activities, sponsoring legislation, and presenting informational programs. All club activities are led by skilled, experienced volunteers, who are dedicated to promoting safe and responsible enjoyment and preservation of the outdoors.

The Mountaineers Books, an active, nonprofit publishing program of the club, produces guidebooks, instructional texts, historical works, natural history guides, and works on environmental conservation. All books produced by The Mountaineers are aimed at fulfilling the club's mission.

If you would like to participate in these organized outdoor activities or the club's other programs, consider a membership in The Mountaineers. For information and an application, write or call The Mountaineers, Club Headquarters, 300 Third Avenue West, Seattle, Washington 98119; (206) 284-6310.

Send or call for our catalog of more than 300 outdoor titles:
The Mountaineers Books
1011 SW Klickitat Way, Suite 107
Seattle, WA 98134
1 (800) 553-4453